He spoke in parables

He spoke in parables

Gordon J. Keddie

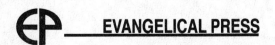

EVANGELICAL PRESS

EVANGELICAL PRESS
12 Wooler Street, Darlington, Co. Durham, DL1 1RQ, England

© Evangelical Press 1994
First published 1994

British Library Cataloguing in Publication Data available

ISBN 0 85234-312-4

Unless otherwise indicated, Scripture quotations in this publication are from the Holy Bible, New International Version. Copyright © 1973, 1978 1984 International Bible Society. Published by Hodder & Stoughton.

Printed and bound in Great Britain at the Bath Press, Avon.

To
the members and friends of
Grace Reformed Presbyterian Church
State College, Pennsylvania.

Contents

Part III: The consummation of the kingdom

Preface

My one brush with royalty was in 1959, when Prince Philip, Duke of Edinburgh, visited George Heriot's School, Edinburgh, on the occasion of its tercentenary. I was a teenage biologist whose task on the great day was to dissect a rat for the royal visitor. In due course, Prince Philip arrived at the lab, looked at my rat and asked very amiably if it had anything wrong with it. It was, of course, a perfectly normal rat, so I had nothing untoward to report. Later, however, it occurred to me that, however normal it might have been, it was also a dead rat. There it was, all opened up, with its internal anatomy neatly pinned out on a board for all to see.

I have since thought that many Bible commentaries do this with the Bible. They dissect its every component, pulling and teasing and cutting, until it is disassembled and pinned down, ostensibly to the end that we might understand what it is all about. But like the dissected rat, it can end up looking rather dead. Martyn Lloyd-Jones used to inveigh against preachers who felt they had to 'share their reading' with their hearers, so that what ought to have been a passionate, experiential exposition of the Word of God ended up being more like a report on a homework assignment. This has come home to me in a new way in the preparation of this exposition of the parables of Jesus. Few portions of Scripture have been subjected to such minute scrutiny as these stories Jesus told. In contrast with their essential simplicity, they have been exegetically dissected this way and that to the point where clarity of meaning and firmness of application have sometimes all but disappeared beneath an overburden of speculation and spiritualization. Footnotes — those ubiquitous markers of the barrenness of so much modern scholarship —

seem increasingly more prominent than the biblical text itself. The 'certain sound' of God's trumpet vanishes amidst a storm of discordant exegetical clamour.

The parables, rightly handled as the word of truth, ought to be a perfect antidote to this deadly tendency of our times. Left to speak for themselves, with only the lightest touch of exposition, they live and move and touch our being with a vibrant immediacy and unmistakable clarity. This is at least the aim of the present volume. Although I have sought to take account of the wider literature available on the parables, the focus throughout is that of the preacher who wants to get the message across. I have twice in twenty years preached through the parables and I hope that something of the pulpit still rings in what I have now committed to writing. This treatment is far from exhaustive, for there are many parabolic sayings and illustrations in the Gospels. What I have sought to do is to cover the main stories that Jesus told in developing his teaching on the kingdom of God — hence their arrangement in three sections, from the nature of the kingdom, to the marks of kingdom life and to the consummation of the kingdom. They are not extraneous and unconnected anecdotes. They unfold the heart of the gospel and the destiny of the human race. For those who want to follow up on the more technical aspects of the parables, I would recommend *The Parables of Jesus* by Simon Kistemaker, currently Professor of New Testa-ment at Reformed Theological Seminary, Jackson, Mississippi.

May Jesus, by his Holy Spirit, make his stories live in our hearts, to the glory of his Father and ours.

Gordon J. Keddie
State College, Pennsylvania
January 1994

Part I
The nature of God's kingdom

The parables of
Jesus' Galilean ministry
(Matthew 13:1-52)

1.
The secrets of the kingdom

The purpose of parables
(Matt. 13:10-17)

'The disciples came to him and asked, "Why do you speak to the people in parables?"' (Matt. 13:10).

Have you ever asked yourself what prompted the disciples to ask Jesus, **'Why do you speak to the people in parables?'** Did they not know the value of a good story? Did they not realize that he was being as simple and as practical as he could be in teaching about the kingdom of heaven? After all, we have known from our earliest days that a parable is a simple 'earthly' story with a profound 'heavenly' meaning. Did the followers of Jesus not know this? We wonder, and we begin to think that this is an example of how undiscerning these men were at this point in their lives and ministries.

What I want to suggest right at the start, however, is that the disciples, far from being ignorant and undiscerning, had asked Jesus a very intelligent question. They knew enough about the usefulness of parables, from the Old Testament, to know that Jesus must have had good reasons for turning to this distinctive method of teaching. Jesus' ministry until now had been more doctrinal and thematic. Although he often used colourful illustrations and figures of speech, only once had he used the story-telling form. That was his story about the wise and foolish builders in the Sermon on the Mount (Matt. 7:24-27). 'What,' the disciples were asking themselves, 'is behind this shift from doctrinal and thematic teaching to parables?' That is the import of the disciples' question, and it reveals them to be thoughtful observers of Jesus' ministry.

We ought to note that although this question is discussed in Matthew 13:10-17, in connection with the parable of the sower (13:1-9), it was actually raised after Jesus had left the boat from which he had addressed the crowd and gone into the house with his immediate disciples (13:36). Matthew records verses 10-23 out of chronological order because Jesus' answer fits in so beautifully with the thrust of the parable of the sower. We shall see why when we look at that parable in the next chapter.

1. Secrets revealed

Jesus characteristically answers the question by stating some basic principles, only then going on to flesh them out with practical explanations and applications. He sets out three principles governing the use of parables in Matthew 13:11-12.

Mysteries revealed

The first principle is that they are vehicles of special revelation from God. 'Why do you speak to the people in parables?' the disciples asked. **'He replied, "The knowledge of the secrets of the kingdom of heaven has been given to you, but not to them"'** (13:11). The focus is 'the secrets of the kingdom of heaven'. The word translated 'secrets' is the Greek *musteria*, i.e., 'mysteries'. We often think of a mystery as something that is so weird and difficult to grasp that it is beyond all explanation, or, as in the literary genre of murder mysteries, something we can figure out if we really work at unravelling it. In the Bible, however, a 'mystery' is neither of these things. It is neither an insoluble problem nor a solvable puzzle. A biblical 'mystery' is always some part of the secret will of God that we cannot know unless he reveals it to us. It is not that it is too difficult to understand. It is just something that is hidden unless unveiled. Biblical 'mysteries' are spiritual truths — truths about spiritual things. Paul, for example, says about the resurrection of the dead, 'Listen, I tell you a mystery: We will not all sleep, but we will all be changed — in a flash, in the twinkling of an eye, at the last trumpet' (1 Cor. 15:51). Similarly, Paul speaks of 'the mystery of the gospel' (Eph. 6:19). Why 'mystery'? Because we only know about the gospel of Christ because God has directly revealed it in his Word and in his Son.

These secrets concerned the 'kingdom of heaven'. We shall learn a great deal about this kingdom as we proceed through the parables. Suffice it to say that this is a kingdom that has come, in the person of Jesus himself, the final King (Eph. 1:22). It is an empire of faith, in and through a divine Saviour. It is not of this world. It is heavenly in nature. It cannot be seen with the eye of sight, only with the eye of faith. It consists in 'mysteries' (NIV 'secrets') which, to be known at all, must be specially revealed by God! Jesus is saying that he speaks in parables precisely in order to make known what would otherwise be unknowable. The parables are vehicles of free grace, bringing light to darkened souls.

Mysteries revealed to particular people

The second, astounding, component of Jesus' answer is his declaration that the 'knowledge'[1] of the mysteries of the kingdom is revealed to 'you', that is, his immediate disciples, but not to 'them', the crowds (13:11). So even though multitudes heard the parable of the sower, its meaning was to be reserved, at least at this point in his ministry, for the inner circle of disciples. Jesus was thereby teaching them that God's grace is particular. We shall come to the detailed explanation of this in a moment. All we need note here is that Jesus is saying, 'Yes, there is a very deep reason for using parables at this time in my ministry, and it is rooted ultimately in the counsel of eternity, in God's plan from before the foundation of the world, in the mystery of sovereign election. It is the choosing of particular sinners to be saved by grace through faith and the passing by of others. The same message that illumines some remains a mystery to others.' Paul later speaks of this effect in relation to the preaching of the gospel in general: 'For we are to God the aroma of Christ among those who are being saved and those who are perishing. To the one we are the smell of death; to the other, the fragrance of life' (2 Cor. 2:15-16; cf. 1 Cor. 2:14-15). Hearing the truth of God requires more than functioning ears. It requires a work of God's Holy Spirit. It requires a work of grace, as God effectually calls, regenerates and converts the lost person upon whom he has set his love from all eternity. For, as Jesus was later to say, 'Many are invited, but few are chosen' (Matt. 22:14).

Mysteries revealed for faithful response

Jesus then turned to his third principle governing the use of parables.
**'Whoever has will be given more, and he will have an abun-
dance. Whoever does not have, even what he has will be taken
from him'** (13:12). Here is where the first two principles touch the
experience of the individual. It comes down to the personal responsibility of each hearer, for the thrust of these words is directed at
what happens when people respond to the message of God's Word.

The disciples knew very well, as we do, that you can never stand
still with respect to any gift, faculty or achievement. The natural
athlete who never trains soon becomes unfit. The brilliant student
who rests on past success in examinations declines to mediocrity
through lack of fresh study. On the other hand, the average person
who works hard can ascend to new heights of accomplishment.
Steady effort is the only way to prevent vegetating spiritually and
physically. Indeed, it is the guarantor of growth and progress. 'Use
it or lose it' is an unbreakable reality in human experience. Everything we don't do, that we ought to do, becomes more difficult to
take up again. In spiritual things, as in business, education and sport,
the lazy lose out and the diligent prosper.

When Jesus speaks of those who 'have', he is talking about those
who truly know the Lord and therefore long for more of his promised
blessing. To keep the Lord's commands from the heart is to cultivate
one's own being. Heart-discipleship always produces richer fruit.
The experience of salvation is, as William Hendriksen puts it, 'an
ever deepening stream'.[2] Growth in grace is the fruit of a believing
response to the teaching of the parables.

In contrast, those who 'have not' are those who have no zeal to
press on actively, lovingly, joyfully and obediently in practical
godliness. Whatever they may say, or even think, about their
devotion to the Lord (assuming they have any concern at all about
such things), the practical evidence of living faith and personal
holiness is simply lacking. They want to stay the way they are. So,
as in the parable of the talents (Matt. 25:14-30), the 'one-talent' man
loses that 'talent' — and not because of some arbitrary sovereign act
of God which prevented him from using it properly, but because he
freely determined to go his own way. Like Frank Sinatra, he can
sing, 'I did it my way.'

2. A vision of the gospel

Jesus further explains the principles set out above by detailing the specific purposes of the parables (13:13-17). He makes three main points. These encompass the past, the present and the future and are rightly understood as setting forth his vision for the work of the kingdom of heaven upon earth.

The past: prophecy fulfilled

Jesus first roots his explanation, and therefore his warrant, in the Word of God revealed in times past. He quotes Isaiah 6:9-10 to show that the very simplicity and clarity of his parables condemned his hearers' unbelieving response and that this was the fulfilment of Isaiah's prophecy.

Why did he speak in parables? He did so in order to expose the hardness of heart of the many in the Old Testament church who thought themselves right with God, when in reality they were determined to resist his claims. **'Though seeing, they do not see; though hearing, they do not hear or understand'** (13:13). Please note that Jesus was not trying to be obscure so as to make sure that people would remain lost in their unbelief.[3] Quite the opposite is true. The Lord was being as clear as he could be, so that there would be no misunderstanding. The point was that those who rejected him knew exactly what they were rejecting and would never forget what it was they were rejecting. Herman Hanko points out that 'Oftentimes the wicked Pharisees understood the meaning of Jesus' parables before the disciples did.'[4] The responsibility for unbelieving incomprehension rests with the sinner and is not attributable to some inherent obscurity in the message. 'It was not darkness and a famine of hearing the word of God that would destroy the nation; it was light, too much light. It is this very light which would blind the people.'[5]

This, Jesus was saying, should not be difficult to grasp. It was predicted centuries before by the prophet Isaiah:

> **'For this people's heart has become calloused;**
> **they hardly hear with their ears,**
> **and they have closed their eyes.**

Otherwise they might see with their eyes,
      hear with their ears,
      understand with their hearts
and turn, and I would heal them'

                                    (Matt. 13:14-15; Isa. 6:10).

Isaiah was predicting how the latter-day Old Testament church would respond to the whole message of the gospel. People would not reject it because the message was too difficult to understand or deeply veiled in obscurity. They would reject it because it was only too clear. This was also the judgement of the apostle Paul, who used the selfsame text as an epitaph for the attitude of the Jewish church to the preaching of the gospel of Jesus Christ (Acts 28:25-27).

Behind this lies the dark but inescapable truth that God *purposed* to pass by those who were hardening their hearts against his Son and the light of his Word. Indeed, God was hardening the hearts of the reprobate lost, in such a way that they were all the more repelled by the gospel of the kingdom. 'In his mysterious wisdom,' writes E. J. Young, 'God had foreordained that this people would not respond to the blessed overtures of the gospel. In His sovereign good pleasure He had passed them by, not ordaining them unto life eternal, and for their sin had ordained them to dishonour and wrath.' Nevertheless, the same writer adds, 'The blindness of the nation is to be ascribed to its own depravity.'[6]

The same mystery is at work today and has its echoes among us. People still keep Christ at arm's length, because his claims are only too clearly unacceptable to them. The clearer and more pointed the preaching of the whole counsel of God becomes, the more offensive it becomes to the unchanged heart (1 Cor. 2:14). Hardness of heart is the rejection of what is obviously true! And hardness of heart produces new hardness of heart. And God himself seals that hardness of heart in the reprobate so that they cannot embrace the message they so wilfully despise. Were the gospel essentially unclear, then to reject it might be no more than 'reasonable doubt'. The Lord allows no such excuse. He will be so clear, so down to earth, so unambiguous, that those who refuse to believe in him will have to sear their own consciences, suppress the truth itself, deny their rationality and contradict the true meaning of their life, in order to protect themselves from being saved! They cannot plead ignorance. Isaiah preached — clearly — and Judah stiffened in their opposition to the message. Jesus taught in parables — equally clearly — and the 'old covenant' people hardened their hearts. Thus was God's purpose fulfilled — a purpose of salvation to those who believed, but a path of condemnation for those who did not (cf. 2 Cor. 2:15-17).

The present: lives are being blessed

For all the past and present resistance of so many to the claims of God, the message of grace was not ineffectual. The disciples and others had opened their eyes and ears to the Lord. 'They saw the glory of God in Christ's person,' writes Matthew Henry, 'they heard the mind of God in Christ's doctrine; they saw much and were desirous to see more, and thereby were prepared to receive further instruction...'[7] Jesus assured them, **'Blessed are your eyes because they see, and your ears because they hear'** (13:16).

Blessing is the happiness and joy that flows from receiving good gifts that were otherwise unexpected and undeserved. The Lord had taken any scales off from their eyes (Acts 9:18; cf. Prov. 20:12). These eyes — the 'eyes of your heart', Paul calls them (Eph. 1:18) — are the portals of the soul. With them, the truth is seen with an accepting, understanding, confiding and trusting spirit. Thus the testimony of believers is often couched in the language of light. When the aged Simeon took the baby Jesus in his arms, he said,

> '...my eyes have seen your salvation,
>   which you have prepared in the sight of all people,
> a light for revelation to the Gentiles
>   and for glory to your people Israel'
>
> (Luke 2:30-32).

When John Newton spoke of his own conversion he could say,

> Amazing grace! (how sweet the sound)
>   That saved a wretch like me!
> I once was lost but now am found,
>   Was blind but now I see.

Everything that was so sad in those with no ears to hear or eyes to see is being turned around in everyone who will listen and look to the Lord. Jesus' parables had this positive purpose. They opened up the real issues of life for all who would believe. They brought understanding to minds that otherwise knew nothing of Christ and his kingdom. They did the work of God in the renewal of lives, kindling a desire for the things of God and an ever-fresh devotion to his Son, Jesus.

The future: a new era has dawned

Jesus also indicated something of the extent of the disciples' privilege when he emphasized that they had been given what had been denied to faithful people in earlier generations: **'For I tell you the truth, many prophets and righteous men longed to see what you see but did not see it, and to hear what you hear but did not hear it'** (13:17).

The upshot of this is that a new era had dawned upon the world. Jesus and his parables stand at the hinge of history. In the past, there were many who did not see because of their own unbelief. But that is not the whole story. 'What is revealed in my ministry,' Jesus is saying, 'goes beyond what was proclaimed before. Even the saints of old, who wanted to know more of the purpose and the promises of God, were not given to know these things.' The new age had come, when the hidden and veiled was being brought into the noonday light of fulfilment. Shadow was giving way to substance.

Specifically, the 'prophets and righteous men' had known about the coming Messiah, but they never saw him. The disciples knew this to be true. What, then, was Jesus saying to them? He was 'clearly and unambiguously' pointing to himself 'as the long-expected Messiah'.[8] The parables, in other words, are part of the self-revelation of Jesus as the Christ, the Son of the living God. The measure of the disciples' privilege is that they were called to be believing eyewitnesses of the ministry of the Mediator of the new covenant, promised so long before (Jer. 31:31-34). They were in on the beginning of a new future for the human race — a future in which salvation would be preached to every nation and the Messiah would save his people from their sins! (Matt. 1:21).

The uniqueness of the disciples' experience only makes our privileges greater still. For them, much remained to be revealed. Christ had still to die and rise again from the dead. The Holy Spirit had yet to be poured out upon the church. The New Testament was as yet still only an intention in the mind of God. For us, the revelation of Christ and his atonement for sin is accomplished reality. How much more ought we to desire to be his followers! How much more earnest should our thirst be for the knowledge of his truth and the joy of his salvation! How much warmer should our love be for the lost and how much more urgent our zeal to reach them for Christ! And for the unconverted, who know nothing of Christ as a Saviour, how much less excuse there is for unbelief! As long as the world lasts, the parables will call people to faith in Christ. Their very simplicity shines brightly with the gracious invitation to repent, to believe and to be reconciled to God, through the same Jesus who first uttered them so long ago. He still calls, 'Hear me, that your soul may live!' (Isa. 55:3).

2.
The message of the kingdom

The parable of the sower
(Matt. 13:1-9,18-23)

'But the one who received the seed that fell on good soil is the man who hears the word and understands it' (Matt. 13:23).

Jesus calls his first recorded parable 'the parable of the sower', but it is more a story about soils than about a sower. Through the interplay of the sower, the seed and the soils, Jesus shows us the different ways in which people respond to the message of the kingdom — the preaching of the gospel. In addition, Jesus gives us his own interpretation of the parable — something he did only twice — and so not only makes it easy for us to understand what he is saying, but also provides us with a model for our approach to his other, unexplained parables. What is striking is that he does not find spiritual truths in every detail of the story, but focuses only upon the central themes. This reminds us that parables are meant to be simple and usually teach one main lesson. Following Jesus' example, we ought to resist the temptation to come up with over-elaborate explanations and applications. Parables are meant to be simple!

Who is the sower?

The parable of the sower did not fall out of a clear blue sky. It was set in a context. Jesus had already been healing the sick and teaching the people. Some had even asked if he were the 'Son of David' (Matt. 12:23). Jesus had identified himself as the 'Son of Man' — the promised Messiah — and told them that 'Whoever does the will

of my Father in heaven is my brother and sister and mother' (Matt.
12:50). It was on **'that same day'** that he preached to the crowds
from a boat (13:1). Everybody there knew what Jesus had done and
said and they were hanging on his every word. It was inevitable that
whatever he said would be a comment on the meaning of the events
of that day. He **'told them many things in parables'**, beginning
with the parable of the sower: **'A farmer went out to sow his seed'**
(13:3).

The seed fell on four main types of 'soil'. The birds got the seed
on the **'path'**; the plants that grew on **'rocky places'** withered for
lack of soil; those that germinated **'among thorns'** were choked;
while the seed that fell on **'good soil'** produced crops, **'a hundred,
sixty or thirty times what was sown'** (13:4-8). Then he added the
earnest call: **'He who has ears, let him hear'** (13:9).

Who, then, is this farmer who sows his seed? Well, who had been
teaching the crowds and healing the sick? Most obviously and
immediately it was Jesus himself! He had been declaring **'the
message of the kingdom'** in word and deed all that day (13:19,37).
He was interpreting his own ministry! He was sowing seed for God.
He was spreading it around — not neatly, in set rows, as with a
modern seed-drill, but widely and promiscuously, as with the
sweeping action of a sower of that time. Perhaps the disciples
wondered why Jesus travelled the country preaching in this place
and that, rather than heading for Jerusalem to take over the world in
a blaze of Messianic power. Perhaps they chafed under the relative
lack of success in Jesus' ministry. For all the miracles and the
crowds, there was also much opposition and Jesus himself kept
retreating from the public eye (cf. Matt. 12:14-15). If that was how
they felt, and they had 'ears to hear', then Jesus was giving them a
dose of realism about the nature of his mission. His kingdom was
coming in with seeds, not swords; with thoughts, not triumphs; with
changed lives, not conquered capitals.

The 'sower' also included by implication the disciples themselves and every one of 'God's fellow-workers' (1 Cor. 3:9). It is the
church in her public ministry — the appointed agents of the Lord
declaring his Word — and encompasses the corporate witness of the
whole church for the truth of God. 'The sower,' says J. A. Alexander, 'is generic, meaning the whole class, or an ideal individual who
represents it.'[1]

What is the seed?

According to the parallel account in Luke's Gospel (8:11), the seed is 'the word of God'. This is the same as 'the message of the kingdom' in Matthew. Therefore, the 'seed' is not to be thought of as just one part of God's message — a so-called 'evangelistic' message extracted from the Word as a whole. One of the most pervasive errors of the modern church is the notion that most of Scripture and the preaching of sermons in the churches is reserved for building up those who have already become believers. 'Evangelism' is then locked up with what happens outside regular worship — with a narrow range of Scripture texts, with personal witnessing, evangelistic 'fish-pond' social events and so-called 'seeker services'. In the New Testament, the seed is the full-orbed message of God's Word, all of it centred in Jesus Christ as the only Saviour of the lost. It was no accident that the two on the road to Emmaus were shown by the risen Jesus himself 'what was said in all the Scriptures concerning himself' (Luke 24:25-27).

It is this seed, says Peter, that brings people to the new birth: 'For you have been born again, not of perishable seed, but of imperishable, through the living and enduring word of God. For,

> '"All men are like grass
>   and all their glory is like the flowers of the field;
> the grass withers and the flowers fall,
>   but the word of the Lord stands for ever"

'And this is the word that was preached to you' (1 Peter 1:23-25; Isa. 40:6-8). The apostle deliberately draws a parallel, by way of antithesis, between the living, eternal fruit of the spiritual word-seed and the transient crops of earthly seeds. This contrast is clearly designed to highlight the point that the Word of God is a life-giving seed to be implanted in the very being of those who hear it and receive the message of salvation in Jesus Christ. It is a seed that saves.

What are the soils?

It is obvious that the 'soil' in general is the human heart, and that the soils in particular represent different states of the human heart.

Soil in general

The soil is the world. It is the human race — the children of Adam in need of a Saviour. More specifically, the soil represents the hearers of the gospel. So the seed of the Word is to be scattered over the world and a hearing to be sought from everybody under heaven. This, then, provides for God's ploughing of the hearers' hearts by his Word and Holy Spirit. The problem is, of course, that the soil is not uniformly ready to receive the seed. There is good soil and there is bad soil. The bad soil is of three types — the 'path', the 'rocky places' and the 'thorns'. The good soil is the soil of the farmer's fields. A parallel is maintained between the bad and the good, in the three levels of fruitfulness in the latter — it yields 'a hundred, sixty or thirty times what was sown'.

Ultimately, this distinction between good and bad soils corresponds to the difference between believers and unbelievers, between the regenerate and the unregenerate, the elect and the reprobate, the saved and the lost. Everyone who steadfastly responds to Jesus Christ in bad-soil ways, never repents and dies in that condition, will be eternally lost. Conversely, good-soil hearers will be saved. Remain a bad-soil hearer, then, and you will stay lost and go to hell for ever under the just condemnation of the holy God whom you have rejected. Standing darkly in the background of the parable is the question of the eternal destiny of sinners. This is true and it cannot be escaped, but it is not the main subject of the parable.

The primary thrust of the parable is not to discuss our eternal destiny as such, but simply to describe how people respond now to the message of the kingdom of God. The fact is that we cannot look into people's hearts. We do not see them as elect or reprobate, but just as sinners responding positively or negatively to the claims of Christ. In any case, sin still clings to the elect, so that in practice even true believers can at times be bad-soil hearers. Jesus' application is therefore all the more pointed, because it does not allow Christians to say that what he says about the bad soil does not apply to them. Rather, it confronts Christians with the questions: 'Are you what you profess to be? Are you in practical reality a good-soil hearer? Do you receive the Word of God with gladness? Is there fruit in you — thirty, sixty or a hundred-fold? Or are there problems to be dealt with?' Jesus wants his hearers to realize where they actually stand with him and, from that point, to go forward to faith and spiritual growth, for fruitfulness is the only proof of a changed and receptive heart. Bad-soil responses are unbelieving — and if you see such attitudes in yourself at all, then Jesus is calling you to repentance and faith. Good-soil response is simply the way in which former bad-soil hearers are brought by God's grace to a new and living faith. Jesus' purpose is at once to explain why people respond as they do and to call any who are listening to him to waste no time in embracing him as their Saviour.

Bad-soil hearers (13:19-22)

Jesus began his explanation of the parable by describing three categories of bad-soil hearers.

1. The path (13:19). Fields in Palestine were small and separated from one another by paths where the soil was beaten flat and hard as concrete under human feet and the summer sun. As the sower walked down the field, some seed landed on this impenetrable soil and the birds would swoop down and pick it up. This, says Jesus, is a picture of the person who **'hears the message about the kingdom ... does not understand it'** and **'the evil one comes and snatches away what was sown in his heart'** (13:19). In such cases, the lack of understanding is the fault of neither the message nor the messenger. In a basic sense, the hearers do know what is being said. They know the meaning of the words, sentences and concepts. The point is that it all means nothing to them, it has no attraction to them, no claim upon them; they are just not interested and are therefore unresponsive.

Many, probably the vast majority, of unconverted people are like this. They can be the nicest people, but to them church is a bore and they just have no interest in the gospel. Their minds are on other things. They have other commitments and they do not listen out of any zeal to learn from Christ or change their ways. They don't even know that they have let Satan come and snatch the seed away!

But professing Christians, too, can take the same attitude. They can be spiritually torpid. Nothing seems to move them, except maybe to switch them off. Maybe it is a particular teaching (or any 'doctrine'?), or certain passages of Scripture (especially from the Old Testament?), or a passionate emphasis on practical godliness. Minds drift, and Satan plucks the seed away. It all eventually comes down to the question: when is a Christian really a Christian?

2. The rocky places (13:5-6,20-21). This was not ground with stones in it, but a thin layer of soil on an underlying layer of rock. Seeds would get into it, germinate and grow, but the plants could never get good roots. When the sun beat down, they withered and died.

This is the hearer who receives the message **'with joy'**. He is so instantly enthusiastic that he almost seems too good to be true. And we rejoice in what seems to be a wonderful conversion to Christ. But wait a minute! He suffers some ridicule at work from his old pals. The cost of being a Christian speedily mounts up. And soon the Lord, the Bible and the church are seen as the source of his troubles. He **'lasts only a short time'**. He never really had the root of the matter in him. Such folks never were 'deeply convinced of sin, nor felt their need of Christ', remarked Charles Simeon, and they renounce their 'profession as speedily as they had taken it up'. They either quietly slip away from their new-found fellowship or 'openly proclaim the disgust, with which their late pretensions [had] inspired them'.[2] Their 'faith' was superficial and temporary, its falsity exposed by the tests of life.

3. The thorns (13:7,22). This was soil that had not been cleared of weeds, so that the good seed never got established. It grew a little, but was soon choked. This is the person who is preoccupied with **'the worries of this life and the deceitfulness of wealth'**. Luke and Mark add a third element, respectively that of 'pleasures', or 'the desire for other things' (Luke 8:14; Mark 4:19). These are the weeds in the soul that leave no place for Jesus. The reason is obvious. Worries, wealth and things are all centred in self. They all relate to personal security and comfort. That it is all illusion, and Christ is the only true security, matters not. The weed-choked man is willing to listen, up to a point. But nothing comes of it. He always puts it off. Like the rich man in the parable of the rich fool, he is too busy worrying about the economics of retirement to give attention to his eternal destiny.

Good-soil hearers (13:8-9,23)

The three levels of fruitfulness in the good soil contrast with the three varieties of bad soil.

1. 'Good soil' does not make itself good. To be 'good soil' in the first place, the ground had to have been ploughed and manured. It was not always good. Indeed, it may once have been hard like the path, infertile like a rocky place, or choked with weeds. It had to be prepared to receive the seed. This is the first work of the Holy Spirit. The soil was made broken and soft, not compacted like the path; it was made deep and fertile, not like the rocky ground; and it was cleared and weeded, in contrast to the weed patch. The human heart that is prepared by the gracious strivings of the Spirit of God is not hard and unresponsive, uninterested in the message, or bored by the Word of God. Neither is it merely impulsive, showing a spurious temporary infatuation with the gospel, while the mood lasts. Nor is it preoccupied by worldly fears and desires. This heart, like the ploughed and harrowed field, is burdened only with an unformed openness to the overtures of grace. Such a person has 'an ear to hear' and he listens. This is never an innate capacity; it is a work of God's sovereign grace.

2. 'Good soil' receives the seed. The good soil **'is the man who hears the word and understands it'**. He accepts it, according to its plain meaning, and he does so from the heart. He understands what he is doing. His is an intelligent faith. He knows the facts of the gospel, he accepts them as true in his innermost being and he trusts the one of whom they speak. He receives Christ as his Saviour and as his Lord.

3. 'Good soil' bears fruit. 'Fruit,' said Jesus, is 'showing your-selves to be my disciples' (John 15:8). It is 'all goodness, righteous-ness and truth ... what pleases the Lord' (Eph. 5:9-10). It is the 'fruit of the Spirit ... love, joy, peace, patience, kindness, goodness, faithfulness, gentleness and self-control' (Gal. 5:22). 'We then bear fruit,' observes Matthew Henry, 'when we practise according to the word; when the temper of our minds and the tenor of our lives are conformable to the gospel we have received, and we do as we are taught.'[3] Grace in the heart and obedience with the hands are the growing points of spiritual fruit.

Finally, Jesus notes that *good soils vary in fruitfulness:* **'He produces a crop, yielding a hundred, sixty or thirty times what was sown.'** Jesus takes us from the sowing to the harvest, from the beginning of faith to the end of the life lived for Christ. The point is that there is always a harvest. He does not tell us why some believers have more richly productive lives than others. His purpose is not to make invidious comparisons, or to suggest that some believers are inherently better than others. His purpose is rather to describe, simply and accurately and without prejudice, the fact that Christians have different experiences of effectiveness in their life and witness, whatever the reasons might be. Some live in times of spiritual revival, others labour as a persecuted minority. Times and personal circumstances vary. True, Christians can sin away much of their potential usefulness. But criticism and blame are not in Jesus' mind.

Rather, encouragement and challenge ring in his assurance that, whatever betide, there will be fruit in every believer's life. 'This final fate of the Word,' says R. C. H. Lenski, ' is shown to us now, so that we may examine ourselves as to how we are treating the Word now, before life is done. And this is done because, though no man can change himself, God has means to change us all (trodden path, rocky places, briar patches) into good soil for his Word. This means of God is the Word itself as exhibited in this very parable. Like all the Scriptural revelations of man's sinful state, this one too, aims at the conscience and repentance, thus opening the soul for the gospel. And the more it is opened, the more fruit will there be in the end.'[4]

Notice also the precise nature of the comparison: one seed gives rise to thirty, sixty and a hundred — of what? Seeds! A little leads to a lot, both inwardly in terms of the fruit of the Spirit, and outwardly in the planting of the seed in other lives. The plants become sowers too, just by their changed lives! Their seed falls on different soils and another generation of good soil is by grace brought into being and, in due course, fruitfulness. The message of the kingdom is the good news of transformed lives, through saving faith in Jesus Christ, the great Sower of the seed. The challenge, of course, is to face the questions: 'What kind of a hearer are you? What kind of soil are you?' You know what your real attitude to God's Word and God's Son is. Whatever other people see, whatever impression you give, you know inside whether you love Jesus and thirst for growth in his grace, or whether, like the bad-soil hearers, you are preoccupied with other commitments. Jesus is calling you to repentance, to faith, to new life, to fruitfulness and, afterwards, to

3.
The two seeds in the kingdom

The parable of the weeds
(Matt. 13:25-30, 36-43)

'Jesus told them another parable, "The kingdom of heaven is like a man who sowed good seed in his field. But while everyone was sleeping his enemy came and sowed weeds among the wheat, and went away"'(Matt. 13:24).

The continuing presence of evil in the world is very troubling to many people. You will frequently hear the questions: 'If God is good, why does evil exist? If there is a God, why is there so much wickedness?' Most often, these questions are asked by those who would reason, with massive illogicality, that the existence of evil proves the non-existence of God. (Think about it — it simply does not follow!) But not infrequently the question why evil is allowed to exist is asked by honest Christians, crying out in the anguish of some terrible personal tragedy. We want to see an end to every evil, because evil is the contradiction of the goodness of God. Evil is not an abstraction. It is inseparable from *people* — people who do wicked things openly and apparently without any conscience, and other people who suffer as a result. Why does a good God allow people to do bad things? Is there to be no end of it, no relief from the oppressiveness of human sin in this world? These are the cries of many a human heart.

This is never more distressing, even bewildering, than when it happens in the church. Manifest, unrepented sin in those who profess to be Christians gives us serious pause. How is it that even in the *church* — the primary visible manifestation of the kingdom of heaven upon earth — we have such contradictions? Why is it that so much of what calls itself the church is so obviously committed to denying that the Bible is truly God's Word and shamelessly

espouses positions and practices contrary to God's revealed will?[1]
Why are there so many false gospels going around? Why does God
permit people to twist and pervert the true gospel of his Son? Why
does God not sweep away all this confusion and error so that the
work of his kingdom can be seen to be what it is supposed to be —
a unified testimony to Christ, making a 'clear call' on the gospel
trumpet? (cf. 1 Cor. 14:8). After all, it would surely be much
simpler, less confusing and more fruitful, if all who claimed to
belong to Christ actually proclaimed the one true gospel and lived
the truly Christian life.

It is to answer questions like these, I believe, that Jesus tells his
hearers the parable of the weeds — better known in the past as the
parable of 'the wheat and the tares'. He does so not merely to inform
us of realities of which we are already well aware — namely, that
the world and the church are awash in sins and contradictions. He
means rather to encourage his followers with the realization that all
these things — false gospels, heresies, cults, evil deeds — cannot
actually hinder the gospel, but are in spite of themselves serving the
purposes of God's plan of redemption for a lost world!

The story, like all parables, has a number of simple elements.
There are two sowers and two seeds, a field and a harvest.

The two seeds and their sowers (13:24-26,37-38)

The story is that a man **'sowed good seed in his field'**, but an enemy
came while he was asleep and sowed **'weeds among the wheat'**.
When this later came to light, the question was raised as to how the
weeds got there and whether they should be pulled up. The farmer's
answer was that this would damage the good plants, so they should
wait till harvest and then separate the crop — the weeds for the fire
and the wheat for the barn (13:24-30).

As with his parable of the sower and the soils, Jesus here
interprets the story (13:36-43). The **'good seed'**, he says, **'stands
for the sons of the kingdom,'** whereas **'The weeds are the sons of
the evil one'** (13:38).

The good seed (13:37,38)

The **'good seed'**, planted by **'the Son of Man'**, represents those who
are truly converted to Christ. They repented towards God and

believed in the Lord Jesus Christ (Acts 20:21). They were saved by grace through faith in Christ as the only mediator between God and man (Eph. 2:8; 1 Tim. 2:5). They love the Lord from the heart (Rom. 5:5). They walk in the light as he is in the light (1 John 1:7). They strive to avoid fellowship with the unfruitful works of darkness (Eph. 5:11). They are the citizens of the kingdom of heaven (Eph. 2:19-20). They confess the lordship of Christ over their lives (John 20:28). They will never be plucked out of Jesus' hand (John 10:28-29). This is what it means to be **'sons of the kingdom'**. These are the elect of God. Jesus is speaking about those whom he is saving from their sins — the redeemed of the Lord.

The weeds (13:38-39)

The **'weeds'** are **'the sons of the evil one'**, sown by **'the devil'**. These are the lost people, although at first they are indistinguishable from the wheat in the farmer's field.[2] As they grow to maturity, it becomes evident they are useless weeds. 'By their fruit you will recognize them,' said Jesus of false prophets (Matt. 7:16). There was no good fruit. These weeds are the reprobate lost, the children of their father, the devil.

Jesus' perspective, you will notice, is the *ultimate destiny* of the lost and the saved. He sees what we cannot see — the heart of every individual — and he gives us the simplified view of the battle between light and darkness in human history. What Jesus is showing the disciples is that, just as God is doing the work of saving sinners to himself in this world, so Satan is actively labouring to claim sinners for himself and keep them lost for all eternity. In practice, this means that where the kingdom of heaven is most active — i.e., where the Lord is changing lives and saving lost people — there the evil one will also be doing his utmost to defeat the purposes of God (Matt. 24:24; 1 Peter 5:8).

Turning opposition into encouragement

Opposition need not engender an attitude of 'gloom and doom'. It is in a sense a proof that the work of God is going forward. 'Woe to you,' Jesus warns us, 'when all men speak well of you, for that is how their fathers treated the false prophets' (Luke 6:26). On the other hand, 'Blessed are those who are persecuted because of righteousness, for theirs is the kingdom of heaven' (Matt. 5:10). The fact that there is a darkness in the world that is resistant to the witness of the light of Jesus Christ must not be treated as a cause for discouragement and frustration, but as a ground for encouragement and a stimulus to persevering discipleship. To the eye of faith, the presence of 'weeds' is a harbinger of victory, not defeat. In the same way that Napoleon's marshals had standing orders to march towards 'the sound of the guns', the presence of blinded, lost and hell-bent sinners is the Christian's call to God's victorious struggle with the enemy of all our souls!

The field (3:24,38)

In the parable, the sower sowed good seed, but his enemy came to the field at night and sowed the weeds. A mixed crop eventually grew up in the field. But what is this field?

Jesus tells us that **'The field is the world'** (13:38). But what is meant by 'the world'? A number of answers have been proposed.

Some have suggested that it is the world *as distinct from the church*. The argument is that since Jesus here teaches that the weeds are *not* to be uprooted, but elsewhere teaches that there *ought* to be discipline in the church, he must be referring exclusively to the world outside the church. On this basis, R. C. H. Lenski argues that it is therefore not the role of the church to purge the world of sinners[3] — an entirely unexceptionable point in itself, because Scripture teaches elsewhere that the sword is given to the civil magistrate and not the church (Rom. 13:1-7). Jesus, however, is not talking about what the *church* may or may not do with respect to the lost. He is discussing why *God* lets 'the world' go on as a mixture of light and darkness, righteous and unrighteous, saved and lost until the very end of history. Those who want to use this parable to teach something about the *policy* that the church ought to adopt towards the unbelieving world are missing the point and reading into the text something that just is not there! The parable simply describes *what* the church has to face while the world lasts, *why* this is so, and *where* it will lead in the end.

It should be clear enough that 'the world' (= the field) is not to be understood in the widest possible sense — the whole created world, planet Earth — as if Jesus were merely teaching that the world consisted of good people and bad people and we should accept that, because we can do nothing about it.[4] The disciples hardly needed to be taught such an obvious lesson — they knew there would be wickedness, and to spare, while the world lasted and did not entertain any airy notions that they would purge the world of it all!

What the disciples did assume was that the Messiah's kingdom would sweep over the whole Jewish community and then lead on to greater things for God's people in the world at large. But Jesus was not sweeping all before him. If his kingdom had come, it was definitely not an all-conquering phenomenon, even among the Jews! Jesus answered the immediate perplexity of the disciples. Accordingly, his reply centred on the narrower question of the condition of the kingdom of heaven as it became an established presence in the world. The 'field', then, is the world viewed as *the sphere of operations of the kingdom of heaven*. Notice that the sowing of the weeds takes place in the particular field in which the Lord is working, and in direct response to his work of building his kingdom. The focus is on what happens in the world wherever the gospel is preached. As the kingdom of God develops, the evil one sees to it that he infiltrates it with his own people! He makes his counter-moves *within* the sphere of the kingdom of God. This sphere is the 'field/world' in the parable. Hence, whenever Christ is preached, antichrists arise (2 John 7). Whenever the truth of God is preached, heresies are proclaimed to draw people away from the Lord. Why is it that what used to be called 'Christendom' is so divided? This is the fundamental reason. What may be called, externally and in the widest sense, God's kingdom upon earth — what calls itself 'the church' — has 'weeds' planted in its midst, weeds that are openly in opposition to the teaching of the Word of God. The Christian's immediate world — not the pagan, unevangelized world yet to be penetrated with the gospel, but the world where Christ is building his kingdom — is a world of wheat and weeds, a world of conflicting voices and contradictory actions *within* the sphere, in the broadest sense, of the kingdom of God.

Turning a confusing situation into hope

Christians do worry about this subject. It bothers them that not all who call themselves 'Christians' bear much resemblance to the Bible's description of real discipleship to Christ. It distresses them that many of the clergy in the dying establishment churches are no better than chaplains of humanism, espousing the going brands of secularism baptized with anti-supernaturalist God-talk — no more than a hollow simulation of the true religion of the Bible. The effect of Jesus' parable of the weeds, however, must be to rebuke our fears. It puts the work of the devil in proper perspective: 'Don't lose hope over the fact that the world is littered with spiritually dead and dying denominations and churches blighted by false teachers and hypocritical members. Your calling is to hold up the truth as it is in Jesus and fight the good fight of faith, with the assurance that God is seeing to it that his light will never be put out, whatever the efforts of the enemy.'

However thick the weeds, the field is *the Lord's*! Christians must never let the confusing and conflicting voices on every hand scare them into thinking that they are engaged in a hopeless struggle. The gospel really is *simple*. The doctrines of God's grace really are *plain*. You *can* grasp the truth, however simple you think you are and however clever the Bible's critics may appear to be. Satan wants us to lose hope and say to ourselves, 'I don't know what to believe!' He wants us to say, 'It doesn't really matter what you believe; we all pray to the same God anyway.' (It does, and we don't!) Satan is out to turn true churches into 'synagogues of Satan' (Rev. 2:9; 3:9). He will try, he will have some spectacular successes, but he will always fail in the end. Our danger is our challenge, but it is also the measure of our victory in Christ our Saviour, for God has 'placed all things under his feet' (Eph. 1:22).

What is the harvest? (13:27-30,40-43)

In the parable, the owner's servants see the weeds growing in the wheat and ask him if he wants them pulled out. He says no, and gives as his reason the danger that pulling out the weeds at this stage would uproot the wheat as well. He would rather '**let them grow until harvest**'.

The problem that the servants discerned is obvious enough in its application to God's kingdom on earth. The kingdom looks as if it needs purging. Side by side in the sphere of God's kingdom work are true churches and false churches, the faithful and the heretical, the ignorant and the confused. Surely error, hypocrisy and confusion should be eliminated and purity established and maintained? 'No!' says the Lord. 'Strange as it may seem, it is better to leave them where they are until harvest.'

Why the weeds can be left till harvest (13:27-30)

The weeds, as we noted above, were to be left to grow among the wheat, because to do otherwise **'might root up the wheat with them'** (13:29). That is to say, the presence of sinners and their sins, of false churches and their heresies, does not harm the true cause of Jesus Christ as much as their attempted extirpation would! Why so? No doubt many reasons could be advanced.

For one, we have seen from history what happened when, in the name of God, even godly powers attempted to extirpate all heresies by the power of the sword.[5] Woes were multiplied, not only for the parties involved but for succeeding generations.

Another answer is that the presence of the 'weeds' causes the true church to refine her doctrine and witness. Real Christians do better at 'working out their salvation' in 'fear and trembling' in a context where opposition is active than they would were there no opposition at all! As the 'weeds' teach, preach and live out their rebellion against the Lord, God's own people see the issues more clearly, form their witness more carefully and give themselves all the more earnestly to the work of the gospel in a world that they see is perishing for want of a Saviour.

Not least, it is simply a fact that Christians are not called to execute God's judgements on the 'weeds'. Notice, however, that this does not contradict the need for church discipline (Matt. 18:15-20; 1 Cor. 5). Jesus' parable does not address the responsibilities of particular churches for the faithfulness of their ministers and members. It looks rather at the broader picture of the professing church in the world, both the true and the false. The point is that God has his own 'reapers', the angels, who are charged with the task of separating the 'sheep' from the 'goats'. This is not our task. We are not capable of searching people's hearts; we are not commissioned to purge the earth of the antichrists and false teachers. That is God's work, not ours.

The harvest of human history (13:40-43)

This harvest, says Jesus, is **'at the end of the age'** (13:40). God 'will send his angels with a loud trumpet call, and they will gather his elect from the four winds' (Matt. 24:31; cf. Rev. 14:14-20). The angels will also **'weed out of his kingdom everything that causes sin and all who do evil'** (13:41). History is maturing to a harvest which, when it is complete, will give way to a final reckoning, a day of judgement.[6] The harvest — pre-eminently the gathering in of the Lord's truly believing people — also involves the filling up of the winepress of God's wrath (Joel 3:13; Isa. 63:3). Three fundamental doctrines of God's Word are taught in these words of our Lord.

The first is the doctrine of *the final judgement*.[7] 'What a wonderful but awful separation will there then be!' wrote Charles Simeon. 'Among the tares [weeds], not so much as one grain of wheat will be found. The ungodly husband shall be torn from the arms of his compassionate wife, and the profane child from the bosom of his religious parent. God will show no respect to one rather than another. The wicked, stript of their veils, will be consigned over to punishment; and the righteous, freed from mutual jealousies, shall unite in perfect harmony.'[8]

The second is the doctrine of *eternal punishment*.[9] The first to go will be the persistent unbelievers, the reprobate lost, those who die in their sins with neither repentance towards God nor faith in the Lord Jesus Christ. **'First collect the weeds and tie them in bundles to be burned... As the weeds are pulled up and burned in the fire, so it will be at the end of the age'** (13:30,40). The 'fire' is not the divine incinerator of the annihilationists,[10] but the undying wrath of God against unrepentant sinners — the same kind of wrath poured out upon the Lord Jesus Christ as he hung upon the cross and took it in the place of all those he would save from their sins. A lost eternity is far from being eternal non-existence. That is precisely what consistent atheists want — a life with no more after it than silent, painless non-being, devoid of justice and the retributive anger of a holy and offended God. The real destiny of the lost consists in palpable, inescapable justice for their high treason against the God who called them to repentance to no avail. There will be **'weeping and gnashing of teeth'** (13:42) — the anguish of unrelieved regret and self-pity, beyond all recall, removed even from the slightest desire to repent, but eternally wedded to the consequences of utter separation from God.

Isaac Asimov, the atheist science-fiction writer, used to say that if there were a heaven, he would not enjoy being there. He was quite correct. Unbelief hates the idea of heaven hereafter, just as it hates obeying the Lord's will here and now. But hell will not go away because sceptics don't like the idea. Sooner or later, but always for ever, God's justice will be served with perfect righteousness.

The third is the doctrine of *the eternal blessedness of believers.*[11] For those who have trusted in Christ as their Saviour, eternity is salvation completed. **'Then the rightcous will shine like the sun in the kingdom of their Father'** (13:43).

In his oratorio, *Elijah*, Felix Mendelssohn brilliantly uses this verse to tie in the career of the prophet with those of the second Elijah, John the Baptizer, and the Messiah to whom he was a forerunner. In this way, he brings out the fact that Christ is the ultimate meaning of Elijah's ministry, and glorious redemption is the meaning of Christ's ministry for all who come to him in faith. So, Mendelssohn has the tenor sing:

> Then shall the righteous shine forth
> > as the sun in their heavenly Father's realm.
> Joy on their head shall be for everlasting,
> > and all sorrow and mourning shall flee away for ever
> > > > (Matt. 13:43; Isa. 51:11).

Then, after a chorus in which prophetic reference is made to the advent of Christ from Isaiah 41:25; 42:1 and 51:2, the contralto sings the very call of the gospel:

> O come, everyone that thirsteth,
> O come to the waters:
> O come unto Him.
> O hear, and your souls shall live for ever
> > > > (Isa. 55:1,3).

The oratorio ends with a mighty evocation of the everlasting blessedness of the saints in heaven: 'And then shall your light break forth...' The composer catches the theological transition in the text with marvellous verve, not to mention discernment. The struggles of Elijah become the victories of Christ. In the parable, the 'wheat' becomes 'light', shining with the unquenchable glory of redemption in Jesus Christ! The shift from the imagery of the field and harvest to that of the sun blazing with glory lifts us from the present experience of the church in a fallen world to the future destiny of the elect in glory and emphasizes the activity of God's people as they participate in the unhindered praise of God, face to face in the presence of his majesty!

The parable of the weeds calls us to fix our eyes on God's purpose of grace and live out our lives from the perspective of the glory yet to be revealed at the end of the age. 'What is your only comfort in life and in death?' asks the *Heidelberg Catechism*. The answer comes: 'That I am not my own, but belong — body and soul, in life and in death — to my faithful Saviour Jesus Christ... Because I belong to him, Christ, by his Holy Spirit, assures me of eternal life and makes me wholeheartedly willing and ready from now on to live for him.' From now on, I can live into the future as it unfolds day by day, because my Saviour is Lord both of all these days and of the harvest at the end of the age in which he will take me to glory with all his people.

4.
The growth of the kingdom

The parables of the mustard seed and the yeast
(Matt. 13:31-33)

'The kingdom of heaven is like a mustard seed, which a man took and planted in his field. Though it is the smallest of all your seeds, yet when it grows, it is the largest of garden plants and becomes a tree...' (Matt. 13:31-32).

It must have disconcerted the disciples that, for all Jesus' preaching about the coming of the kingdom of God, there was little evidence of its growth and development into any kind of a tangible presence. People were suitably amazed at Jesus' preaching and healing, but this did not translate into any apparent, cohesive, emerging power for the kingdom of which he spoke. This, as we know, continued throughout Jesus' ministry and certainly contributed significantly to the discouragement of the disciples at the time of his death on the cross. Even then, after three years of ministry, no more than 120 believers were to be found in Jerusalem! We can understand the disciples asking why large numbers of people did not believe Jesus' message; or why the kingdom of darkness was allowed to exist alongside God's kingdom (this was answered by the parable of the weeds, Matt. 13:24-30); or why God's kingdom was not growing and beginning to take over society.

These are, of course, the kind of questions Jesus anticipated, and answered, in his parables. The parables of the mustard seed and the yeast form a pair that give us two closely related perspectives on the question of the growth and advancement of God's kingdom and should therefore be considered together. The former — the mustard seed — deals with the visible, outward growth of the kingdom, while the latter — the yeast — focuses on the kingdom's invisible, inward extension.

Promise of growth

The parable of the *mustard seed* (13:31-32) has the same basic elements as the two earlier parables — those of the sower and the weeds. The sower stands for the ministry of the Word of God, the seed is the Word and the field is the world in which the work of the kingdom of God is being done. This sees the impact of the gospel of Christ in history as a 'farmer's year', from sowing, through the growing season, to the harvest. The present age — from the first advent of Christ to his second coming at the end of the age — is that growing season, in which the little seed becomes a great tree. All of human history, then, offers a prospect of visible advance for the kingdom of God.

The parable of the *yeast* (13:33) views this same progress in terms of its inward aspect. There is a 'sowing' — an implantation — of the yeast in a large lump of dough. By analogy with the agricultural model of the mustard seed story, the yeast is the Word of God, while the dough is the world. This contrasts with the use of yeast elsewhere in Scripture as illustrative of a corrupting influence (Matt. 16:11; Luke 12:1; 1 Cor. 5:7-8; Gal. 5:9), because here it represents the transforming influence of the gospel. This quietly and invisibly proliferates and extends itself inexorably throughout the dough until its work is complete. The emphasis is surely upon the transformation of human hearts, by the regeneration of the Holy Spirit and sanctification by the Word, accompanied by the Spirit. 'The leaven must be hid in the heart (Ps.119:11)...,' observes Matthew Henry. 'When the woman hides the leaven in the meal, it is with an intention that it should communicate its taste and relish to it; so we must treasure up the word in our souls, that we may be sanctified by it (John 17:17).'[1]

The overall thrust of both parables is quite plain: *from small beginnings* the work of God in the world grows and extends until his eternal purpose is completed. The Lord Jesus Christ then returns to judge the living and the dead and inaugurate the final and eternal glory of his consummated kingdom. From one perspective, this growth will be *phenomenal* — Jesus' dominion would eventually extend from sea to sea and to the uttermost ends of the earth (Ps. 72:8). This was all in the future as far as Jesus' immediate disciples were concerned, and so had the distinct character of a promise yet to be fulfilled. For us, the promise remains, but in the context of two thousand years of God's mighty works in human history and a fearful, ongoing, see-sawing battle between the powers of darkness and the light of saving grace in the gospel of Jesus Christ. From another perspective, the kingdom grows *quietly* in the hearts of people who come to believe in Christ as their Saviour. The absence, much of the time, of spectacular gains for the gospel, is never to take away from us the assurance that God is at work, his kingdom is on the move in the world and that each day brings us closer to the completion of the work of redemption and the Second Coming of Jesus Christ.

Patterns of growth

Jesus may have assured the disciples that God's kingdom was growing, but they might well have asked, 'Where is the evidence of this growth, even now, even admitting we are at the beginning of this great work of God?' No doubt anticipating this question, Jesus sketched out for them a threefold pattern by which the kingdom would advance in the world: from insignificant beginnings, through substantial growth to eventual maturation. Here was what to look for, in assessing the progress of the gospel.

Insignificant beginnings (13:31-32)

'The kingdom of heaven,' says Jesus, **'is like a mustard seed, which a man took and planted in his field'** (13:31). The mustard seed was proverbially the **'smallest'** seed in the farmer's inventory (13:32); hence the saying: 'If you have faith as small as a mustard seed, you can say to this mountain, "Move from here to there" and it will move' (Matt. 17:20).

The idea of *smallness* is the vital element. The mustard seed is the Word of God — the same as Peter's 'incorruptible seed' by which sinners are 'born again' (1 Peter 1:23-25) — and the diminutive character of the seed conveys the practical truth that the gospel always has small, relatively inconspicuous beginnings. The historical emergence of the apostolic church would later confirm this truth, but it is also true with every new beginning of the gospel in the lives of people and communities. How did you, if you are a Christian, first come to be influenced by the gospel? Was that first contact almost imperceptibly insignificant at the time?

I can trace my own eventual coming to faith to a moment a year or two earlier, when it first crossed my mind that I just might not be the Christian I had always imagined myself to be. It was in a shop-front meeting-place used by the Edinburgh University Christian Union, borrowed on Friday afternoons by George Heriot's School Scripture Union group, of which I was then a brand new attender.[2] I heard the speaker say — it was from Ephesians 2:1, 'You were dead in your transgressions and sins' — that there were live people walking around in the streets who were actually dead. That went through me like an arrow. Maybe I was spiritually dead too! I managed to set this disquieting thought aside at the time, but it came back to niggle me until, in a different setting altogether I came, I believe, to trust in Christ as my Saviour.[3]

Even those who have had a dramatic conversion to Christ can look back and see that the first seeds of gospel truth were planted years before, perhaps in a mother's quiet testimony, a verse of Scripture memorized, a 'chance' encounter on the street or in any of a myriad of ways.

This is the way, Jesus says, that the gospel of the kingdom starts out in the world. Jesus himself did not arrive as a king, but as a carpenter's son. How triumphant did his kingdom look at Golgotha? Yet soon there was a Pentecost and, down the centuries, millions have been gathered into the kingdom. And seeds are being sown somewhere all the time.

Furthermore, you will notice that this was *a* mustard seed — just *one* seed! Christ plants the one gospel of salvation in and through his perfect atoning sacrifice for sin. From that 'one act of righteousness' flows 'justification that brings life for all men' for whom he died (Rom. 5:18). Christ's cross did not seem like an earth-shaking event to most of the people who stood around watching his dying agonies. Yet it was the seed that changed the world.

Significant growth (13:32)

The mustard plant — probably the black mustard, *Brassica nigra*, is the variety in view — is an annual, belonging to the cabbage family, the Cruciferae. It grows very rapidly and can attain a height of three metres (nine to ten feet) in the right climate — **'the largest of garden plants,'** Jesus calls it. Furthermore, although described as **'a tree'**, it is not a woody, but a herbaceous plant, yet one that is sturdy enough **'that the birds of the air come and perch in its branches'** (13:32).

So it will be with the kingdom, says Jesus. There will be tremendous growth by harvest-time. To be sure, the mustard will never seem as impressive to the world as the great oaks (that 'from little acorns grow'), or the cedars of Lebanon, but grow it will as the Lord transforms people's lives, one by one, generation by generation. The point is that the growth of the church, however visible, however much it affects people's lives, is never going to look very terribly grand in the world's eyes. Jesus' kingdom 'is not of this world' (John 18:36). It is a movement that is despised and opposed by the world — a movement finding its strength and permanence not in organizations and institutions, but in the rule of Christ in the heart.[4]

Even great spiritual revivals, such as the Reformation or the Great Awakening, were not attended by worldly magnificence and power, but by the quiet fruit of the Spirit, shining forth against a background of sometimes bitter resistance from a watching and hostile world.

Eventual maturation (13:33)

The maturation of the work of the kingdom is perhaps most aptly illustrated by the yeast in the dough: **'The kingdom of heaven is like yeast that a woman took and mixed into a large amount of flour until it worked all through the dough.'** When its leavening is done, the result is a loaf of bread, the fruit of an unobtrusive penetration of an otherwise inedible lump. This gives us a picture of the eventual completion of God's plan to gather a people to himself from all the four corners of the earth.

The yeast and the dough ought not to be taken to mean that the entire world will be Christianized and the planet largely dominated by Christians and their principles and institutions. The point of the yeast illustration is limited to the methodology of penetration — the almost imperceptible spread of the gospel throughout the masses of humanity — the yeast being kneaded into the lump of flour, and the fact that there will come a time when the evangelization of the world is complete.

The 'mustard' is always a herbaceous plant, never a great oak. 'Even at maturity,' writes Herman Hanko, 'the kingdom of God looks small and insignificant if measured against the standards of the world.'[5] As we learned from the parable of the weeds, Satan's crops will also be maturing and they will not go into the fire without a struggle. There will still be 'powers' and 'super-powers' on the political scene; there will still be a large antichristian pseudo-church; unbelievers will still be marrying and giving in marriage, planning for a godless future that does not exist. Yet the kingdom of God will be completed; the world will be ripe for its last contest with the will of God; the church will be prepared to enter the glory of the heavenly state. Even in the last moments as the 'mustard' matures, when the yeast has done its work and the people of God — still 'strangers and aliens' in the world — await the coming of the Lord, the world will still despise the Lord Jesus Christ and his true church. Kings will still be taking counsel against the Lord (God the Father) and his Anointed (Jesus). Martyrs will still cry from under the altar, 'How long, O Lord?' And the reprobate lost will be shocked and terrified to learn that *the end* has really come! It will, however, be a day of joy and indescribable blessing for those who love the Lord. For them the age will end, not with a whimper, but with a bang — the glorious revelation of the consummated kingdom of God, brought in by the coming of Christ to gather his redeemed people to himself.

Patience for growth

The practical implications of Jesus' teaching are not at all difficult to discern. Let me suggest three lines of application.

Expectant realism

The parables of the mustard seed and the yeast preach expectant realism to modern Christians. As we give ourselves to the work of the kingdom of Christ, we must not pin our hopes on false and, indeed, carnal, expectations of easier times for the church. We are not called to worldly glory, political dominance and a pain-free utopian existence. Even the spiritual growth and revival which we ought prayerfully to expect, and for which we are diligently to labour, will not mean the abolition of all our problems. The advance of the gospel always brings intensified opposition. Victories are the fruit of battle.

Even the growth of Christ's kingdom will not turn the earth into a problem-free paradise. We will not abolish poverty and war — only the return of Christ will do that. But we will preach Christ, help the poor and strive for peace, because it is our mission and calling to point a lost world to the redeeming love of our risen Saviour. To be sure, the blessings that God pours on his children here and now are wonderful and inexpressible, but still our ministry is to point men and women to the way to that 'better country — a heavenly one' that awaits those who are being saved by the blood of Christ (Heb. 11:14-16). We are engaged in the warfare of ultimate peace. The mustard and the yeast show us the way, with the hope-filled realism that arms us to look this dark world in the face — and expect blessing!

Patient witnessing

The mustard and the yeast also teach us *patience* in our witness for Christ. They just grow away quietly, doing their work with unspectacular normality. Even in maturity, the mustard is not a California redwood and the yeast is all but invisible! Yet how impatient we can be! We want results, not just now, but yesterday! We expect evangelistic programmes to 'work' — and quickly. We are today so results-orientated, so attuned to the consumer-society lust for instant gratification, that we tend to tie our enthusiasm for the gospel and the church to some predetermined short-term goals. When they fail to come to pass as we planned, we become speedily discouraged, say, 'It isn't worth it,' and either give up, or go on to invent new schemes that will supposedly produce the rewards we seem to think we ought to get. Well, Jesus calls us to *patient* faithfulness. The yeast teaches us this. Keep on working, keep on praying, keep on being quietly and steadily obedient to the Lord's revealed will, and keep on with patient assurance that his will will indeed be done. Faithfulness is for *now*; the harvest is for the end of the age.

'Delight yourself in the Lord
   and he will give you the desires of your heart...
Be still before the Lord and wait patiently for him...'

                                                        (Ps. 37:4,7).

Confiding certainty

Unlike government economic plans and business projections, the
growth of Christ's kingdom is a great deal more than clever planning
sprinkled with fond hopes that all will go well. The King of this
kingdom is absolute Sovereign of both our present and our future.
The final success of the gospel of the kingdom is assured by the
authority of the King, Jesus Christ, who, when he comes again, will
'[hand] over the kingdom to God the Father after he has destroyed
all dominion, authority and power. For he must reign until he has put
all his enemies under his feet' (1 Cor.15:24-25).

   His kingdom cannot fail;
   He rules o'er earth and heaven;
   The keys of death and hell
   Are to our Jesus given:
       Lift up your heart, lift up your voice;
       Rejoice; again I say, 'Rejoice.'

   Rejoice in glorious hope;
   Jesus the Judge shall come,
   And take his servants up
   To their eternal home;
       We soon shall hear the archangel's voice;
       The trump of God shall sound, 'Rejoice.'

                                        (Charles Wesley, 1707-88)

5.
The value of the kingdom

The parables of the hidden treasure and the pearl of great price (Matt. 13:44-46)

'The kingdom of heaven is like treasure hidden in a field. When a man found it, he hid it again, and then in his joy went and sold all he had and bought that field. Again, the kingdom of heaven is like a merchant looking for fine pearls. When he found one of great value, he went away and sold everything he had and bought it' (Matt. 13:44-46).

Of the seven 'parables of the kingdom' recorded in Matthew 13, only the first four — the sower, the weeds, the mustard seed and the yeast — were delivered by Jesus to the crowds. The last three — the hidden treasure, the pearl and the net, together with the explanations of the parables of the sower and the weeds — were given in private to the disciples only. The reason for this shift from public to private ministry is evident from the content of these latter parables, for Jesus has in them specific instruction for the disciples, in order to prepare them for their future ministries.

The disciples had very foggy notions about this 'kingdom of heaven' that Jesus was proclaiming. They tended to think of it more in material than spiritual terms. They thought of its benefits rather than the cost of its responsibilities; hence, on one occasion, they argued about which of them would be first in this kingdom (Mark 10:35-45). They expected triumphs for Jesus and would become discouraged, even uncomprehending, when he told them of his coming death (Mark 9:31). In other words, they just did not yet understand either the nature of God's kingdom, or the work of Christ as the Saviour of sinners.

The parables of the hidden treasure and the pearl speak of the value or worth of God's kingdom and so, by implication, indicate something of the cost of becoming followers of the Lord Jesus. Together, they teach us three things about the kingdom of heaven:

it is a great treasure (13:44,45); it is worth everything we have (13:44,46); and it is a discovery of grace (Isa. 65:1).

A great treasure (13:44,45)

The basic perspective of both parables is clear enough. Two men, one way or another, find great treasures and, because they recognize them for what they are, they are ready to give up everything they have in order to possess them. There is no mystery about this: we can all understand a super-bargain and why we waste no time in taking advantage of it! Our hearts pound away within us as we scrape together the cash necessary for our purchase! Jesus applies this to the kingdom of heaven. What is the greatest once-in-a-lifetime bargain? It is the Christian salvation, the gospel of saving grace through the blood of Christ and the rule of the risen Jesus in human hearts and lives — the message of the kingdom of heaven.

Hidden treasure

In both stories, the treasure is **'hidden'** to begin with (13:44). The **'field'** in which it is hidden is the world,[1] as in the earlier parables, while the treasure itself is the gospel of the kingdom. The two men are sinners who embrace the gospel in saving faith. The only difference between them is that the one man appears to have stumbled on the treasure by accident, while the other was looking for **'fine pearls'** when he found the **'one of great value'** (13:45-46). Leaving aside the question as to how people find the Lord — see our third main point below — we shall focus on the significance of the treasure itself.

The most basic point is that the gospel of the kingdom is now *in the world*. In Jesus, the kingdom had come. This was a mystery, 'for ages past … kept hidden in God,' but now beginning to be made 'plain to everyone' (Eph. 3:9). It was still veiled as long as Jesus ministered on earth, but with his death, resurrection, ascension and sending of the heavenly Comforter, the Holy Spirit, at Pentecost, it became an ever-present reality in human experience, more obvious with every passing generation. Whether it is read about in God's Word, or heard of in the preaching by God's ministers, or seen in the daily lives of God's people, it is to be found in this world. It is in the church of Jesus Christ, in her message, worship and fellowship, and in the witness of believers as they penetrate human society in all sorts of ways. This is the work of the kingdom of heaven upon earth.

Nevertheless, the *hiddenness* of the kingdom remains a factor in the lives of unconverted people (1 Cor. 2:14). The spiritually blind cannot see the light by themselves. The need for personal unveiling — the Spirit opening blind eyes and renewing dead minds — remains an ever-present reality. In this sense, the gospel remains hidden treasure to many who otherwise are aware of its presence in the world and, indeed, the thrust of its claims. Jesus shows that this was the problem with many in his day: 'You diligently study the Scriptures because you think that by them you possess eternal life. These are the Scriptures that testify about me, yet you refuse to come to me to have life' (John 5:39-40). The great need of sinners is to see the gospel of Christ for the 'treasure' it is and to desire to be saved by his free grace. And those who are already Christians must always come to the Lord and his Word with the attitude and prayer: 'Open my eyes that I may see wonderful things in your law' (Ps. 119:18).

Redeeming treasure (Eph. 3:8)

The treasure and the pearl represent all the goodness of God's saving grace, received by grace through faith in Jesus Christ. The gospel is the **'unsearchable riches of Christ'**, which in **'ages past was kept hidden in God'** (Eph. 3:8). Its fruition for all who believe is a new heart, a new record and a new life. It is the entrance upon the way of salvation (what theology calls the *ordo salutis*) — effectual calling, regeneration, conversion (repentance and faith), justification, adoption and sanctification.[2] It is nothing less than the knowledge of God in the face of Jesus Christ, the indwelling power of the Holy Spirit, the hope of glory, true peace and joy, even in a dark world and a life's work of serving the Lord as a citizen of his kingdom.

This is marvellously illustrated in the experience of the apostle Paul. In Acts 8:1 we see Paul (Saul) approving the stoning of Stephen. Paul had heard the martyr defending himself from the Word of God and saw him, manifestly full of the Holy Spirit, looking up to heaven where, unseen by Paul and the crowd, Stephen beheld God's glory and Jesus standing at his right hand. He heard

Stephen cry out, 'Look, I see heaven open and the Son of Man standing at the right hand of God.' And as Stephen died under the stones, he heard him say, 'Lord Jesus, receive my spirit,' and 'Lord, do not hold this sin against them' (Acts 7:54-60). A little later, in Acts 9, Paul was converted to Christ on his way to Damascus. Still later, he would testify to the Christians in Philippi, 'If anyone else thinks he has reasons to put confidence in the flesh, I have more: circumcised on the eighth day, of the people of Israel, of the tribe of Benjamin, a Hebrew of Hebrews; in regard to the law, a Pharisee; as for zeal, persecuting the church; as for legalistic righteousness, faultless. But whatever was to my profit I now consider loss for the sake of Christ. What is more, I consider everything a loss compared to the surpassing greatness of knowing Christ Jesus my Lord, for whose sake I have lost all things. I consider them rubbish, that I may gain Christ and be found in him' (Phil. 3:4-9).

Worth everything we have (13:44,46)

In both parables the men marshal all their resources in order to possess their prize finds. They sold everything they had and **'bought'**, respectively, the field and the pearl. The merchant who bought the pearl also showed diligence in his quest, for he knew what he was looking for and went after it with a single-minded zeal.

An unaffordable purchase

The fact that the men *bought* their treasures with their own money does not mean that we may purchase or earn salvation by our own unaided efforts — our 'good works'. The Bible teaches an unassailable doctrine of salvation by grace alone: 'For it is by grace you have been saved, through faith — and this not from yourselves, it is the gift of God' (Eph. 2:8).

Indeed, when the figure of 'buying' is employed in Scripture with reference to the gospel, it is made absolutely clear that it is the 'buying' of free grace. It is the purchase of the unaffordable by the indigent. The helpless, resourceless sinner 'buys' that which he cannot conceivably afford. This theme is found elsewhere in Scripture. Through Isaiah, the Lord reaches out to lost people:

'Come, all you who are thirsty,
   come to the waters;
and you who have no money,
   come, buy and eat!
Come, buy wine and milk
   without money and without cost'

                                        (Isa. 55:1).

The same note is struck by the Lord Jesus Christ, who says to John, 'It is done. I am Alpha and Omega, the Beginning and the End. To him who is thirsty I will give to drink without cost from the spring of the water of life' (Rev. 21:6-7). 'Buying,' in this scriptural usage, is an earnest, urgent, believing response to the free grace of God. It is called 'buying' because such response to the gospel involves the surrender of everything we hitherto held dear, in the interest of cementing a new relationship with the Lord.

A costly purchase

Many a man has made a fortune by sinking everything he had in some project he was sure would be a success. The men in the parable did just that. They went all out to get their new-found treasures. It is idle to dissect the details — such as the morality of the fellow who covered over the treasure until he bought the field. Jesus was not discussing the ethics of the man, but simply used a basic fact of human life — namely, self-interest in action — to illustrate what it means to find the gospel for what it really is.

    Neither man thought that everything he had was too high a price to pay. They both would have understood very well the sentiment of James Graham, Marquis of Montrose, when he wrote with reference to seeking the favours of a young lady,

He either fears his fate too much
Or his deserts are small;
To dare to put it to the touch,
To win or lose it all.

Like Moses, who left the life of a prince in Egypt to suffer with the Lord's people, they had regard to the recompense of the reward. They made sure they would not lose their prizes.

Coming to Christ in faith is, to be sure, 'buying' a great prize 'without money and without cost' — because salvation is indeed all of God's free grace. But it is also, in another sense, the costliest transaction a person can ever make, because it is the unconditional surrender of not only all that he *has*, but of all that he *is*! It is leaving everything, including one's old self, for the sake of following Jesus. It is becoming 'captive' to Christ! (Matt. 10:37-39; Mark 10:29-30; 2 Cor.10:5).

An acquirable purchase

Similarly, becoming a believer in Christ means casting oneself unreservedly upon the Saviour, realizing that glorious gospel paradox: 'Whoever finds his life will lose it, and whoever loses his life for my sake will find it' (Matt. 10:39). The way of real life — life in a risen Saviour — is the path of dying to self. God only fills empty vessels. Christ is pure water to a thirsty soul. To come to Christ at all is a confession that he is too good to miss, that he is the real treasure and that all else is but another species of poverty. Non-Christians often think that people become Christians out of fear, or guilt, or desire to appear more holy than others. Faith and personal holiness, even basic morality, are so unattractive and repressive to them that they find it almost inconceivable that anyone could have a really positive enthusiasm for such a way of life. But the truth is that a true Christian *loves* God as his heavenly Father and his Son, Jesus, as his Saviour and Lord, and *delights* to do the will of the Lord in his daily life. Believers are animated by the most positive motivation in the universe! They don't feel forced to believe in Christ. They don't feel dragooned into following the Bible's pattern for holy living. This to them is the freedom of the children of God! (Rom. 8:21; James 1:25).

A discovery of grace (Isa. 65:1)

A common misinterpretation of these parables is that they teach that all men and women are really searching for the truth of God. The theological liberals, who are universalistic to the core, think everybody has something of the truth already, whether 'Christian', Buddhist, Jew or Marxist. It has been fashionable for over a century now to see scepticism and heresy as legitimate avenues in the search for 'truth'. But this has even percolated down into the litany of fundamentalist evangelistic technique in the assertion, for example, that there is 'a God-shaped space inside every sinner'. If this kind of teaching were true, our evangelistic task would be much easier than we know it to be. The truth-vacuum inside lost people should readily suck up the truth we proclaim. The evidence is, however, that while people *do* recognize the gospel when they hear it, they do not trample over one another in a rush to embrace it! The world is not full of people looking to receive Christ as he is offered in the gospel!

Rightly understood, these parables show that our discovery of the value of the kingdom of heaven is a discovery of grace. That is to say, the process of discovery is a work of God's grace in our lives. The hunger after, the search for and the discovery of the unsearchable riches of Christ do not arise from autonomous man deciding unaided what is best for himself, but from the secret movements of God's love, drawing the sinner to himself, one step at a time and often against his will.

Seekers?

It is true, as Augustine has said, that human hearts are restless till they find their rest in God. That, however, is not the same thing as saying that we are restless *for* a rest in God. Augustine's restless sinners are like the men in the doomed eighth-century B.C. kingdom of Israel (Samaria) who

> '... stagger from sea to sea
> and wander from north to east,
> searching for the word of the Lord,
> but they will not find it'

(Amos 8:12).

They might have gone *south* to Jerusalem, where the truth was actually to be found, but they were only willing to search anywhere and everywhere but in the right direction!

Not every restless human being is thirsting for the Christian salvation. Sinners in fact do *not* yearn for God — that is the characteristic of saints (Ps. 42:1). But God graciously and sovereignly draws lost people to himself. Sometimes, like the man in the field, they are surprised to find the Christian gospel. Such was the case with the woman of Samaria (John 4), the apostle Paul (Acts 9) and the Philippian jailer (Acts 16). C. S. Lewis was 'surprised by joy'. God says,

> 'I revealed myself to those who did not ask for me;
>   I was found by those who did not seek me.
> To a nation that did not call on my name,
>   I said, "Here am I, here am I"'
>
> (Isa. 65:1).

Sometimes God prepares people's hearts so that they start to seek him, even though they do not quite know what they are doing. The Ethiopian eunuch (Acts 8), Cornelius (Acts 10) and Lydia (Acts 16) are cases in point. They searched because of God's grace and they found, also by God's grace.

Finders?

What is really important in life? In *your* life? Jesus says we are to 'seek first his kingdom and his righteousness,' adding the promise that he will supply all our other material needs 'as well' (Matt. 6:33). The converse is the hardest truth for sinners to accept: that if they live for 'things', they will ensure the loss of the most important treasure in the world — reconciliation to God through the blood of the everlasting covenant in Christ Jesus. When Christ is the most important person in our lives, we let go of the idols we once worshipped. That necessarily involves real sacrifices. Old ways, old thinking, old loyalties, old relationships undergo radical re-evaluation and change. But like the men in the parable, we can not only face that, but welcome it, because we are truly persuaded that Christ is the Lamb of God who takes away our sins and is worthy of all 'honour and glory and praise' (Rev. 5:12).

We are not told what the two men did with the treasures they had so enthusiastically acquired. Clearly, the first man did not buy the field just to leave the treasure in the ground. The pearl was not acquired to be hidden in a vault. These were to be adornments to the lives of both men in some productive way. The knowledge of Christ is to be lived. Being saved changes people. They put on Christ (Rom. 13:14; Gal. 3:27). They are visibly transformed and become new creations, new people (Col. 3:12; Eph. 4:24; 2 Cor. 5:17). They shine like the sun in their heavenly Father's realm (Matt.13:43). This is why the kingdom of God is a pearl of great price. This is why Christians would 'rather have Jesus than silver or gold'. 'You believe in him,' says the apostle Peter, 'and are filled with an inexpressible and glorious joy, for you are receiving the goal of your faith, the salvation of your souls' (1 Peter 1:8-9).

> I with my lips have oft declared
> The judgments which thy mouth has shown,
> More joy thy testimonies gave
> Than all the riches I have known.[3]

6.
The ministry of the kingdom

The parable of the net
(Matt. 13:47-52)

'The kingdom of heaven is like a net that was let down into the lake and caught all kinds of fish' (Matt. 13:47).

The parable of the net is the seventh and last of the 'parables of the kingdom' recorded in Matthew 13. Because of its obvious similarities to the parable of the weeds, it is often treated by Bible commentators as a twin of that earlier story. Hence David Brown, in the old and famous *Jamieson, Fausset and Brown* commentary, simply deals with it in connection with the 'weeds'. More recently, William Hendriksen can find nothing distinctive about it, has nothing to say on it, and almost seems embarrassed to have to comment on it at all![1]

This ought not to be, for the Lord never wastes words. Even when, as in the present case, he *seems* to be covering the same ground as he covered before, a close examination shows that he has a distinct purpose in view. Part of the reason for so many missing this is perhaps because the key to understanding this parable lies, not so much in the parable itself, but in Jesus' challenge to the disciples that immediately followed it (Matt. 13:51-52). He asks the disciples, 'Have you understood all these things?' and then tells them what the task of a disciple involves. It is to bring 'new treasures as well as old' out of the storeroom; that is to say, to go ahead to teach the whole truth of God, old and new, as it has come from the mouth of the Lord. It is to cast the gospel net into the world. The followers of Jesus are called to a new, ongoing ministry of the kingdom of heaven upon earth. Their task is to fish for lost people and to catch for the Lord the very population of heaven! In the earlier parables, the focus was on the content of the message, or on how it was received. Here the scope is even wider, for the disciples are brought face to face with their future ministry as the messengers sent out by the Lord to proclaim the gospel of the kingdom.

The meaning of the parable (13:47-50)

The kingdom of heaven is like a **'net that was let down into the lake and caught all kinds of fish'**. The 'net' would have been something like what we call a seine-net — a long net suspended from cork floats and held straight down by weights on the lower edge. Swept in a great arc, it would catch the fish within its path. The 'lake' is, of course, the world and the 'fish' that are 'caught' are those who become part of the visible manifestation of the kingdom — that is, the people of God, the church of Jesus Christ, externally considered. Not all of those who are called Christians are true believers.

When the net was **'full'** the fishermen **'pulled it up on the shore'** and collected **'the good fish in baskets'**, while they **'threw the bad away'** (13:48). Like the parable of the weeds, that of the net and the fish gives us a picture of the last judgement at the end of this age, particularly as that judgement is applied to the professing church of God. As there will be 'wheat' (true believers) and 'weeds' (pseudo-believers) in the field until the harvest (13:30), so there will be 'good fish' and 'bad fish'. Within the visible kingdom of God throughout the course of history, there will be both the truly converted and those who are not, the faithful and the hypocritical, the saved and the lost, the elect and the reprobate.

One might well ask what is different about the parable of the net. This general truth pervades the Lord's teaching in all the parables of the kingdom. A closer look, however, will reveal several distinctive emphases.

Casting the net — fishing for people

There is an obvious focus on what would be an ongoing work of gathering people into the kingdom of heaven. The parable of the weeds viewed the advance of the kingdom in relation to satanic opposition that planted antichrists and their false gospels wherever

God was saving sinners through the preaching of the gospel. The 'net' employs a hunting, as opposed to a farming, motif and shows what happens as the gospel message sweeps through history catching the attention and the commitment of masses of people.

This not only describes the effect of the gospel in history, but the task of the ministers of the gospel in particular and the church's witness in general. Peter and Andrew were called from their nets to do just this. '"Come, follow me," Jesus said, "and I will make you fishers of men"' (Matt. 4:19). Jesus was telling the disciples about their future work as ministers of the gospel. Much later, Paul set it down in the clearest terms. How can people call on a Jesus in whom they do not believe? No, before that, 'How can they believe in the one of whom they have not heard? And how can they hear without someone preaching to them? And how can they [those who are to bring that message] preach unless they are sent? … Faith comes from hearing the message, and the message is heard through the word of Christ' (Rom. 10:14-17).

Make no mistake about it: the Christian church is a mission to reach the whole world for Christ by proselytizing the maximum number of people. The Christian faith is not some inner light for the exclusive use of a limited circle of secret initiates. It is not an 'option' — one among many and all legitimate — for people who feel the necessity of a spiritual crutch of some kind. The gospel and its ministers are trawling for souls. Christ is looking for converts. God means to save lost people. The task is an imperative if people are not to descend into hell in their unbelieving droves! This does not sit well in today's world of individualism and pluralism — the 'I'm all right ; you're all right' world in which all viewpoints are to be accepted all round. God is not a pluralist; the wicked, of all varieties, will be turned into hell, and all the nations that forget God (Ps. 9:17). This is the background against which the ministers of the kingdom of heaven must preach the uncompromising but exclusively redeeming message of the gospel of Jesus Christ. The world, like the fishes, will have to be found, caught and landed. This is why, Christian friends, you are here!

The good fish and bad fish in the church

The parable of the net also shows that it is inevitable that those who are 'caught' by the gospel will be a mixed multitude of 'good fish' and 'bad fish'. That is to say, not all who claim to be Christians will be the real thing. The preaching of the gospel, and even the proper, necessary exercise of church discipline, does not, cannot and is not designed to make God's kingdom on earth 100% pure! The perfection of the church must await the Day of Judgement and the glory yet to be revealed in heaven.

You will notice that, while this is the teaching of the parable of the weeds, the distinctive perspective of the parable of the net lies in the fact that this mixture within the kingdom comes about as a result of the very means by which the kingdom operates in the world as it faithfully executes its mission, namely through the outward *acceptance* of Christ by people who are not inwardly committed to him.

There is no way that even the best leadership in the church can read the thoughts and intentions of people's hearts, so as to purge the church of hypocrites and dissemblers. The truth is that until God's final separation of the good and bad fish (also known as wheat and weeds, sheep and goats, saved and lost, elect and reprobate), the visible church cannot but be, as the *Westminster Confession* puts it, 'subject both to mixture and error'.[2] 'For not all who are descended from Israel are Israel,' says Paul (Rom. 9:6). This is just as applicable today. The administration of the covenant community — accepting people for membership, administering the sacraments (baptism and the Lord's Supper) and the exercise of church discipline — does not infallibly decide who are the true Christians and who are not. The reality is that the gospel 'net' by its very nature will always come up with more than just 'good fish'.

All kinds of fish

The parable of the net also indicates the universal scope of the gospel. The net catches fish of **'all kinds'** (13:47). This means at its most basic 'all sorts of species'. The later division between the good and the bad fish cuts across all these 'kinds'. The point is that the kingdom of God would no longer be the preserve of the old covenant people, the Jews, but extend to all the peoples of the world. Whereas God until now had said, 'You only have I chosen of all the families of the earth' (Amos 3:2), he would now fulfil the true scope of the original promise to Abraham: 'All peoples on earth will be blessed through you' (Gen. 12:3).

In summary, we may say that the parable of the net has certain distinctive emphases that are not to be found in the other parables of the kingdom. These are: first, that the ministry of the gospel involves the active pursuit and proselytization of lost people for the kingdom of God; secondly, that faithful ministry will not prevent hypocrites from coming into the church before the last judgement; and, thirdly, that salvation will extend to all peoples in the world. It can hardly be dismissed as just another version of the parable of the weeds.

The application of the parable (13:51-52)

We must remember what Jesus was doing in his ministry at this point. He opened his mouth in parables to 'utter things hidden since the creation of the world' (13:35; Ps. 78:2). He was revealing new things about the redemptive plans of God for the world. And for those who see what he is saying, he says, 'Blessed are your eyes because they see, and your ears because they hear. For I tell you the truth, many prophets and righteous men longed to see what you see but did not see it, and to hear what you hear and did not hear it' (13:16-17).

This is why Jesus, having told the seven parables of the kingdom, asks his disciples the question: **'Have you understood all these things?'** (13:51). They answer in the affirmative — rather weakly, when one considers the evidence of their actual grasp of Jesus' ministry at this point in their lives — and Jesus then tells them what it must mean for them in practice to understand truly his teaching about the kingdom: **'Therefore every teacher of the law who has been instructed about the kingdom of heaven is like the owner of a house who brings out of his storeroom new treasures as well as old'** (13:52). What he is saying is that since they have been trained and instructed as to the mind of the Lord, both old (the Old Testament Scriptures) and new (the preaching of Jesus), they have a stewardship to take these treasures to the world. The truth, some of it 'hidden since the creation of the world', but now revealed to them, is to be proclaimed and to be lived out in the hearing and the sight of the widest audience! Cast wide the gospel net! Sweep across the sea that is the world! Gather in the 'catch' of each generation, all the while looking in unquenchable hope to the end of the age, when

God will seal up his work of salvation in the last judgement and the consummation of the kingdom!

The parable of the net certainly confirms the specific lessons of the earlier parables, but in a real sense it draws them together in terms of a personal, practical thrust for the future task of the ministers of God. Why was Jesus teaching them these things about the kingdom of God? It was to the end that they would get on with the business of spreading the good news of that kingdom. Yes, seed might fall on bad soil; Satan might sow antichrists in the church; children of believers might reject the faith of their parents; false converts might insinuate themselves into the body of Christ; but the kingdom would grow like the mustard seed and mature like the farmer's crops. The work of redemption would be completed one day, as the net is drawn in on human history. How would this happen? Through the disciples of Jesus and their spiritual descendants in every generation of the New Testament church getting the message out to lost people!

The work before us is to preach the cross of Jesus Christ — to proclaim salvation from sin in a substitute who bore the penalty for sinners in his own body on the cross — and to proclaim it until the knowledge of the Lord covers the earth as the waters cover the sea. The net is drawn tighter every day. God's work of redemption is that much nearer completion every night when we go to bed. Let us therefore cast the gospel net, while it is still called 'today'. Let us call men and women to the only one who is able to save them for time and eternity!

> O Christ! He is the fountain,
> The deep, sweet well of love;
> The streams on earth I've tasted
> More deep I'll drink above:
> There to an ocean fulness
> His mercy doth expand,
> And glory, glory dwelleth
> In Immanuel's land.

> (Anne Ross Cousin).

Part II:
The marks of kingdom life

The parables of
Jesus' Perean ministry
(Matthew 18; Luke 10-18)

7.
Forgiveness

The parable of the unmerciful debtor
(Matt. 18:21-35)

'Then Peter came to Jesus and asked, "Lord, how many times shall I forgive my brother when he sins against me? Up to seven times?"' (Matt. 18:21).

One day, Jesus' disciples had an argument about which of them would be the greatest in the kingdom of heaven. They couldn't come to any agreement among themselves, so they asked Jesus. Jesus answered by standing a child in their midst. First he rebuked them: 'Unless you change and become like little children, you will never enter the kingdom of heaven' (Matt. 18:3). He then exhorted them, 'Whoever humbles himself like this child is the greatest in the kingdom of heaven.' To be childlike in spirit and to receive little children in his name was to welcome the Lord himself. Jesus then went on to make two important points of application.

Firstly, in the parable of the lost sheep (which we shall look at later in connection with Luke 15:1-7), he emphasized that *God* would seek and save even the very last of his lost little ones. They are never so low and insignificant that God would be willing to let them go (Matt. 18:10-14).

Secondly, Jesus pointed out that *we* must be humbled and loving enough to reach out to the brother who has sinned against us so that he may be won over and restored to full fellowship (Matt. 18:15-20). This reaching out therefore cannot be one of merely seeking vindication, but one that is clothed in a spirit that offers forgiveness from the heart, towards the goal of reconciliation with that estranged person.

Peter picked up on this and had a question for Jesus: **'Lord, how many times shall I forgive my brother when he sins against me?**

Up to seven times?' (Matt. 18:21). 'Is there some limit to this forgiving attitude?', Peter was asking. To this, Jesus gave a twofold answer. First, he said, **'I tell you, not seven times, but seventy-seven times'** (18:22). That is to say, 'Go on forgiving your brother. Never stop reaching out to him in kindness.' Then he illustrated his point with the parable of the unmerciful debtor.

The unmerciful debtor

The parable itself

The gist of the story is this: a powerful king wanted to settle accounts with his servants. One of these servants owed him 10,000 talents. This was an astronomical figure — equivalent to many millions in the hard currencies of today. The point is that it was so great as to be an *unpayable debt*. The king, following the usual practice of the time, decided to sell the servant and his family and his goods in lieu of the debt. The servant thereupon **'fell on his knees'** and promised to pay back the debt, if given time. The king knew very well that this was impossible, but he **'took pity on him, cancelled the debt and let him go'** (18:23-27).

Thus forgiven, the servant went off and promptly found a fellow-servant who owed him 100 denarii — the equivalent of about three months' wages, but a trivial debt in comparison to the one he had just been forgiven. He accosted the man violently and in spite of his entreaties — identical to his own towards the king — he had him thrown into a debtor's prison.

The other servants were upset and told the king, who summoned the man to appear before him and rebuked him in no uncertain terms: **'"You wicked servant," he said, "I cancelled all that debt of yours because you begged me to. Shouldn't you have had mercy on your fellow-servant just as I had on you?"'** He then handed the man over to his **'jailers to be tortured'** until the debt was paid (18:32-34). The thought here is that since the debt was essentially unpayable, his suffering of the penalty would be without end.

The interpretation of the parable

The king is God. The servants are those who profess to be the citizens of his kingdom. The contrast is drawn between the unpayable debt that we owe to God in virtue of our being sinners by nature, and the relatively trivial debts we owe to each other. This is not designed to minimize the sins we commit against our brothers and sisters. Rather, it emphasizes that if God has truly forgiven our unpayable debt, it ought to be relatively easy for us to forgive the debts of others. The point laid on the Christian's conscience is simply this: that a vital evidence that our sins are forgiven through Christ is that we freely forgive the sins of others. If we do not forgive others their sins against us, it says of us that we have not grasped the meaning of gospel forgiveness and that we are not as right with the Lord in our hearts as we would like to believe we are.

The application of the parable

It is this central theme that we must understand and apply to our own attitudes and actions. We may do so in terms of three main points: God's forgiveness of us; a forgiving disposition in us; and the example of Christ as the path of obedience for us in our relationships with God and others.

God's forgiveness of us

1. We owe a tremendous debt to God. God's forgiveness of our sins comes before our forgiveness of others. Indeed, the former is the engine which moves the latter. The parable reminds us that we are debtors to God in the matter of our personal sin and that the debt is unpayable by us. Good deeds do not cancel out the bad; they are only what ought to be done (Luke 17:10). Paying your electricity bill this month does not atone for your failure to do so last month. Present righteousness cannot atone for yesterday's sin. In any case, 'There is no one righteous, not even one' (Rom. 3:10; Ps. 14:1).

> 'All our righteous acts are like filthy rags;
>   we all shrivel up like a leaf,
>   and like the wind our sins sweep us away'
>
> (Isa. 64:6).

We are inevitably and unavoidably helpless to save ourselves by our own best efforts. Even if we were sinlessly perfect in thought, word and deed for the rest of our lives — an utter impossibility anyway — we could still never cancel out the sins of the past.

Yet these must be paid for. God's perfect justice must be served. Sins must either be forgiven, or the guilty must suffer the penalty that is due them. The penalty for unforgiven sin is eternal separation from God and unending bondage to the corruption and miseries of unrestrained evil. Hell is evil embraced for ever. This is why Scripture speaks of the eternal destiny of the reprobate lost in terms of 'wailing and gnashing of teeth' and 'the lake of fire'. Hell is not 'other people', as Jean-Paul Sartre claimed. It is endless unrelieved abandonment to the consequences of commitment to the contradiction of God. In the end, God takes the unrepentant and unbelieving at their word: 'You did not want me in your life on earth. Your wish is granted for eternity. Depart from me, you who are cursed, into the eternal fire prepared for the devil and his angels.'

2. God's forgiveness of this debt is sovereignly and unconditionally given. The king cancelled the unpayable debt. In gospel terms, the debt of sin is paid by Christ for all who believe in him. Believers 'are justified freely by his grace through the redemption that came by Christ Jesus' (Rom. 3:24). 'God made him who had no sin to be sin for us, so that in him we might become the righteousness of God' (2 Cor. 5:21).

Salvation is free, in Christ. It is sovereignly given. It is unmerited and unearned. It is received through the exercise of faith, which is 'not from [our]selves, it is the gift of God — not by works, so that no one can boast' (Eph. 2:8). God forgiving his people means that he looks at them and does not see their sins, because they have been washed away by the blood of Christ. Christ went through the punishment of a lost eternity in his own person in the place of all who will truly believe in him. God does not see the sins of these believers because they are covered. Sin forgiven is sin forgotten. It is sin rendered invisible, even in the very mind of the omniscient God! God forgives, in Christ, before ever the sinner has done anything that is righteous in his eyes. This is forgiveness, sovereignly given and unconditionally applied.

A forgiving disposition in us

The parable also clearly teaches that the knowledge of God's mercy can only produce in us a forgiving disposition.

1. There is a proper way to receive forgiveness. The unmerciful servant knew the king had cancelled his debts, but it is quite clear that he did not receive this with any genuine contrition. In other words, for him 'being forgiven' was no more than 'getting away with it'! He was unchanged. He had no conception of the true nature of mercy as an act of free grace. He had merely lived to steal another day. That is why, in the parable, the king reverses his cancellation of the debt, when the servant is unmerciful to his brother. This does not teach that God reverses his decision to forgive a man his sins. The purpose of the story is to illustrate that there is no experiential knowledge of forgiveness in a heart devoid of a forgiving spirit. Real confession of sin, genuine repentance and saving faith in Christ produce, and cannot but produce, a sincere desire to forgive others, just as we have been forgiven.

We receive forgiveness only through confession of sin and true repentance. 'If we confess our sins, he is faithful and just to forgive us our sins and cleanse us from all unrighteousness' (1 John 1:9). The experience of grace from God is the motivating force of graciousness towards others.

2. The evidence of being truly forgiven is a forgiving spirit. If the infinite, eternal and unchangeable God has forgiven the unpayable debt owed to him by those who become believers, it should be very much easier for believers to forgive the lesser debts that other people owe them.

Why, then, is it so difficult to be forgiving? We know this is a great problem in the Christian life. The urge for revenge, or at least a decisive vindication, is so deeply embedded in our make-up. Getting justice appeals to us more than showing mercy — assuming that the justice is coming down on someone else. Justice is certainly important. Immediately before our parable, Jesus tells how it is to be achieved in disputes between Christians (Matt. 18:15-17). First, you take your grievance to the one who sinned against you. If that fails to effect repentance and reconciliation, you take one or two witnesses. If that fails, you go to 'the church', i.e., to the elders, who are responsible for the spiritual leadership and discipline of the body of Christ.

You will notice that this is not merely a blueprint for arriving at the punishment of an offender. The aim is renewal, restitution and reconciliation for both the individuals immediately involved and for the fellowship as a whole. The aggrieved party therefore cannot fulfil Jesus' intentions in mandating this three-step process if he comes with only a desire for vindication in his soul. Clearly, he must go to the brother who sinned with a forgiving spirit in his heart. Yet how many who invoke Matthew 18 church discipline ignore this side of the equation altogether? How many use it out of a legalistic desire to get even? How many go without a scrap of forgiveness, intent primarily on personal satisfaction?

Forgiving is very hard, because it cuts against the grain, not merely of sinful human nature, but against even a right desire for justice in every human heart. Forgiving is a spiritual exercise, flowing from the grace of God. It takes being first forgiven by Christ, to go out to others wanting to forgive them.

Jesus' example for us

It is impossible to leave Jesus' teaching about forgiveness without reflecting on the fact that he is the supreme example for all who would follow him. He not only taught us perfect righteousness, he lived it every minute of his days. In every aspect of his person and work he shows us the way we are to go. He leads his people from the front. He begins with 'Follow me' and only later says, 'Therefore go...' (Matt. 4:19; 28:19).

1. Consider the *spirit* exhibited in Christ. Jesus came to save. His motive was to seek and to save lost people. 'God did not send his Son into the world to condemn the world, but to save the world through him' (John 3:17). So many Christians are engaged in what we might call ministries of outrage. They are all steamed up about the moral wrongs around them — so much so, sometimes, that the gospel gets lost in gales of wrath and judgement to come. When it is proclaimed at all, the gospel is set in the context of law, instead of setting law, as Jesus does, in the context of the gospel.[1] Thus he calls for repentance and faith and tells us, 'Go and sin no more.' And even when he pronounces judgement on the reprobate lost, who would not come to him that they might have life, he passionately laments their self-generated destruction (Matt. 23:37). Jesus came that we might have life and have it abundantly.

2. Consider, too, the *sacrifice* of Christ. The means by which Jesus obtained redemption for sinners was by giving himself as the

sacrifice for sin. He was able to cry from the cross, 'Father, forgive them ...', because he was at that moment dying in the place of all he would save. He bore the penalty due to them, by taking their sin as his. 'God made him who had no sin to be sin for us, so that in him we might become the righteousness of God' (2 Cor. 5:21). His death was a substitutionary atonement. Christ died for our sins according to the Scriptures. His death, and only his death, effected that pardon in which the justice and mercy of God perfectly coincided. Jesus took the justice; believers receive the mercy.

3. Finally, consider the *salvation* won by Christ. Salvation of particular lost people is accomplished by the death of Christ in their place. One by one, generation after generation, that salvation is applied to them as they come to Christ in faith and repentance, receiving him as he is offered in the gospel. The experience of being saved by grace comes in the exercise of a sincere belief in the Lord Jesus Christ as Saviour and Lord. Jesus emphasized this frequently in his own ministry: 'Whoever believes in him ... is not condemned ... has eternal life ... will never be thirsty ... streams of living waters will flow from within him ... [and] he will do even greater things than [Christ did in his earthly ministry]' (John 3:18,36; 6:35; 7:38; 14:12). The message remains the same today: 'If we confess our sins, he is faithful and just and will forgive us our sins and purify us from all unrighteousness... He who has the Son has life; he who does not have the Son of God does not have life' (1 John 1:9; 5:12).

The parable of the unmerciful debtor teaches us that a forgiving spirit is an essential mark of kingdom life — of a saving knowledge of Jesus Christ. It takes us to the heart of the gospel. Those who are forgiven much want to follow their Saviour in forgiving the lesser debts they are owed by others. 'Forgiveness' is no abstract, religiously neutral character trait. True forgiveness is the fruit of being forgiven, in Christ, by our Father God, and all experienced through the work of the Holy Spirit. That is why real Christians can echo from the heart A. M. Toplady's great confession of faith:

A debtor to mercy alone,
Of covenant mercy I sing;
Nor fear, with thy righteousness on,
My person and offering to bring.

The terrors of law and of God
With me can have nothing to do;
My Saviour's obedience and blood
Hide all my transgressions from view.

8.
Caring about others

The parable of the good Samaritan
(Luke 10:25-37)

'Which of these three do you think was a neighbour to the man who fell into the hands of robbers?' (Luke 10:36).

Perhaps you have noticed that when Jesus was asked leading questions, he usually did not give straight answers. Very often, he would reply with a question of his own, or make some statement that at first glance seemed totally unrelated to the original enquiry. Just look at his famous conversations with Nicodemus, the woman of Samaria and the rich young man, and what stands out is the unconventional brilliance with which our Lord interacted with people.

The reason is not difficult to discern. Jesus not only knew how to 'get to the point'. He also knew that people with questions have their own agendas in mind. So to get to his point — the real point — he had to get away from the other person's question. Jesus rarely gave a straight answer 'off the bat' because he rarely got a straight question. He wasted no time, however, in redirecting the conversation, homing in on the real issues and bringing them into the clear light of God's truth. To avoid dealing with Jesus' personal claim to be the source of 'living water', the woman of Samaria was willing to talk denominational politics all day (Jews v. Samaritans; Jerusalem v. Mt Gerizim), but the Lord blew away her evasions by revealing his knowledge of her adulteries! (John 4:9-26). Jesus was *the* master of the art of bringing a conversation around to the heart of the matter!

This is what he did in the conversation of which the parable of the good Samaritan is the centre-piece. The passage consists of three conversational exchanges between Jesus and the lawyer, by means of which the questioner became the questioned and was led to the truth that Jesus wanted him to grasp. The first is the lawyer's opening gambit — an attempt to trip up Jesus with a leading theological question (10:25-26). In the second exchange, Jesus makes a countermove by very gently exposing the lawyer's hypocrisy (10:27-29). Finally, in telling the parable of the good Samaritan, Jesus administers a checkmate and shows what it means truly to care for others (10:30-37).

Opening gambit: a leading question (10:25-26)

As Jesus became better known, his enemies sought to trip him up, by trying to get him to say things they could use to discredit him. One day a lawyer, probably a 'scribe', tried to do this by asking him the apparently simple question: **'Teacher, ... what must I do to inherit eternal life?'** Jesus replied, not with a direct answer, but with a counter-question: **'What is written in the Law? ... How do you read it?'** (Luke 10:25-26).

What was going on here? It is obvious that the lawyer was not asking about eternal life because he felt himself in need of some enlightenment. It is equally obvious that Jesus did not regard this, coming as it did from a lawyer, as an honest question. So what does it all mean?

Why, then, was the lawyer's enquiry, in this context, a trick question? A clue to this is in Jesus' answer. Jesus directs the man to 'the Law' — that is, the Scriptures. This quietly implies that the questioner was not looking for an answer from the Law. He was looking for Jesus to give him an answer that was outside of the strict doctrinal confines of the Law. Had Jesus, for example, given Paul's answer to the Philippian jailer when he asked, 'What must I do to be saved?', the lawyer would have had his heart's desire. Answering, 'Believe on the Lord Jesus Christ and you will be saved,' would have done the trick! Jesus could then have been condemned for blasphemously claiming to be the Messiah promised in the Scriptures. Later, he would be nailed to the cross for this very reason.

We can see, then, why Jesus answered as he did. He was not yet ready to reveal himself to an extent that would result in his death at the hands of the Jewish authorities. This had two major consequences.

Let the Scriptures speak for themselves

Firstly, notice that Jesus was content to let the Scriptures speak for themselves at this point and in this context. He carefully paced his self-revelation as the promised Messiah and the Son of God who would die for the sins of his people. That is why he pointed the lawyer to the law of Moses by asking him, 'What is written in the Law?' The test of truth is 'the law' and 'the testimony' (Isa. 8:20). The general principle for us, of course, is that we must always endeavour to let the Word of God speak for itself. Unlike Jesus, we have no new revelations to offer. We nevertheless do have a tendency to make our opinions sound like revelations. Our task is, however, to point to what God has said and let his Word speak to the issues of people's hearts and daily lives.

Lay it upon the consciences of the hearers

Secondly, Jesus clearly wanted the lawyer to answer his own question. Hence the follow-up: 'How do you read it?' He intended to oblige the man to face himself, his motives and his sin. He did not let the lawyer pose as an honest enquirer. He exposed him to himself as a dissembler out to entrap the very man he called, with simulated respect, a 'Teacher'. Again, there is a general principle for us to apply. It is that if anyone is to be truly convicted of his sin and come to repentance, he must be brought to the place of convicting himself in his own conscience. No one repents until he can honestly and openly declare himself guilty. A fair trial, an open and shut case and the power of the law can put a man in prison for years, but he will never accept his guilt until his own heart condemns him. That is why biblical preaching and counselling are directed at the heart and conscience, that the Holy Spirit might accompany the Word of God to the root of a sinner's rebellion, in the innermost being, and bring true conviction of lostness and need of a Saviour. Sinners need to stew in their own juice a little and feel the heat of conviction of sin.

Countermove: the spirit of the law (10:27-29)

The lawyer knew very well what the law of Moses said and quoted
Deuteronomy 6:5 and Leviticus 19:18: **"'Love the Lord your God
with all your heart and with all your soul and with all your
strength and with all your mind"; and, "Love your neighbour as
yourself"'** (10:27).

He had of course delivered himself into the Lord's hands. Jesus'
answer completely disarmed him by seizing the initiative and
focusing firmly on the Word of God. From that point, Jesus could
direct the conversation into a path of his choosing and apply the truth
to the man's conscience. When the Lord replied, it was with a
master-stroke. He *simply agreed* with his questioner. **'You have
answered correctly... Do this and you will live'** (10:28). This
classically simple answer accomplished several important things.

First, Jesus touched the man's life at a vital point of contact *for
him*. Where do you take a legalist? To God's *law*. Why? Because
that is what he thinks he knows, when in fact he has been ignoring
its true meaning and spirituality. Had the man been an antinomian
or a libertine — like the woman of Samaria — Jesus would have
focused on the practical fruit of his lawlessness rather than the law
itself. Jesus adapted his approach to the specific outlook of the
person he was addressing. That is what we ought also to do in our
evangelism. Too often, however, we train people to be gospel
parrots, who trot out the same well-rehearsed set of questions,
answers and Scripture quotations, as if all non-Christians were a
uniform caste of evangelistic targets — one script fits all! There is
none of this in the ministry of Jesus or the apostles. They applied
spiritual discernment to the people they evangelized and respected
their individual integrity as human beings. They met people where
they were in their particular spiritual state and personal circumstances and addressed that with wisdom born of a sound grasp of
both human nature and divine truth.

Secondly, Jesus went straight to the *real point* at issue. In this
case it was the spirituality of the law. The man knew very well that
no one could really keep the law. He knew that no one could be saved
if this depended on sinless perfection (Ps. 130:3). The idea that
salvation was attainable by man's best efforts needed to be exploded
and the (Old Testament) scriptural emphasis on the necessity of

salvation by grace alone revived. Jesus never allowed himself to be hung up on the other fellow's agenda. He always, as the Americans say, 'cut to the chase'. So, when people ask you about your church, don't give a lecture on the differences between you and the other twenty denominations represented in town, and what happened in the last 300 years to get you there. Go to the lifeblood of your faith and task — Christ and him crucified! People can talk denominations and history all the way to hell. Jesus never indulged such diversions. He made people face up to their real need and drove them towards a decision.

Thirdly, he exposed the lawyer's true intentions for any discerning person to see. Anybody present would have understood that the lawyer was looking for more than an opportunity to quote two basic biblical texts for Jesus. So he was left looking rather silly and must have felt somewhat mortified at being so easily outflanked. Jesus humbled him — without, let it be noted, humiliating him completely — and left him with a keen awareness that he was being challenged right to the depth of his being.

How do we know this? Because he responded by asking a question, which can only be regarded as an attempt to evade the implications of the very truths Jesus had obliged him to quote. Luke observes, **'But he wanted to justify himself, so he asked Jesus, "And who is my neighbour?"'** (10:29). This can only mean that he suddenly felt the force of the Word of God about loving one's neighbour as oneself, and realized that it did not find a loving answer in his heart. Therefore he wanted Jesus to define the limits of this injunction, by saying who were his neighbours and who were not.

Notice, too, that this represents a total reversal of his initial purpose. He had come gunning for Jesus, so to speak, but now he felt as if Jesus was blowing him out of the water. The hunter had become the hunted. The attacker was on the defensive. And it all happened so quickly and so gently. Jesus led the man to condemn himself by replying simply, politely and without the slightest hint of a raised voice or a combative spirit. Truth courteously stated has this kind of effect. The idea that Christians should march in the streets and wave placards, and shout the Scriptures at the world — which has become so fashionable in our confrontational age — did not come from Jesus' teaching or example. Our Lord shows us the way to witness for him — and it is with serenity rather than stridency.

Checkmate: the practice of caring (10:30-37)

In replying to the question, **'Who is my neighbour?'** Jesus gives no direct answer. Instead he tells a story — the famous parable of the 'good Samaritan' — and uses this to illustrate one of the marks of the spirituality of the kingdom of God, namely the practice of caring for others in their need (10:30-35). Again, Jesus obliges the lawyer to face his own sin by having him, in effect, interpret the parable (10:36-37).

The man who fell among thieves

That lonely eighteen miles from Jerusalem to Jericho was a great place for bandits to waylay travellers. A certain man was set upon, beaten up, robbed of all he had and left to die in the hot Judean sun. A while later, a **'priest'** and then a **'Levite'** came along, but both **'passed by on the other side'** (10:31-32). Neither man wanted to get involved, in spite of the fact that it was their calling to serve God and, of course, to 'love [their] neighbour as [themselves]'. Indeed, the priest may well have been going up to Jerusalem (or returning) in connection with his annual term of duty in the temple. We are not told, but this we do know, that for all their official positions, the two men showed nothing of the love of God for lost people that was signified in the temple sacrifices they knew so well. Who knows what excuses they came up with to justify passing by? The point is that they did not really care a whit for the poor fellow who lay crumpled and bloody at the roadside. The very people who might be expected to care went on their way.

'But,' said Jesus, along came **'a Samaritan'**. The very use of the term was profoundly meaningful to Jesus' Jewish hearers. To call a man a 'Samaritan' was not merely to identify his ethnic origin. It was more like calling an Irishman a 'Mick' or a German a 'Hun'. It cast an aspersion. It indicated a prejudice against him. It affected a certain superiority. Worse — to call a man a 'Samaritan' was tantamount to saying he was 'demon-possessed' (John 8:48). The Jews despised the Samaritans.[1] Accordingly, when Jesus cast the Samaritan in the role of the one who shows mercy to the thieves' victim, the callousness of the Jews would have become all the more shockingly obvious. Jesus' point was thus made crystal clear.

What it means to love your neighbour (10:33-34)

First, the Samaritan *felt* compassion for the man: **'When he saw him, he took pity on him'** (10:33). The suffering of another human being moved him to pity. He in a sense suffered with him. He felt his pain. And since the essence of compassion is to drive out all selfish considerations, he resolved to help him as best he could. He didn't worry about the bandits getting him if he stopped. He didn't think about the probability that this man was a Jew, who perhaps shared his countrymen's habit of despising Samaritans. He gave himself to the simple task of helping a man who was suffering and in deep trouble.

Secondly, the Samaritan *acted* on that compassionate impulse. He **'went to him and bandaged his wounds…'** (10:34). Love is not a theory; love acts. Love is tangible and palpable. Love expends resources in the interests of others. God loved lost people — and sent his only begotten Son to be their Saviour, by dying for them upon a cross. 'Greater love has no one than this,' said that Son, 'that he lay down his life for his friends' (John 15:13). Jesus did more — he died for his enemies, to make them, by grace through faith, into his friends, brothers, sisters, even the very children of God! The Samaritan risked himself for his Jewish 'enemy' and so is a living example of what love is really all about. 'Love binds up and soothes the wounds of life,' writes Herman Hanko. 'Love helps until it is no longer within one's power to help. Love forgets about one's self and thinks only of the other.'[2] 'If you love those who love you,' asked Jesus, 'what reward will you get? Are not even the tax collectors doing that?… Be perfect, therefore, as your heavenly Father is perfect' (Matt. 5:43-48).

Thirdly, the Samaritan *persisted* in his care for the robbers' victim. Some people's charity is like an Exocet missile — they 'fire and forget'. Churches will send money to support good causes at a distance, but rarely 'get their hands dirty' in caring for needy people on their own doorstep. The Samaritan took the man **'to an inn and took care of him'** and then left money for his bills, with the promise that he would **'reimburse [the innkeeper] for any extra expense'** on his return journey (10:34-35).

Love is defined by the apostle Paul as patient and kind. Negatively, love is not given to envy, boasting or pride; not rude, self-seeking, easily angered, bearing grudges or delighting in evil. Positively, love rejoices with the truth and always protects, trusts, hopes and perseveres (1 Cor. 13:4-7). This is not some abstract idea of love — a mere collage of fine-sounding words. It is a practical manifesto for Christian life. It is rooted in Christ and his love for his people — Paul had just been speaking about worship, the Lord's Supper and the nature of the church as the body of Christ (1 Cor. 11-12). It is that love which elsewhere he says is 'the fulfilment of the law' (Rom. 13:10). It is that love which flows practically from having been transformed by the love of God in Jesus Christ. It is pre-eminently the love of Christ as he hung on the cross and said, 'Father, forgive them, for they do not know what they are doing.' It is the everlasting love of God as he continues to call the lost to redemption and newness of life through the gospel of his own dear Son. Love is more than a feeling; it is acting on that feeling and persevering in that acting and feeling. Love is spending oneself for the Lord and for one's neighbour.

Are you a neighbour to those in need?

You will recall that this story was Jesus' response to the lawyer who had asked the question: 'Who is my neighbour?' (10:29). Jesus now looks the lawyer in the eye and asks him, **'Which of these three do you think was a neighbour to the man who fell into the hands of robbers?'** (10:36). The answer was, of course, inescapable. But he could not bring himself to say 'the Samaritan'. It 'stuck in his craw', as the Americans say, so all the lawyer could say was that the true neighbour was **'the one who had mercy on him'** (10:37). Now, what is Jesus teaching us here?

First of all, he is stressing that we can assume that our neighbour is *anyone in need that we can help.* The Samaritan didn't ask, 'Is he *really* my neighbour?', 'What nationality is he?', 'Do I know him?', 'Can I afford it?', or, 'Is it safe?' He simply did all that he could to help a human being in trouble. He showed the love that the priest and the Levite only talked about. Who is your neighbour? Anyone in need that you can help at the time! That means, at its simplest, responding to the needs that you meet up with in the day-to-day providence of God. Sending contributions for foreign relief and the like is fine, but what really tests our mettle is how much compassion we feel and show in practice for those who are feeling hurt close to hand. James made it clear that the essence of true religion was to 'look after orphans and widows in their distress and to keep oneself from being polluted by the world' (James 1:27). We are too used to leaving the orphans and widows — even the Christian ones in our own churches — to the ministrations of the welfare state, when they are, in truth, often the most immediate neighbours who need our help.

Secondly, Jesus' question is a direct challenge to the *conscience.* He was virtually asking the lawyer: 'Are *you* a neighbour to those whose paths you cross in daily life?' You see, the question, 'Who is my neighbour?' can be a wonderful theoretical question — the kind of question that can be discussed and debated in endless seminars and retreats, without ever getting round to dirtying a single hand in real mercy work.[3] Jesus surely discerned something of this attitude in the lawyer. That is why he rephrased the question in a personal way and shot it right at the fellow's conscience. That is why Jesus backed him to the wall with a question that forced him to confess that the man who *showed* the love was the real neighbour. And that was designed to teach him that being a neighbour starts with love and compassion in your heart and reaches out in practical help with your hands. Jesus therefore told him, **'Go and do likewise'** (10:37) — no frills; no elaborate explanations; no lengthy discussion on the 'parameters of the problem', as we might say. Just 'go' and 'do' — like the Samaritan! Do the best you can. But 'do'!

Jesus himself was, in a sense, the ultimate Good Samaritan. He came to lost people. He came as their neighbour and treated them as his neighbours. He died in the place of sinners. He died to heal their wounds and restore them to real and never-ending life, received and enjoyed through repentance towards God and faith in himself as Saviour and Lord. It is therefore a mark of kingdom life that God's people love others and care about them — because Christ first loved them when they were blind, naked, helpless and condemned.

He has dispersed his wealth abroad
   and given to the poor,
His horn with honour shall be raised,
   his righteousness endure.[4]

9.
Prayerfulness

The parable of the persistent friend
(Luke 11:5-13)

'I tell you, though he will not get up and give him the bread because he is his friend, yet because of the man's boldness he will get up and give him as much as he needs'(Luke 11:8).

It is a general truth that the best way to learn how to do something is to watch somebody else do it properly. So it was that, one day, Jesus was observed at prayer by one of his disciples. The disciple must have been mightily impressed by the spiritual power of the Lord's communion with his Father, no doubt in relation to his own lack of such intensity and depth in his personal experience of prayer, so that he asked Jesus, 'Lord, teach us to pray, just as John taught his disciples' (11:1).

This question, and Jesus' answer, teaches us that prayer is not something that comes naturally, but is learned from Christ, by grace through faith. It is therefore no mere mastery of a technique, as one might memorize a mathematical theorem or outline a speech. It requires being taught by God, in the heart, through the influences of the Holy Spirit and the Word — being taught and learning something that, once acquired and faithfully exercised, becomes a growing means of experiencing the love of Jesus Christ in the one who so prays. In this sense, then, we need to learn and practise the grace of believing prayer. Prayer is a world into which the Christian must and will strive to grow. It is not difficult to be a virtually prayerless Christian. Prayer has to be worked at in faith and cultivated and nurtured, so that it becomes more precious to us than fresh air and more vital to our life and happiness than the choicest of everyday pleasures. The truth is that Christian growth begins — or ends — in our private prayer lives. Prayerfulness is a vital mark of the kingdom of heaven in your heart and mine. It is this theme that is the subject of Jesus' parable of the persistent friend.

The parable of the persistent friend (11:5-8)

Jesus first answered the disciple's question by giving a model prayer — Luke's version of the Lord's Prayer. This is briefer than the one which Matthew recorded in the Sermon on the Mount. The differences just serve to underline the fact that Jesus is not interested in the mere repetition of some correct form of words, but in organized, though otherwise free, prayer (11:2-4).

The parable that immediately follows this prayer takes up the subject of answers to prayer. This is the subject of verses 5-8. In verses 9-13, Jesus applies the lessons of the parable, making clear the certainty that every Christian's prayers will be answered and that the answer will become plain in God's own good time to the one who prays in faith.

The unexpected nocturnal visitor (11:5-7)

In the first part of the parable, Jesus proposes a scenario to his disciples. Suppose you have an unexpected visitor late one evening and you are totally unprepared. You want to be hospitable and give him a meal after his travels, but you don't have a thing in the house. It is nearly midnight, but you have a friend who lives down the street and you are sure he will help in an emergency like this. So you go and knock on his door. You blurt out your request: **'Friend, lend me three loaves of bread, because a friend of mine on a journey has come to me, and I have nothing to set before him.'**

Your friend, however, is a little put out. He is all locked up. Everybody is asleep in bed. He is half asleep himself. It is all a bit unreal. So, with that groggy irritability of the half-awake, he whispers loudly from inside, **'Don't bother me. The door is already locked, and my children are with me in bed. I can't get up and give you anything.'** There is no need to ascribe bad motives to the man. You know how difficult it is to cope with midnight phone-calls. You can hardly remember your own name, far less deal rationally with the fellow on the line! Your body just cries out to be left alone!

Since Jesus begins the story with an interrogative — **'Which of you…?'** (11:5, AV; Greek: *tis ex humon*) — it is proper to see the whole parable as one long rhetorical question asking, 'What would you do in this situation? Would you give up and go home, or keep on trying till you got the food you needed?'

Persistence pays (11:8)

Jesus did not wait for the disciples to respond. He immediately gave an answer: **'I tell you, though he will not get up and give him the bread because he is his friend, yet because of the man's boldness he will get up and give him as much as he needs.'** Friendship isn't even going to do it, says Jesus. But sheer boldness and persistence will! Is this not true to life? That is why a child who wants mum to give him some sweets keeps nagging away until he gets them (or is sent packing!). Persistence is a normal and necessary ingredient in achieving any goal in life. Persistence is proof of commitment and the essence of effort. No one is commended for giving up after one try. Every good Boy Scout knows that the basic maxim is: 'If at first you don't succeed, try, try and try again!'

What, then, is Jesus' point? He was not just giving the disciples a lesson about 'persistence' as if it were an abstraction or a virtue in itself. He had a concrete spiritual purpose. He had in mind something to do with life in his kingdom — with the nature of a faith-driven discipleship towards God. Surely it is this: if our friends will certainly help us when we are persistent and importunate in seeking their help, how much more will God supply our needs when we are persistent and importunate in prayer, as we seek his help? Yes, we may need to 'nag' a friend or a spouse, because he or she doesn't seem very sympathetic to our need. In contrast, the Lord knows what we need before we even ask for it (Matt. 6:8) and has a sympathy for his people that is infinitely deeper than anything we may feel for our most beloved friends. 'So,' Jesus is saying, 'when you pray as I have taught you, persist in that prayer, all the time believing as an unmovable article of your faith that your heavenly Father will hear and answer according to his perfect will for your life. Even though he may delay an answer — like the friend at midnight in the parable — be assured that the answer will come as you persist in crying out to him.'

Another point relates to the nature of the prayer itself. In his excellent book, *The Mysteries of the Kingdom,* Herman Hanko notes three elements in the parable which 'must be applied to the relationship between God and his people which is expressed in prayer'.[1]

First, there was *true need.* The man's request was not frivolous, casual or unnecessary. Neither was it of earth-shattering importance. It was just the need of that moment and, for all that it was an unusual time and circumstance, it was a *normal* kind of need. The God who marks the fall of sparrows is interested in the things that happen in our ordinary lives.

Secondly, the request was made out of a *selfless love.* The man would not have disturbed his neighbour for himself. He did it out of love for the weary traveller. Compare the hypocrite who is the subject of Robert Burns' poem, 'Holy Willie's Prayer', who after praying for the judgement of God on all and sundry, then has the gall to say,

But, Lord, remember me and mine
Wi' mercies temporal and divine,
That I for grace and gear may shine
Excelled by nane
And a' the glory shall be Thine—
    Amen, Amen!

Last and not least, there was *no other source of help.* The man had nowhere else to go. The shops were closed. Only the neighbour could help. Some people pray when they should be working instead. 'I'll pray about it,' is too often a pious excuse for not *doing* what needs to done. For example, you don't need to pray about 'going to church' — you just need to go! Prayer is a lifeline for God's saving power, in Jesus Christ, to pour into the experience of each child of God.

'I love the Lord,' says the psalmist, 'for he heard my voice;
    he heard my cry for mercy.
Because he turned his ear to me,
    I will call on him as long as I live.

The cords of death entangled me,
    the anguish of the grave came upon me;
    I was overcome by trouble and sorrow.
Then I called on the name of the Lord:
    "O Lord, save me'''

(Ps. 116:1-4).

At the very heart of prayer, as a mark of kingdom life, is the awareness that without the Lord we are lost. Every real Christian can only cry with Augustus Toplady,

Foul, I to the fountain fly;
Wash me, Saviour, or I die.[2]

'So I say to you...' (11:9-13)

Jesus immediately offered the practical application of his parable. **'So I say to you'** indicates that a declaration is about to be made that has all the force of divine authority. The minds of men are being confronted by the mind of God. That declaration concerns the *imperative* to persist in prayer (11:9-10) and the *promise* that God will richly bless persistent prayer (11:11-13).

'Ask ... seek ... knock' (11:9-10)

We must notice that this is not an exhortation to offer up a prayer now and again — far less an encouragement to recite prayers like pagan mantras. God is not impressed by a lot of mere words (Matt. 6:7). Persistent godly prayer is what is called for.

1. Prayer must persist towards its goal. Jesus gives a threefold encouragement to pray: **'Ask ... seek ... knock.'** Underlying this is an unspoken assumption that we may find quite disturbing. It is that God rarely gives us what we ask for right away. Sometimes he does, but mostly he does not. Hence the need for Jesus to emphasize persistence. Why is this so? It is simply because asking once doesn't cost a thing. Anybody will try something once. I saw a billboard somewhere in America that just said, 'Try prayer.' That is *not* what Jesus has in mind. Anybody can 'try' prayer — but what kind of prayer, and to whom, and for what purpose? Jesus first gave an outline for the ordering of our prayers *to his Father* and then exhorted persistence in the practice of such God-centred prayer. To persist, on and on, until the Lord brings the blessing in *his* time, takes genuine, humble Christian faith. Pride and unbelief give up when they do not get their way. 'God isn't there. It didn't work!' they say. It takes love, faith, trust and holy confidence to persevere. We know this to be true in our dealings with people. 'Well, I asked him once before,' we say of the person from whom we sought a favour. It takes some commitment to keep on trying.

2. Prayer must escalate in intensity of commitment. The three verbs (which are all in a tense which implies repetition), 'Ask..., seek..., knock', also indicate that our prayers must not stop with the barest request. Asking must be followed by seeking and seeking by knocking. These are not mere synonyms. They represent a deepening involvement in the process of believing prayer.

We must *'seek'*; that is, we must exercise ourselves more fully to the end that we pray aright and be heard in our praying. This means reflecting upon what we have already asked. Was it something clearly in accord with God's will as revealed in the Bible? Is there some impediment in me, remembering that the psalmist once testified, 'If I had cherished sin in my heart, the Lord would not have listened' (Ps. 66:18). Is there a problem I need to go and deal with? Do I need to be reconciled to a brother and then come back and seek God's blessing in this matter I've been praying about? (Matt. 5:24). God's silences are always pregnant with invitations to examine ourselves to see whether we are really living the life of faith as we should (2 Cor. 13:5).

Then we must *'knock'*. We must continue with the intensity of a Jacob as he wrestled with the pre-incarnate Son of God at Peniel — 'I will not let you go unless you bless me' (Gen. 32:26). A salesman who tramps the streets and knocks on doors is saying something about his commitment to the job. He is prepared to give all he has got! Likewise, persistence is the proof of a true spirit of prayer. Think of the Canaanite woman who asked Jesus to heal her demon-possessed daughter, only to hear him say, 'I was sent only to the lost sheep of Israel,' and 'It is not right to take the children's bread and toss it to their dogs.' Did she go away angry or dejected? No! She cried all the harder, 'Yes, Lord, ... but even the dogs eat the crumbs that fall from their master's table.' 'Woman,' said Jesus, 'you have great faith! Your request is granted' (Matt. 15:21-28). Think of the blind beggar, Bartimæus, who, the more the bystanders tried to shut him up, shouted out all the louder, 'Jesus, Son of David, have mercy on me!' Jesus said to him, 'Go, your faith has healed you' (Mark 10:46-52). Think too of the apostle Paul, who prayed three times for the removal of that 'thorn in the flesh' that perennially afflicted him (whatever it was). The blessing came after persistent prayer and consisted not in the removal of 'the thorn', but in the increase of the grace to endure it! 'My grace is sufficient for you, for my power is made perfect in weakness' (2 Cor. 12:7-9).

'Ask, seek' and 'knock' and **'It will be given ... you will find ... the door will be opened.'** God answers prayer.

'How much more will your Father in heaven?' (11:11-13)

Jesus' final word is an encouragement about the certainty of God's promises with respect to answering our faithful prayers. It is an appeal to the character of God as our heavenly Father. Jesus introduces this in such a way as to heighten the force of his message. In the parable itself he spoke about a friend-to-friend situation (11:5-7). Here, he moves to a father-and-son relationship. From that he drives home his point by taking us on to consider the attitude of God towards his believing children. The argument is from the lesser to the greater. If our earthly fathers know how to give good things to their children, **'How much more will your Father in heaven give the Holy Spirit to those who ask him?'** (11:13).

If a son asks his father for **'bread ... will he give him a stone?'** (11:11, AV).[3] The bridge to the parable is obvious. If a friend will give three loaves at midnight, what kind of a father would give a stone to a hungry boy? Would you give your son a **'snake'** instead of a **'fish'**, or a **'scorpion'** instead of an **'egg'**? 'No father mocks his child in such heartless ways,' remarks R. C. H. Lenski.[4] The reality is that some fathers do abuse their children in all sorts of cruel and bizarre ways, but those who do are rightly regarded as criminals of the lowest order.

The argument is unanswerable. **'If you then, though you are evil'** (and we know very well in our hearts that we are sinners, even though saved by grace) **'know how to give good gifts to your children, how much more will your Father in heaven give the**

Holy Spirit to those who ask him!' (11:13). A holy God cannot do
otherwise than love *his* children! And notice something else. From
bread — both in the Lord's prayer ('Give us each day our daily
bread', 11:3) and in the parable of the persistent friend — Jesus has
now taken us to the gift of the Holy Spirit! Yes, we can and should
pray for our daily bread! But there is far more to be asked of the Lord.
He will give his Holy Spirit. He will give himself! In other words,
the certainty that he will answer prayer is absolute. The assurance
that believers may come to enjoy is likewise complete and unassailable. Jesus does not say it here, but it is a fact that in the Holy Spirit
we have come to the one who is the beginning of believing prayer
as well as the highest gift that Christ can give in answer to prayer.
He is the 'Spirit of adoption, whereby we cry, Abba, Father', the
Spirit who bears 'witness with our spirit, that we are the children of
God' (Rom. 8:15-16, AV). He is the reason why prayer is the
Christian's 'native air'.

10.
Rich towards God

The parable of the rich fool
(Luke 12:13-21)

'But God said to him, "You fool! This very night your life will be demanded from you. Then who will get what you have prepared for yourself?" This is how it will be with anyone who stores up things for himself but is not rich towards God' (Luke 12:20-21).

You can tell a great deal about a person from the questions he asks and the requests he makes. Jesus had been encouraging his disciples to trust in God in the face of potential danger. They were not to worry about what to say, when called upon to defend themselves before the authorities, 'for the Holy Spirit will teach you at that time what you should say' (12:12). Suddenly, a man in the crowd blurted out a demand. **'Teacher,'** he said, **'tell my brother to divide the inheritance with me'** (12:13). This was the plea of a man who felt strongly that he had been wronged and was seeking justice for himself.

Jesus discerned, however, that the man's concern for justice was only part of the problem. He saw a man who was so wrapped up in his problem that he *had* to bring it up, however inappropriate the situation. He saw this consuming passion for resolving the inheritance dispute as an indication of a deeper spiritual problem that needed urgently to be addressed. Jesus' reply is in two parts.

First, he denied any jurisdiction in the case: **'Man, who appointed me a judge or an arbiter between you?'** (12:14). Jesus was not a civil magistrate and was not about to be drawn away from his preaching of the kingdom of God. His answer implied that there was a proper court where the man might seek redress for his grievance. The most basic point is that the inheritance dispute itself was only a symptom of a deeper underlying spiritual problem in the man's life. Jesus was willing to tackle the root problem. The inheritance was a matter for the civil courts. Jesus wanted men's hearts and minds.

Accordingly, he refocused the man's attention — and that of his audience — on the personal, spiritual aspect of the case, namely the man's obvious obsession with the lost inheritance. Jesus does this by first stating a general principle and then going on to illustrate it with a story — the parable of the rich fool. The principle is in the latter part of Luke 12:15: **'Watch out! Be on your guard against all kinds of greed; a man's life does not consist in the abundance of his possessions.'** Jesus goes straight to the heart of the matter: money and possessions are not the meaning of life! He was saying to the man, 'You need to stop running around like a chicken on hot bricks and recognize that your real problem is an inordinate desire for "things"! You are acting as if this inheritance is the most important thing in your life ... which it certainly is not! The *real* problem is that you think this inheritance is the problem!' Jesus then tells his story about the rich fool to explain the point (12:16-20). After that, he drives it home to the man's conscience (12:21).

The rich man's problem (12:16-17)

The parable of the rich fool is about a man whose life revolves around material things. He is a living illustration of Solomon's adage, 'Whoever loves money never has money enough; whoever loves wealth is never satisfied with his income' (Eccl. 5:10). He was a successful farmer and his crops had outgrown his capacity to store them. **'What shall I do?'** he thought to himself. **'I have no place to store my crops'** (12:17).

In these days of socialistic wealth-redistribution through taxation and welfarism, the very idea of being 'rich' is regarded by many people with suspicion, if not downright hostility. 'Tax the rich,' for example, was a leading slogan in the 1992 American presidential campaign that propelled Bill Clinton to the White House. The politics of envy have clothed success and wealth with an aura of grasping selfishness. To not a few, success equals *excess*!

It must be said, however, that the honest production of wealth is not a sin. It is the fruit of our labours. We have no reason to think that the rich man was anything but a hard worker and an intelligent farmer. Furthermore, we can say that God had blessed him. Success was the Lord's rewarding of his good work. God has promised his people: 'You will eat the fruit of your labour; blessings and prosperity will be yours' (Ps. 128:2). The converse is that if you know these blessings, you ought to praise God for them. And you ought not to feel guilty about it. Success like this is a wonderful problem for anyone to have. The real issue is how you handle it.

The rich man's solution (12:18-19)

The rich man had asked himself the right question. He did not have space to store all of his grain. He had to do something with it. His solution would have delighted the mandarins of Brussels — he decided to build bigger barns for his version of the EEC 'grain mountain'.

He could have chosen to *give away* his bonus crops, but he decided to shut up these potential alms in his storehouse. It evidently never entered his head to use it to do some good for needy people. No! He saw *security* in this extra grain. It was his ever-expanding savings account, his certificates of deposit, his pension fund. **'And I'll say to myself, "You have plenty of good things laid up for many years. Take life easy; eat, drink and be merry"'**(12:19). Here was the man's fatal flaw: not his success as a producer of wealth, but his attitude to, and use of, his riches. Notice three points in which he went completely wrong, all of which show that, like Jesus' original questioner, he centred his whole life around material things. He was self-centred, security-centred and satisfaction-centred.

Self-centred

Have you noticed how often the rich man spoke about *himself*? There are no fewer than thirteen references to himself: six 'I's and seven assorted 'my's and 'you's. He talks to himself about himself: 'I'll say to myself...' It is all 'me, me, me, me'! It is a trifle trite to say that 'I' is at the centre of 'sin'. But it is true that all sin begins with self. All sin seeks to put me first and enthrone me, myself, as the prime object of my concern. Sin is doing things *my* way, as opposed to God's way. It is me being my own god and doing what

I want. The rich man acted as if he were the lord of all his possessions. He was completely preoccupied with self. Nothing else figured at all in his calculations.

Security-centred

He also believed that riches provide security. **'You have plenty of good things laid up for many years.'** What is it that men and women crave for, but security? They want to know for sure, don't they, that they will be comfortable for as long as they live — and even for eternity, just in case there is a God after all? And that is what our God-denying society tries to provide! Insurance, banking, political promises, social security, national health, public assistance, defence spending, not to mention a universalistic state church — all offer hopes of cradle to the grave and to the great beyond (if there is one) security! We are bombarded with promises of security — security without sweat; most of all, security without God. Christian prudence is always commendable, but the rich man's thirst for security was an idol.

Satisfaction-centred

The rich man also had satisfaction from his riches. This was not the normal satisfaction we should have in a job well done or a kindness given or received. The Greek text says that the man said to himself, 'I will say to my *soul* [Gk, *psuche*], "*Soul*, you have plenty of good things laid up..."' (12:19). Archbishop Trench noted, 'There is an irony as melancholy as profound in making him address this speech, not to his body, but to his *soul*; for that soul, though capable of being thus dragged down to the basest service of the flesh ... was also capable of being quickened by the divine Spirit, of knowing and loving and glorifying God.'[1] The point is that the rich man felt *spiritually* satisfied because of his riches. He fed his inner being on earthly things: 'Soul ... take your ease.' But the truth is, comments Herman Hanko, 'The soul cannot find rest in corn, ... the soul cannot eat and drink money and houses, ... the misery of life cannot be drowned in drinking the cup of worldly joy and carnal pleasure.'[2]

This is why God called him a **'fool'**. In everyday speech, a fool is someone who makes mistakes out of ignorance — things that are silly but in a way excusable. In the Bible, however, foolishness is a distinct spiritual condition. It is sin rooted, not in ignorance, but in a depraved heart. The fool refuses to face God's realities. He says in his heart, 'There is no God' (Ps. 14:1). He lives his life without reference to the will of God. He prefers his own way and his world is an unreal fabrication — a web of self-deceit in which he distorts reality and makes it fit his Christ-denying plan for his life. The rich fool was sincerely satisfied, but his whole system, from the foundation up, was completely out of touch with the true scheme of things, namely, God's plan and purpose. This kind of foolishness is not buffoonery; it is a lethal disregard for the most important truths about life, time and eternity.

God's response to the rich man (12:20)

As we have already seen, God's first response was to call the man 'You fool!' He then underscored this characterization by stating the proof for it: **'This very night your life will be demanded from you. Then who will get what you have prepared for yourself?'** The language is heavy with irony, highlighting the arrogance of a man who thought he was in control of his own life.

'This very night ...'

The rich fool thought he had plenty for 'many years' (12:19). Like virtually all of us, no doubt, he assumed he would wake up tomorrow morning. People in apparently good health never expect to die tonight. All but the very elderly have plenty of plans for the future. The rich man was looking forward to a new life. The truth was that he had no future at all! As a matter of fact, not one of us really knows what a single day will bring forth (Prov. 27:1). He never prepared for eternity, because wealth and ease were his whole life. This is the rule for all unbelievers, for they are all going to be surprised by death and judgement, as by a 'thief in the night' (1 Thess. 5:2-4; 2 Peter 3:10). It is impossible to prepare effectively for something you do not believe in. The rich fool lived as if there were no tomorrow — and no reckoning with God. But tomorrow did come, as it will for everyone, for 'It is appointed unto man once to die, but after this the judgement' (Heb. 9:27, AV).

'Your soul is required of you ...' (12:20, NASB)

The use of the word **'soul'** (Gk, *psuche*) takes us back to the rich man's words in 12:19. That same *psuche* that he had told to rest easy was now called into eternity, while his body was left lifeless, surrounded by the bulging barns that he had trusted to guarantee a long and happy retirement. The departure of his *psuche* proves the folly of attachment to earthly things. Shrouds don't have pockets. Naked we come into the world, and naked we go out. Trust in the transitory and confidence in the corruptible are patently ridiculous.

'Then who will get what you have prepared for yourself?'

> 'Man,' says the psalmist, 'is a mere phantom as he goes to and fro:
> he bustles about, but only in vain;
> he heaps up wealth, not knowing who will get it'
>   (Ps. 39:6).

'I hated all the things I had toiled for under the sun,' observed the Preacher, 'because I must leave them to the one who comes after me. And who knows whether he will be a wise man or a fool?' (Eccl. 2:18-19). Riches are supposed to be meaningful and a blessing, but to experience them in this way requires lying very light to them — seeing them as a stewardship from God. 'What do you have that you did not receive?' asks the apostle Paul (1 Cor. 4:7). God gives his gifts to us that we might use them in the work of his kingdom. With this is the assurance to those who are faithful that 'In all things at all times, having all that you need, you will abound in every good work' (2 Cor. 9:6-9).

This, sad to say, was a closed book to the rich man. He believed in himself and his 'things' — trusting the Lord was never in his mind.

'You fool!'

Now we can see the force of God's first words to the man. They contrast radically with the man's opinion of himself. He was well pleased with his own genius. He was going to enjoy the fruits of his brilliance — or luck, call it what you like — for 'many years'. Such is the folly of the fool. God is not in all his thoughts.

Jesus' application to us all (12:21)

Jesus' application could hardly have been more direct: **'This is how it will be with anyone who stores up things for himself but is not rich towards God.'**

'Be on your guard against all kinds of greed' (12:15)

Negatively, this is a warning against the danger of *greed*. Jesus had warned against this before telling the parable:'Watch out! Be on your guard against all kinds of greed; a man's life does not consist in the abundance of his possessions' (12:15). We are therefore called to search our hearts as to our attitude to good things. Are we consumed with desire for a bigger house, a better-paid job, a newer car, expensive clothes or foreign holidays? These are not bad things in themselves. All could be blessings. But they can also be snares, if not put in their proper place in the scheme of our ambitions. They can become the focus of discontent and lead us away from Christ. Greed is in the end a discontent with the providence of God, because it arises from the conviction that we do not have what we think we deserve. And that is sin and therefore ultimately self-destructive.

Positively, we ought to recognize that God's warning is essentially an act of *grace*. It is easy to portray God's role in the parable as merely vindictive. I once heard a prominent evangelical preacher interpret God's action this way. Just when the rich man was ready to take his ease and do some serious thinking, this preacher said, down came the judgement of God. It was as if God was only willing to let the man be materialistic, but as soon as he was ready to consider spiritual things — that was it! 'Can't have him becoming a believer now!' This kind of interpretation twists the passage to gain a maximum 'scare' effect for preaching the gospel. While this may stir some emotions, it does a disservice to the Lord and his Word. In fact, the rich man gave no indication of giving attention to the things of God after his barns were built.

More importantly, God is not capricious and merely vengeful.

He takes no pleasure in the death of the wicked (Ezek. 33:11). His every warning is an overture of grace that invites repentance. Such warnings are his 'Exit' signs and under each one there is a gospel door to the fresh air of new life in his Son. The world hates the Bible's rebukes of sin and affects such high-minded offence that Christians are made to feel guilty that they have any moral standards at all. It is as if the only real sin is calling sinners what they are. But God's warnings are pleadings of grace. They say, in effect, 'Flee the wrath to come!' They rebuke in order to redeem.

'Be rich towards God'

Being 'rich towards God' is the opposite of the materialism of the rich fool. Money and security filled his horizon. Mammon was his god. He was intent on laying up for himself treasures on earth (Matt. 6:19). He was rich towards riches. 'The greatest error of all is that he is in no care to be *rich toward God*, rich in the *account of God*, whose accounting us rich makes us so (Rev. 2:9), rich in the *things of God*, rich in *faith* (James 2: 15), rich in *good works*, in the *fruits of righteousness* (1 Tim. 6:18), rich in graces, and comforts, and spiritual gifts.'[3]

The rich man needed to die to his bigger barns and find his true wealth in the things of God. He needed 'treasure in heaven that will not be exhausted, where no thief comes near and no moth destroys' (12:33). And what is this spiritual treasure, but a saving interest in the Saviour of the world? Christ is the true treasure. In him 'are hidden all the treasures of wisdom and knowledge' (Col. 2:3; 2 Cor. 4:7). Only in the context of knowing Christ as Saviour and Lord do the material blessings of this life come into their own. Our God will supply all our needs (Phil. 4:19). He will bless the work of our hands (Ps. 90:17). 'Seek first his kingdom and his righteousness, and all these things will be given to you as well' (Matt. 6:33).

The sad end of the rich fool asks each of us, 'Where is your treasure? For what are you living your life? Where will you spend eternity? What is your relationship to Jesus Christ and the things of God?' Jesus himself tells us that 'Where your treasure is, there your heart will be also' (12:34). Remember Moses? He counted 'disgrace for the sake of Christ as of greater value than the treasures of Egypt'. Why? 'Because he was looking ahead to his reward' (Heb. 11:26).

Moses had saving faith in the Lord and knew the true value of things. Those who love the Lord Jesus Christ, who are the citizens of his kingdom, live lives that are marked by being 'rich towards God'.

> Thy Word I've treasured in my heart,
> That I give no offence to thee.
> Thou, O Jehovah, blessed art,
> Thy statutes teach thou unto me.
>
> I with my lips have oft declared
> The judgements which thy mouth has shown,
> More joy thy testimonies gave
> Than all the riches I have known.[4]

11.
Bearing fruit

The parable of the fruitless fig-tree
(Luke 13:1-9)

'But unless you repent, you too will all perish' (Luke 13:5).

People are never more interested in 'the news' than when it is bad. Our family lived in Britain during the Falklands War of 1982 and in America during the Gulf War of 1991. At no time in our lives have we felt so compelled to 'watch the box' as during these 'television wars'. News of terrible things *is* compelling and this cannot but be so. Events enthral us, the fearful fascinates, the terrible titillates, the important intrigues and the momentous mesmerizes. 'Bad news' grabs our attention. The other side of this is that when the news is good, it can pass over us with scarcely a flutter, as if it were hardly news at all.

Part of the reason for this phenomenon is surely that there is something in human nature that attracts us to the bad news. What is the genesis of all bad news but human sin or, in the case of natural disasters, the fallenness of a world marred by human sin? There is even a word in German for this gruesome fascination with dark deeds. *'Schadenfreude'* is 'a malicious joy at the misfortunes of others'. Even among Christians, who you would have thought would be most interested in the good news of the work of God in people's lives, it is the gossip about people's problems that moves most quickly from mouth to ear and ear to mouth.

There is, however, sometimes an even more sinister element in this enjoyment of bad news. It is the idea that those who have been crushed by these reported calamities deserved to suffer in this way, whereas I, who have been spared such things, must be a better person than they. Some people came to Jesus and told him about an atrocity committed by Pilate, the Roman governor. Pilate's men had entered the temple, it seems, and killed some Galileans who were there to offer sacrifices. Their blood was **'mixed with their sacrifices'** (13:1). Jesus caught their meaning right away and asked them, **'Do you think that these Galileans were worse sinners than all the other Galileans because they suffered this way?'** (13:2).

Jesus discerned in this the tendency to self-righteously slap oneself on the back in the face of someone else's misfortunes. Perhaps they were thinking to themselves, 'What terrible sinners these fellows must have been for God to allow such an awful thing to happen to them! And how thankful I am that I am apparently in a better spiritual state before God!'

Well, if this was how they were thinking, Jesus soon set them straight! His uncompromising reply was, **'Unless you repent, you too will all perish'** (13:5) They were looking on the surface of these events, that is, on the *methodology of other people's deaths* and its supposed significance for their eternal destinies. Jesus took them to the substance of the matter, namely the *fact that everybody dies* and the true significance of that for their eternal destinies. Forget other people's terrible sins, and remember that every human being 'is destined to die once, and after that to face judgement' (Heb. 9:27). Death *is* 'the wages of sin', but that goes for everybody, not just disaster victims! (Rom. 6:23).

At its most basic level, bad news in anybody's life is an invitation to reflect on, first, the fact that I too will soon die, and, second, that I must answer to God for the life I have lived. It calls me to reflect on my own spiritual condition and realize that if I do not repent towards God, then I will soon go down the same road to a lost eternity that I so readily assigned to the victims of Pilate's soldiery and the Siloam tower!

The necessity of repentance (13:5)

Several vital assumptions underlie Jesus' response and since they form the theological context for a proper understanding of the parable that follows, we must get them clear in our minds.

Everyone is condemned already

The first and most obvious assumption behind Jesus' statement in verse 5 is that everyone is 'condemned already' (John 3:18) and will only escape the just judgement of God through faith and repentance. Guilt, lostness, rebellion against God and just condemnation under his righteous law are all inseparable from the human condition. A long and quiet life is not proof that you do not need a Saviour.

Circumstances are not the whole story

A second assumption is that what happens to people is not *ipso facto* the result of their attitude to God. The fact that calamities overtake some, while others have a quiet life, says nothing about the merits of the individual. It is a fallacy to conclude that those who die because of accidents or atrocities are greater sinners in the sight of God than those who die in their beds at a great old age. We should therefore be very careful before identifying personal disasters with particular sins. We should never, for example, make illness an index of relative wickedness, even if certain illnesses are associated with certain excesses or immoral lifestyles. Not all AIDS deaths result from sodomy. Not all who die of cirrhosis of the liver are drunkards.

There are instances where connections have been made between a particular illness or death and a specific judgement of God. The death of the Herod who was 'eaten by worms' and the sicknesses and deaths in the Corinthian church are cases in point. We only know about these because they are the subjects of special revelation in Scripture (Acts 12:22-23; 1 Cor. 11:30) The general rule, here established by Christ himself, is that we cannot make such connections. The manner of death is simply not determinative of eternal destiny. Read Psalm 73, where David reflects on the prosperity and long life of the wicked, and Ecclesiastes 7:15, where the Preacher sees 'a righteous man perishing in his righteousness, and a wicked man living long in his wickedness'. We thirst for an easy test by which to tell the good from the bad (especially if it makes *us* feel good about ourselves!). But we 'all share a common destiny — the righteous and the wicked, the good and the bad, the clean and the unclean...' (Eccl. 9:2).

God is faithfully dealing with us

A third assumption is that God is dealing sovereignly and faithfully with every human being. If, in the case of manifestly wicked people, he appears to delay his judgements, it is not that his justice is being thwarted. If, in the case of genuinely godly people, he allows tragedy to cast its shadow over their lives, it is not because he loves them any the less. It is just that God is working out his purposes of redemption and of judgement in a way that, while it often baffles us, is wholly consistent with the purposes of his perfect will. So if some Galileans are killed in the temple and some people die in Siloam when a building collapses, or somebody is killed in a traffic accident down the street from where you live, don't jump to false, self-serving, self-righteous conclusions. You can live to be 100, die in your bed and still go hell — 'unless you repent'! God is dealing with us all, and in such a way as to bring us to himself with broken spirits and contrite hearts. The real issue for every individual is repentance and new life versus rebellion and eternal death. Don't misread the signs! 'Repent,' says Jesus, '… or perish.'

Having set forth the necessity of a saving change in one's heart and relationship to God, Jesus then drove home the point in a most searching way in the parable of the fruitless fig-tree.

The peril of fruitless lives (13:6-9)

A farmer had a fig-tree in his vineyard. He looked for fruit on his tree, **'but did not find any'** (13:6). He had a right to expect some fruit on that tree. The fig is one of the great fruit-bearing trees of the East and its reason for being in his vineyard was to produce fruit.

For **'three years'** he had come looking for fruit on this tree, but he had found none. Accordingly, he told the vine-dresser, **'Cut it down! Why should it use up the soil?'** (13:7). As in the American game of baseball, it was a case of 'three strikes and you are out'! The tree was a dud! It had to go!

The vine-dresser, however, interceded for the fig tree. He asked for one more year — a year in which he would cultivate the soil around it and put down fertilizer. **'If it bears fruit next year,'** he said to the farmer, **'fine! If not, then cut it down'** (3:8-9). The farmer clearly agreed. The tree was spared — for now!

The vineyard is probably the world, although, as Herman Hanko observes, 'It is quite likely that the Lord intended no definite analogy between the vineyard and a reality in life.'[1] The fig-tree is surely the nation of Israel, the Old Testament church (cf. Isa. 34:4; Jer. 5:17; 8:13; Hosea 2:12; Joel 1:17).[2] The farmer is God, while the vine-dresser is the Mediator, Jesus the Messiah, as he intercedes for these fruitless 'people of God'.

The implications of the parable are not difficult to discern, but they are very searching. Three points stand out.

1. God has a right to see spiritual life and fruitfulness in our lives

The specific focus is upon those who are already inside his vineyard. This is a word for those who profess to be God's people, who are within the bosom of the church and think, in whatever way, that they are right with God. Well, says Jesus, that which calls itself the church, whether of the Old or New Testament, and professes some sort of faith in the living God, ought to show some evidence of actually belonging to the Lord. God had repeatedly poured out his blessings upon Israel and shown his great love towards his people. Yet they just as repeatedly turned away from his ways and will. The same is true of the New Testament church throughout her history. Ruin and revival have chased one another down the centuries. Today in the West, the gospel is on the defensive as it has not been since before the Reformation. And, as in Jesus' day, it is the leaders of our ecclesiastical establishments and the erstwhile shepherds of the people that have led the Gadarene rush to the theological suicide and practical fruitlessness that have devastated the churches of our time and condemned whole generations of ordinary people to ignorance of the truth and spiritual darkness.

The fruit looked for is that of a living faith, evidenced by true personal holiness. Do those who claim to be believers have a heart-persuasion of the truth of the inspired Word of God as the rule of faith and life? This is the fruit that alike weighs down the boughs of godly old saints and forms the aspirations of young believers (Ps. 92:14; 119:9). But what does the Lord often find in the so-called churches of this world? External religion and unchanged hearts; forms of words and empty rituals; easy assurance of God's favour combined with unrepented sin and darkened minds; sham religiosity at Christmas and Easter. Where, pray, in all this, is the evidence of real love for the Saviour?

2. *God has set a limit to his long-suffering of our rebellious fruitlessness*

The tree was not going to be allowed to be fruitless for ever. This is true of daily life. Modern academics must 'publish or perish'! Workers must produce the goods, or they are laid off. There is a law of results in operation in every job situation under heaven (see Prov. 6:6; Eccl. 5:18-20; 2 Thess. 3:10). All these different patterns of accountability reflect the ultimate fact that we are accountable to God. The other side of God's expectations of us in time will be his disposition of us for eternity. When God revealed himself at the second giving of the Ten Commandments on Mount Sinai, 'He passed in front of Moses, proclaiming, "The Lord, the Lord, the compassionate and gracious God, slow to anger, abounding in love and faithfulness, maintaining love to thousands, and forgiving wickedness, rebellion and sin. Yet he does not leave the guilty unpunished; he punishes the children and their children for the sin of the fathers to the third and fourth generation"' (Exod. 34:6-7).

There is a definite point at which the Lord ceases to 'contend with man' (Gen. 6:3). The apostle Peter warned his readers about 'scoffers' in 'the last days' who would flaunt their utter contempt for this truth, especially as it was expressed in the teaching about the Second Coming of Jesus Christ and the Day of Judgement (2 Peter 3:3-10).

The parable of the fruitless fig-tree reminds us of this truth, albeit in a compressed fashion. As with the tree, so with *you*! And notice, too, that the parable is directed, not simply at the church as a collection of individuals, but at the church as *a body, set in a specific historical context*. Jesus was speaking to apostate Israel in the last generation of its existence as the Old Testament church. He had earlier pointed out that this generation would 'be held responsible for the blood of all the prophets that has been shed since the beginning of the world, from the blood of Abel to the blood of Zechariah, who was killed between the altar and the sanctuary'. He was especially emphatic about it, 'Yes, I tell you, this generation will be held responsible for it all' (Luke 11:50-51).

John Owen, that greatest of English theologians, points out that Jesus goes far beyond his Father's revelation to Moses at Sinai. There, God spoke of a collective responsibility extending to three and four generations. Here Jesus applies it to 'the sins of a *hundred* generations'. Owen observes, 'And whereas this generation was to *slay Christ himself*, and did so, they did, therein, approve of and justify all the blood that was shed in the same cause from the foundation of the world; and made themselves justly liable unto the punishment due unto it. Hence our Saviour tells them (Matt. 23:35) that they, the men of that generation, slew Zechariah, who was actually slain many hundred years before.'[3] In other words, the parable's immediate thrust was to the impending destruction of the unrepentant apostate Old Testament church and the final end of the Old Testament order. This took place in A. D. 70, with the destruction of Jerusalem.

The same principle applies to the New Testament era. Owen notes that 'The blood of all that suffered under the Old Testament was expiated. Abel's blood cries no more; nor doth God look any more on the blood of Zechariah to require it. But the same voice and cry is now continued by another sort of men; namely, those who have suffered in the cause of Christ since his coming, according to the promise (Rev. 6:9,10). And this cry shall be continued until the appointed time doth come for the utter destruction of the *antichristian, apostatized church-state.*'[4] The fruitless fig-trees of this world have a day of reckoning ahead of them. God has drawn a line in their path, and when they reach it, the cup of their sins will be full and their end will have come. This truth is no more palatable to today's clerics and church members than it was to those who heard it from Jesus' lips with their own ears. But it is still true and the day will dawn when God will suffer them no more (cf. Gen. 15:16).

3. God has ordained that the gospel be proclaimed for a season

It is only of God's mercy that we are not all consumed (Lam. 3:22). This is the fundamental meaning of the intercession of the vine-dresser and of the extra year's cultivation he won for the tree. Israel was apostate and in a state of condemnation before God, her days were indeed numbered, but God was prepared to give, as it were, a stay of execution, for the sake of his Messiah. Thus the fig-tree illustrates Jesus' charge: 'Unless you repent, you too will all perish!'

If we are inclined to listen to the Lord's solemn warning, it is a word of grace with a promise of salvation to all who repent. That is why the 'gospel' is, literally, 'good news'. When all appears irretrievably lost, when a sinner is convicted that he really is a sinner and cannot save himself, then comes a word that says that Christ has died to save sinners such as he is and that, upon repentance towards God and faith in the Lord Jesus Christ, he will be saved!

On the other hand, to be warned and to disregard it is to intensify guilt all the more and seal the justice of God's wrath against the unrepentant. 'The state is so with us', writes John Owen, 'that, unless we repent, we shall perish. I do not prescribe unto the sovereignty of God in his providential administrations. He can, if he please, suffer all his warnings to be despised, all his calls neglected, yea, scoffed at, and yet exercise forbearance toward us, as unto a speedy execution of justice. But woe unto them with whom he so deals; for it hath only this end, that they may have a space to fill up the measure of their iniquities, and so be fitted for eternal destruction (Rom.9:22).'[5]

Our great need

The unfruitful fig-tree had only one hope. He was the vine-dresser. Had he not interceded, the tree would have been firewood. To those who heard Jesus, the implication would not have been missed. The Pharisees certainly knew what he was saying, and they hated him for it. Jesus *was* the vine-dresser in the parable. They and their Israel were the unfruitful fig-tree. Only in and through him would they be saved from the judgement that was coming upon them.

All of this is designed, of course, to reach down through history and confront every generation with its greatest need. You remember the people who told Jesus about the death of the Galileans. They had misinterpreted God's dealings with men, especially with respect to calamities. They had not grasped the twin truths of God's just wrath against the sin of all men and women and the absolute necessity of repentance and faith if anyone is to be saved. They needed to be gripped by the urgency of becoming reconciled to God. They needed to realize that the necessity for repentance and faith transcends all else in this life. They needed to be consumed by a passion for being right with the Lord — both for themselves and for others.

The apostle Paul understood the message of this parable with an incisiveness no doubt born of his own marvellous conversion from spiritual blindness of the most pernicious kind: 'I speak the truth in Christ — I am not lying, my conscience confirms it in the Holy Spirit — I have great sorrow and unceasing anguish in my heart. For I could wish that I myself were cursed and cut off from Christ for the sake of my brothers, those of my own race, the people of Israel. Theirs is the adoption as sons; theirs the divine glory, the covenants, the receiving of the law, the temple worship and the promises. Theirs are the patriarchs, and from them is traced the human ancestry of Christ, who is God over all, for ever praised! Amen' (Rom. 9:1-5).

Then, reflecting, surely, on how the bulk of Israel rejected Christ, he comments, 'It is not as though God's word had failed. For not all who are descended from Israel are Israel' (Rom. 9:6). The issue is Christ and what you do with him. Not to repent, not to believe, not to hear his call is to be like the fruitless fig-tree — and perish endlessly and for ever. 'But unless you repent, you too will all perish.'

12.
Humility

The parable of the best seats
(Luke 14:7-11)

'For everyone who exalts himself will be humbled, and he who humbles himself will be exalted' (Luke 14:11).

One Sabbath day, Jesus was invited to a meal at the home of a leading Pharisee. In those days, at a feast in a wealthy home, the table was arranged in a 'U' shape, with the couches on which the guests reclined arranged around the outside. The chief guest — in this instance it was no doubt Jesus — sat in the centre. On either side were the places of honour — depending on their proximity to the guest of honour.

Jesus noticed that **'the guests'** were vying with each other for **'the places of honour'**. Discerning in their actions the evidence of over-weening pride, he took occasion from this to teach them a parable about humility of heart.

You may wonder why this is called a **'parable'** (14:7), since it is not so much a story with a deeper spiritual meaning, as a straightforward piece of moral instruction. For this reason, some commentators treat it as an 'honorary' parable — not a true parable, but a gobbet of teaching with something of the characteristics of a parable. David Brown, for example, says that this 'is called a "parable", as teaching something deeper than the outward form of it expressed — because His design was not so much to inculcate mere politeness, or good manners, but underneath this, universal humility.'[1] More careful consideration reveals, however, that the missing 'story' aspect of the parable is not missing at all. The feast itself *is* the story. Jesus treats the event as a living tableau, in which

the actors are the guests who compete with one another for the best
seats!

Jesus makes this spectacle speak for itself, modifies it slightly by
referring to a 'wedding feast' (14:8), and fleshes it out with plain
moral teaching. In this way, the Lord teaches something, for those
who have ears to hear, about that leading mark of the life of his
kingdom in the souls of men and women — evangelical, or, gospel-
wrought, humility. As before, Jesus tells the parable (14:8-10) and
then makes his point of application (14:11).

The parable of the best seats (14:8-10)

Jesus, as already noted, alludes to a **'wedding feast'**. On such
occasions, then as now, the seating arrangements are made according to carefully crafted protocols. The host arranges the seating in
accordance with the particular relationship each guest bears to the
bride and the groom. In this story, it is not the seating arrangement
as such that forms the core of Jesus' illustration, but rather the
jockeying for position in which so many of the guests had been
engaged upon their arrival.

Jesus' advice

With this undignified spectacle in mind, Jesus offers two pieces of
practical advice. Negatively, he enjoins his hearers to resist the
temptation to make a bee-line for the best seats. After all, if they
'take the place of honour' and **'a person more distinguished than
[they]'** has been invited, they are likely to end up having to
relinquish the seat and, **'humiliated, ...will have to take the least
important place'** (14:8-9). Positively, they ought to **'take the
lowest place, so that when [their] host comes, he will say to
[them], "Friend, move up to a better place."'** They would then be
publicly honoured by their host. Jesus was simply reiterating
Solomon's injunction:

> 'Do not exalt yourself in the king's presence,
>   and do not claim a place among great men;
> it is better for him to say to you, "Come up here,"
>   than for him to humiliate you before a nobleman'
>
> (Prov. 25:6-7).

So far, Jesus' words have been no more than what used to be called 'common sense'. There is no explicit reference to the kingdom of God or the life of true godliness. There is nothing distinctively Christian in what he says. On the face of it, it is just good policy. The context, however, was one in which the table-talk could be expected to focus on matters of a scriptural and spiritual nature. The gathering was in the house of a 'prominent Pharisee'. Jesus had already been raising questions about the interpretation of the law of God, particularly with respect to the keeping of the Sabbath. He had miraculously healed a man of his 'dropsy'. And so, knowing full well that this challenged the straitened sensibilities of the legalists, he took the opportunity to remind them very gently of some important considerations relative to living for God and his kingdom.

1. Examine the attitudes of your heart

No one at the feast would have imagined that Jesus spoke as he did about places at the table merely because he was interested in promoting etiquette and good manners. Nor would they have concluded that he was encouraging a kind of false modesty. No doubt there are those who, like Charles Dickens' character Uriah Heep, always affect to being terribly humble and self-effacing, when inwardly they are exactly the opposite. To such folk, taking the 'lowest place' is a mere stratagem designed to impress people and perhaps gain their trust against a later day when it might be exploited to advantage. This is not what Jesus had in mind and they knew it. Jesus was putting his finger on the roots of human pride.

He was pointing to the need for a genuine humility of heart in our relations with one another. Ultimately this had to come down to being humble before the Lord, but in this context Jesus simply and quietly pricked the bubble of pride by exposing the essentially graceless way they competed with one another for the places of honour. It was a general rebuke of an obvious lack of that inward humility which is alone wrought by the Spirit of God. These 'religious' people had revealed by their behaviour that their 'religion' was no more than a veneer laid over a solid core of selfishness and pride. Jesus was saying that what was really important was what was inside, in their innermost being. God had told them long ago, 'Above all else, guard your heart, for it is the wellspring of life' (Prov. 4:23).

2. Put other people first

The positive principle is that we ought to operate on the practical assumption that others are better than ourselves. Jesus' injunction is later given an explicit doctrinal form in the Pauline epistles. In Romans 12:3 we are told, 'Do not think of yourself more highly than you ought, but rather think of yourself with sober judgement, in accordance with the measure of faith God has given you.' Again, in Philippians 2:3 we are exhorted, 'Do nothing out of selfish ambition or vain conceit, but in humility consider others better than yourselves.' The emphasis is once more upon humility from the heart, which is a Christian grace flowing from the love for others in Christ, not a false modesty concerned with self.

3. Let others bestow the honours

If you are to receive one of the best seats, then let the one who has the right to give it to you put you in that place. 'Self-praise is no honour,' says the common proverb. This is just as true in spiritual things. 'Let another praise you, and not your own mouth; someone else, and not your own lips' (Prov. 27:2). Leave it in the Lord's hands and be content to be quietly and humbly faithful to the Lord's will for your life.

The spirit of service

All of these points come together in our Lord's words to his disciples on the occasion when the mother of James and John asked for places of honour for her boys in God's future kingdom. Jesus informed her that whoever wants to be great must be a servant, and whoever wants to be first must become a slave. He also pointed out to her the basis for this proposition: the 'Son of man did not come to be served, but to serve, and to give his life as a ransom for many' (Matt. 20:26-27). Jesus himself is our example. He took the place of ultimate dishonour — the cross of shame — in order to serve the saving purpose of his heavenly Father and the eternal joy of those for whom he died. This is the holy denial of self which believers are to reflect in their relationships with others. Peter tells us to 'clothe' ourselves with humility 'towards one another'. 'Humble yourselves, therefore, under God's mighty hand,' he adds, ' that he may lift you up in due time' (1 Peter 5:6).

Jesus' application (14:11)

In summing up the matter, Jesus made it inescapably clear that he was not thinking of table manners, but the pride of human hearts in rebellion against God. **'For everyone who exalts himself will be humbled, and he who humbles himself will be exalted.'** This is the great truth of which the parable is only an illustration.

Jesus first pronounces sentence on *carnal pride*. 'God is an enemy to all who desire to exalt themselves,' says John Calvin, 'as all who claim for themselves any merit must of necessity make war with Him. It is a manifestation of pride to boast of the gifts of God, as if there were any excellence in ourselves, that would exalt us on the ground of our own merit.'[2]

The Lord admits no exemptions. 'Everyone' who exalts himself 'will be humbled' (14:11). The verb is a future passive, indicating the involuntary nature of the fall that lies ahead for proud hearts. It is an inevitable judgement, that no amount of effort will forestall. 'God opposes the proud but gives grace to the humble' (James 4:6; Prov. 3:34). The history of proud people is sufficient testimony to the fulfilment of Jesus' words. 'Sceptre and crown must tumble down,' as the poet said. We naturally think of how so many arrogant politicians and crooked financiers get their come-uppance. But the abuse of wealth and power by no means defines the parameters of human pride. The rejection of Jesus Christ as the only Saviour is far and away the most high-handed act of human pride. To attempt to be one's own saviour, or to decide to trust in another, is to make a god of one's own best judgement and exalt oneself over the living God and the gospel of saving grace in his Son. Unbelief is the ultimate blasphemy.

On the other hand, Jesus declares the blessing of *evangelical humility*. Humbling oneself is the way to true exaltation — by God, not self. True humility is evangelical, that is, gospel-produced. It is dying to self. 'Humility,' in John Calvin's unmatched definition, 'must be not only an unfeigned abasement, but a real annihilation of ourselves, proceeding from a thorough knowledge of our own weakness, the entire absence of lofty pretensions, and a conviction that whatever excellence we possess comes from the grace of God alone.'[3]

This, of course, runs counter to the perennial tendencies of human nature. 'Self-esteem' has been touted as a 'buzz-word for the '90s', the theory being that more self-esteem will result in 'decreases in teenage pregnancy, crime, welfare dependency, eating disorders, substance abuse, employee absenteeism and professional and academic failure'.[4] It is true that depressed and defeated people need a renewal of confidence and a sense of usefulness and achievement, but it is misguided to seek it through the exaltation of self — an autonomous, secularized focus on self, in which man is the measure of things.

When Jesus said that the man who 'loses his life for my sake will find it', he was not just referring to a literal martyrdom, but to the whole process of letting go of ourselves and giving our lives in total service to him (Matt. 10:39). To be humbled under God — Calvin's 'annihilation of ourselves' — is not a despairing, defeated, self-destruction of our being (modern 'low self-esteem'), but a discovering of our destiny as the children of God. The paradox of evangelical humility is that when we give up ourselves to the Lord and die to human autonomy and pride, we then come to know the power of God in a myriad of vital and exalting ways. That was why Paul was enabled to 'delight in weaknesses, in insults, in hardships, in persecutions, in difficulties' — the kind of experiences that very quickly get most people down — 'For when I am weak, then I am strong' (2 Cor. 12:10).

Humility in Christian experience

This humility is a fruit of saving grace. It is an evidence of saving faith. Coming to know the Christ of the Bible and the cross cannot but involve a deep awareness of being humbled before God. You needed a Saviour desperately. You became deeply conscious of sin in your life and the need for deliverance from its power and penalties. As a Christian you are now much more sensitive to sin. You feel the shame of your failings more keenly. What the world laughs off as quaint or trivial, you feel to be deeply offensive to God. You are humbled under the awesome holiness of God.

The Christian also lives in constant amazement over his receiving the favour of God. Here is where humility begins to uplift and exalt the believer. Being converted to Christ, translated from spiritual darkness into his marvellous light, and providentially sustained and blessed through daily life, all contributes to that sense of undeserved favour that issues in exultant expressions of praise to the

Lord for all his love and grace. A genuine, heartfelt sense of wonder lies at the heart of Christian humility. 'And can it be that I should gain an interest in the Saviour's love?' is a question that arises, not from doubt, but from being constantly surprised by joy.

Humility in Christian fellowship

The corporate dimension of Christian experience is also powerfully affected by the reality of evangelical humility in the lives of individuals. There are perhaps two ways in which this is most practically evidenced.

1. Putting others first

The first is surely the heartfelt sense in which each Christian identifies with Paul's sense of being 'less than the least of all saints' (Eph. 3:8, AV). The apostle was poignantly aware that he was saved in spite of being a persecutor of the church and a murderer of Christians. He was a trophy of God's grace and he knew it. But who will be so bold as to put him or herself higher that Paul's rating of himself? And if, truly, we see ourselves as saved 100% by God's free grace in Jesus Christ, how shall we ever justify exalting ourselves above others in the fellowship of believers? Yet, we do just that — so frequently that it is a rare church that is spared no squabbles between members who feel they are not being properly appreciated by other members. Petty jealousies ruin the lives of too many professed Christians and blight the joy that otherwise ought to be shared in the life of the church fellowship. Are you willing to take 'the lowest place'? Or do you itch for recognition and influence? Are you ready to be unheralded and unsung? Or do you burn with the conviction that you are God's gift to this church, and that everybody ought to be seeing that and honouring you for what you have 'done for the church'?

2. Enjoying others in the fellowship

Another way in which Christian humility touches the body-life of God's people is the realization of a shared joy in the covenant fellowship of redeemed people. This is the point, surely, behind

Jesus' use of the 'wedding feast' as the context of his parable. To know the Lord is to be an honoured guest at his table, enjoying his bounty. The life of God's people is called

> 'a feast of rich food for all peoples,
> a banquet of aged wine—
>   the best of meats and the finest of wines'
>
> (Isa. 25:6).

The heavenly fellowship of the church in glory is described as 'the wedding supper of the Lamb' (Rev. 19:9).[5] This is the reward of the humble — to be with the Lord and his people, both in time and in eternity and always in the glory of salvation received and enjoyed. Herman Hanko captures the heart of the matter when he writes, 'When at last we arrive with God's people in glory one of the things which perhaps shall surprise us most is exactly the truth that Jesus set forth in this parable. The lowly and despised here on earth have a special place of exaltation in glory. The exalted ones, the powerful ones, the men of position and honour and fame, here in the world, are the ones, if they enter the kingdom, who even there receive the lower places. But then publicly, before the eyes of all the world, the people of God will be taken into the house of their Father. They sit down with Christ at the right hand of God. There they will enjoy the feast of God's covenant of grace for ever. There they will never again boast in anything which they did, for all eternity they know they deserved nothing. They glory in their God! And in the cross of their Lord!'[6]

Jesus had really asked the ultimate question, which is, in effect, 'Where will you spend eternity?' For that is the import of his challenge in the parable of the best seats: 'Everyone who exalts himself will be humbled, and he who humbles himself will be exalted.'

13.
Reconciled to God

The parable of the great banquet
(Luke 14:15-24)

'Go out to the roads and country lanes and make them come in, so that my house will be full. I tell you, not one of those men who were invited will get a taste of my banquet' (Luke 14:23-24).

Jesus was invited one Sabbath day to the home of a prominent Pharisee. This was to be the occasion of his miraculous healing of 'a man suffering from dropsy' (14:2-3) and some very pointed teaching on what it means to live the life of the kingdom of God. Jesus told two parables that afternoon: the parable of 'the best seats' and the parable of 'the great banquet'.

The first of these — 'the best seats' — taught that *humility* is a fundamental mark of those who are truly the citizens of God's kingdom. As we saw in the previous chapter, this was summarized in the principle that 'Everyone who exalts himself will be humbled, and he who humbles himself will be exalted' (14:7-11).

Jesus then urged his hearers to invite the needy to their dinners, rather than their relatives and rich friends. Why? Because, he said, the very fact that the needy could not repay them would bring true blessing to their souls. Indeed, the Lord declared that they would be 'repaid at the resurrection' (14:12-14). This thought struck a chord with one of the guests, because he suddenly exclaimed: **'Blessed is the man who will eat at the feast in the kingdom of God'** (14:15). What was in his mind we are not told. What we do know is that Jesus took this as his cue to deliver a second and even more searching parable about one of the marks of kingdom life — the parable of 'the great banquet'.

The parable of the great banquet (14:16-24)

The parables of Luke 14 assume the notion that the perfected kingdom of God (in heaven) is appropriately symbolized by a great feast. It is no accident that God's people commemorate the Lord's death in a supper, for they share a meal that symbolizes his atoning sacrifice for their sins and celebrate his goodness towards them as the adopted children of their heavenly Father. In the Bible, sharing a meal is repeatedly used as a figure of fellowship in our risen Saviour — both spiritual communion with Christ here and now and heaven itself hereafter are likened to a feast (Isa. 25:6; Matt. 8:11; 22:1-14; Rev. 3:20; 19:9).

In this second parable, Jesus addressed himself to the subject of 'the feast in the kingdom of God' and focused upon the vital question as to how God would make up his guest-list for heaven. The story unfolds in three parts.

A great banquet arranged (14:16-17)

It seems that in those days a double invitation was often given. The first secured an acceptance — the promise of attendance — while the second confirmed this nearer the time. We do this today in a more informal way, when we remind our guests that we are looking forward to seeing them at such and such a time. This is our way of saying, **'Come, for everything is now ready.'**

The original guests excuse themselves (14:18-20)

Despite their promises, the guests for the great banquet all began to excuse themselves from attending. One had just bought a field (14:18), another wanted to try out his new team of oxen (18:19) and yet another pleaded that he had just been married and could not come (14:20). These bear the obvious odour of convenient excuses. Did the first man really need to look at his field? Did the new team of oxen really need to be tried out? Was a new wife truly an obstacle to attending the dinner? Clearly, the excuses given were a smoke-screen to obscure the fact that they simply did not want to go to the banquet. In the end, their promises meant nothing. They just did not want to be bothered.

New guests are invited (14:21-23)

To replace the vacancies in his guest-list, the host sent out his servants, first into the town and, when that did not fill all the places, out into the country, to invite **'the poor, the crippled, the blind and the lame'** (14:21; cf. 14:12-14). In this manner, a new, needy and more appreciative complement of dinner guests was assembled. On the other hand, the original guests were now totally excluded. **'I tell you,'** said the host, **'not one of those men who were invited will get a taste of my banquet'** (14:24).

In this way a remarkable reversal occurred. All the fashionable guests who begged off were replaced with a collection of needy strangers who would never have expected an invitation to that table had they lived to be a hundred!

The meaning of the parable

The key to understanding this parable lies in the fact that Jesus was ministering at this point to Pharisees. They were the party of legalistic 'orthodoxy' within Judaism. They were known for their meticulous attention to the details of religious observance. They regarded themselves as the true keepers of the Jewish flame.

In the person of Jesus, God had sent out his summons to his covenant people to receive with repentance and faith his Son as the promised Messiah. They were, as a people, engaged by covenant to be the Lord's. To them belonged, as Paul later testified, 'the adoption as sons ... the divine glory, the covenants, the receiving of the law, the temple worship and the promises'. They also had 'the patriarchs', from whom 'is traced the human ancestry of Christ, who is God over all, for ever praised!' (Rom. 9:4-5). They did not, however, embrace the ministry of Jesus. 'He came to that which was his own, but his own did not receive him' (John 1:11). The Pharisees, though great students of God's law, were arguably the most vigorous in their rejection of Jesus.

Their excuses were as varied and as spurious as those given by the guests in the parable. Archbishop Trench may be a trifle speculative when he suggests that the new field, the new oxen and the new wife respectively represent pride, the cares of the world and the pleasures of the flesh, but there is no doubt that these are the basic categories of reasons that people will not come to Christ.

The parable, then, speaks of the rejection of the covenant-breakers who comprised the original guest-list for the great banquet. The **'certain man'** who hosts the meal is God. The **'great banquet'** is the final perfection of the kingdom of heaven — the 'wedding supper of the Lamb' of Revelation 19:9. The period in which the invitations are sent out is the history of the world viewed in terms of the outworking of God's plan of redemption as he gathers in his elect from the 'ends of the earth to the ends of the heavens' (Mark 13:27). Those self-righteous Pharisees who believed themselves to be the 'chosen', but had no time for the true implications of their own Scriptures and their own promised Messiah, would find themselves passed by as those who had in fact wilfully denied the faith. They rejected Jesus and called him 'a glutton and a wine-bibber', 'demon-possessed' and a 'blasphemer'. They spat on him and eventually nailed him to a cross. Accordingly, the ultimate judgement of the crucified, risen Son of God upon the unbelief of the Old Testament church is the one stated in the parable: 'I tell you, not one of those men who were invited will get a taste of my banquet' (14:24).

For all that there are legions who reject the gospel of Jesus Christ, God's purpose of redemption will not be thwarted. His house **'will be full'** (14:23). To that end, the Lord sends his servants into the world to gather in a people who *will* come when called.

The destitute and the needy are called

In the parable, the final guests are also the most unlikely to be so honoured. The same is true in terms of the gospel of saving grace. The physically destitute in the parable represent the spiritual destitute in the world. The correct parallel is not that of the old 'social gospel' liberalism, or the new crypto-Marxist 'liberation theology', which sees the poor in the parable as the poor in the world, as if there is some virtue in poverty that God will reverse and reward. The true parallel is that of *felt need*. The poor in the parable *knew* they were poor and the invitation therefore fell on hearts prepared. The people who will come to embrace the gospel are those whom God is also bringing to an awareness of their need. In contrast, the guests who had received the invitation, but begged off, felt no particular need to go to the banquet. Their socio-economic status is beside the point.

This is not a rich-poor divide as such. They felt no need of the invitation and all that it promised. They were satisfied with their own lives.

The irony is, of course, that the people who do come to Christ are often the kind of people looked down upon by the lofty and self-righteous 'Pharisee' type of religious person and the modern secularized cultured despisers of the faith. 'I have not come to call the righteous [i.e., those who *feel* themselves to be 'righteous' although they are not] but sinners unto repentance,' says Jesus (Luke 5:32). 'Brothers,' writes Paul, 'think of what you were when you were called. Not many of you were wise by human standards; not many were influential; not many were of noble birth. But God chose the foolish things of the world to shame the wise; God chose the weak things of the world to shame the strong. He chose the lowly things of this world and the despised things — and the things that are not — to nullify the things that are, so that no one may boast before him' (1 Cor. 1:26-29).

The fact that God calls the 'nobodies' of the world is clear proof that salvation is by grace. He gives to those who are nothing, who feel themselves to be nothing, who have nothing and deserve nothing. His goodness is thereby seen to be all the more wonderful. And those who have received its bounty are all the more impelled to glory in the Lord.

They will be called from all over the world

The servant in the parable is first sent to **'the streets and alleys of the town'** and then to **'the roads and country lanes'** (14:21,23). This is nothing less than a foretaste of God's plan for world evangelization.

The 'town' represents the Jewish people. The gospel was preached in the apostolic period, 'first for the Jew, then for the Gentile' (Rom. 1:16). Notwithstanding a Nicodemus here and a Joseph of Arimathea there, Jesus' successes were among the ordinary people — Galileans, 'sinners', tax collectors and tradesmen — the people neglected by the hierarchy of the Old Testament church. Whereas it is fashionable, if not indeed the norm, for churches today to emphasize evangelizing, or even merely lobbying, the leaders and celebrities of society, Jesus just quietly went about seeking the lost, wherever he could gain a hearing and without any evident bias towards one group or another. He did have access to the upper echelons of the Jewish establishment, but the warmest scenes of his ministry are populated by ordinary, needy, hungry, sick and otherwise despised people. And it was from among ordinary Jews that he called both the founding membership and the chosen leadership for the apostolic church.

The 'roads and country lanes' represent the Gentile world, beyond the 'town' of the Jewish Old Testament church. If the Pharisees looked down on some of their own people, they utterly despised the Gentiles. These they called 'Gentile dogs'. No more proudly prejudiced people ever walked the face of the earth. All but they were 'dogs'. Well, Jesus is saying that the places at his feast vacated, as it were, by their apostasy would be filled by people drawn from the furthest reaches of the earth.

While this is rightly seen as a charge to the church to evangelize the whole world — anticipating the terms of the 'Great Commission' of Matthew 28:18-20 — it is nevertheless true that evangelism is only ancillary to Jesus' main focus in the parable.

His first concern was to lay on the consciences of his Pharisaic company that those whom God welcomes to heaven — to the great banquet — are people who come to love him and do not make excuses for lukewarm commitment or outright unbelief. The primary issue is *reconciliation to God.* When God summons you, you must respond. When Christ calls, you must go! No excuses will do! Simon Kistemaker points out that the 'objective of enumerating these excuses [in the parable] was to show their insufficiency and flimsiness. No one could take them seriously. They simply did not stand up. Besides, everyone in Jesus' day knew the prevailing custom of honouring an invitation to a banquet. To refuse a second invitation constituted an outright insult to that host... The invitation had to be honoured as if it were a command.'[1]

The gospel call to repentance, faith and new life in Jesus Christ is not like the latest 'offer' on the back of a cereal packet. It is not an option, to be mulled over at leisure in 'the privacy of your own home'. The gospel is *a command.* Those who treat it as an option, and decide not to trust Christ right now, are liable to discover later that it was a decision for eternity. That is the force of the servant's foray into the city and the country lanes. God is shaking the dust from his feet at those who rejected his repeated invitation and is letting them know that no amount of unbelief (especially among so-called 'believers') will derail his plan to populate heaven with an elect people, reconciled to himself through the blood of Jesus Christ his Son. God 'now ... commands all people everywhere to repent' (Acts 17:30).

They will be compelled to come in

The servant in the parable was to **'make'** the newly invited guests come to the feast. Calvin is surely right in seeing this as a simple use of whatever force was necessary in order to fill up the places at the banquet. 'By these words,' says the French Reformer, 'Christ declares that he would rake together all the offscourings of the world, rather than he would ever admit such ungrateful persons to the table.'[2] What this means with respect to being reconciled to God is that God will save people out of the world by the invincible force of his saving grace.

When juxtaposed with the rejections by the original guests, this indicates the necessity of the application of the *force* of divine grace to sinners' hardened hearts, if they are ever to be saved from their sins. Becoming a believer in Christ involves a transformation — the good old expression was 'a saving change' — in the innermost being, that is, nothing less than a radical reversal of nature. This change, defined as being 'born again' in Scripture and 'regeneration' in theology, is not self-generated, but requires the secret, compulsive, renewing power of the Holy Spirit. He makes us willing in a day of his power (Ps. 110:3). Every true conversion to Christ results from divine compulsion in the new believer's innermost being. The sinner's will has to be renewed by the power of God, before it will be freely exercised in the direction of saving faith.

God does not compel anyone to profess faith in Christ *against* his will, as for example has happened when tyrannical rulers have forced people to adopt a particular religion or political philosophy on pain of death or torture. What God does do is compel a change, by the supernatural intervention of the Holy Spirit, in the will itself, so that it has the freedom it formerly lacked to desire and to embrace the Lord willingly. Every human will is exercised freely, within the parameters of its own moral and spiritual horizon, but that horizon of freedom is constricted by the bondage of sin and its effects. This reality — the bondage of the will in its fallenness and spiritual deadness (Eph. 2:1) — is what necessitates the application of

sovereign regenerating renewal of the sinner's nature. That is what
it means to be saved by *grace*. It means becoming a Christian
because God has sovereignly applied his invincible grace to an
otherwise hopelessly spiritually dead and resisting heart. To be
saved by grace *through faith* means that, having been made willing
by God's invincible grace, the responding sinner freely exercises his
renewed will to believe in Christ with a glad heart.

In this sense, then, the work of the gospel in the world is an
exercise in divine *force majeure*. Every conversion to Christ is a
supernatural transformation of a lost cause. The **'poor, the crippled, the blind and the lame'** are the spiritually helpless and the
hopelessly lost who, left to themselves, would go on their way to a
lost eternity. They are us — normal human beings — everyday
sinners, 'without hope and without God in the world' (Eph. 2:12).
This is the human condition in its need of a Saviour.

In closing...

This brings us back to the exclamation that triggered Jesus' telling
of the parable in the first place: 'Blessed is the man who will eat at
the feast in the kingdom of God' (14:15). This was a true statement,
and we have no reason to doubt the man's sincerity and write it off
as a 'mere Jewish platitude'.[3] It did, however, beg the question as to
who would actually eat at the feast in the kingdom of God.

Jesus makes it plain in his parable that *a vital personal experience of saving faith in the Lord* is the essential requirement for
fellowship with God in his kingdom. The guests who would not
come to the feast are to be found in or around churches today. They
are nominal, twice-a-year church-goers; they are weekly attenders
who never talk about the faith and have no discernible piety; they are
highly articulate theologians and scholars who devote their lives to
explaining away historic orthodoxy and the inspiration of Scripture;
and occasionally, they are hard-nosed defenders of a type of
orthodoxy that teaches for doctrines the commandments of men, but
is painfully lacking in the peaceable fruit of righteousness. They are
also found throughout the society of the openly godless. They once
went to Sunday School. They once heard Billy Graham. They once
heard an Anglican bishop deny the resurrection of Jesus on TV and
reckoned that Christianity couldn't be worth the trouble (unless you

were drawing your pay from it, like the bishop!). The world is full of excuses for not coming to Christ. God still calls and it is still appointed to man to die once and then face judgement. And a heartfelt love for the Lord, an earnest testimony to saving faith in Christ as Saviour and an open-faced keeping in step with the Holy Spirit in obedience to the Word of God in daily life is evidence of one who has become reconciled to God and knows it and lives it. This is what the life of God's kingdom is about. God's people are reconciled to God, through the death of his Son (Rom. 5:10). This is an irreducible mark of kingdom life.

Jesus also makes clear in the parable that the great banquet he is talking about is not simply the final banquet — the wedding supper of the Lamb and the fellowship of the redeemed in heaven — but is *the life of the kingdom of God here and now*, in this life and in this world. The man whose statement occasioned the parable seems clearly to have been thinking about that future feast in heaven, but Jesus portrays the great banquet as beginning when the invited guests are brought in, first from the streets of the town and then from the country lanes. In receiving the call of God in the gospel of Christ, the new believer enters into the life of the kingdom. Christ is the bread of his life and as he feeds on him, he never goes hungry again. In Christ, he find a table prepared for him in the presence of his enemies and he comes to dwell in the house of the Lord for ever. Although the filling of the Lord's house is *not yet,* and will only be completed when all of the elect of God have been gathered from the four winds and Christ returns to consummate the kingdom and deliver it up in its final form to the Father, it remains a fact that his kingdom is *now* in the experience of his people in every generation.

Finally, there is a tremendous sense of *urgency* in the parable of the great banquet. In the comment of the man at the table, the 'feast in the kingdom of God' not only clearly refers to heaven, but seems very far off into a distant future. This is not so with the parable. 'Kingdom come' becomes kingdom now. 'I tell you,' says the apostle Paul, 'now is the time of God's favour, now is the day of salvation' (2 Cor. 6:2).

'We implore you on Christ's behalf: Be reconciled to God. God made him who had no sin to be sin for us, so that in him we might become the righteousness of God' (2 Cor. 5:20-21).

14.
Seeking the lost

The parables of the lost sheep and the lost coin
(Luke 15:1-10)

'I tell you that in the same way there will be more rejoicing in heaven over one sinner who repents than over ninety-nine righteous persons who do not need to repent' (Luke 15:7).

The human race is lost: lost by nature, morally lost, spiritually lost and in imminent danger of being eternally lost. The basic premise of the Word of God in general and the parable of the 'lost sheep' in particular is the utter lostness of a sin-blighted humanity that is 'without hope and without God in the world' (Eph. 2:12). This idea is vividly captured in the picture of a lost sheep wandering alone and miserable and helpless among the rugged mountains of Judea. It illustrates what Archbishop Trench called the 'centrifugal tendency' of sin: the force of sin tends to take us further and further away from the Lord and his revealed will for our lives. The longer we stray — like the sheep in the parable — the deeper is our predicament; in other words, we become more lost than ever and are utterly dependent on the shepherd taking the time and enduring the danger to seek us out and bring us back.

The over-arching theme is, of course, the love of the shepherd who finds the sheep. Utter lostness in the sheep is met by utterly selfless love in the shepherd. However desperate the human condition, there is a 'great Shepherd of the sheep' who loves his sheep enough to go out into the darkness and terror — *their* darkness and terror — to find them and save them. It is a picture of the love of God for his lost, but elect, people. His is a love that will not let them go.

There is a word here for all who have ears to hear. To the unbelieving this is a word to convince them of their lostness and need of a Saviour and call them in the gospel to embrace Jesus Christ as that Saviour who has lovingly given himself for his sheep. To the already converted, it is a word to call each believer to hear afresh the voice of the Lord, who says of those whom he has saved and who love him, 'I know my sheep and my sheep know me ... and I lay down my life for the sheep' (John 10:14). God's people love to hear the voice of the Lord Jesus and count it a joy to follow him as his disciples.

The lost sheep (15:1-6)

The story could not be simpler. Jesus asked his hearers to imagine being a man who had a hundred sheep. **'Ninety-nine'** are grazing contentedly in the 'open country', but one has wandered off into the hills and is alone and in great danger. The shepherd sets off to find this lost sheep, eventually does find it and brings it back to safety on his shoulders. He then throws a party to celebrate his success. **'Rejoice with me,'** he says to his friends, **'I have found my lost sheep'** (15:6).

The shepherd — the Saviour of sinners

The shepherd represents the Lord in his work of redemption. He is the 'great Shepherd of the sheep' (Heb. 13:20). He is the 'Shepherd and Overseer' of the souls of those who have believed in him (1 Peter 2:25). Jesus is really speaking about what he was doing in his ministry at the very time he was telling the story. He was reaching out to **'tax collectors and "sinners"'** (15:1) — people whom the ecclesiastics of the time, the Pharisees and teachers of the law, despised and avoided. So Jesus was setting up a sharp contrast between their lack of attention to 'lost sheep' and his mission as the Messiah come to save his people from their sins. The Pharisees were *supposed* to be the undershepherds of Israel, but were no more than self-serving clerics, living off an ecclesiastical milk-cow.

The ninety-nine — the bosom of the church

The whole flock together is surely the people of Israel, the covenant people of God. In Scripture, God often calls his people 'sheep'. This is clearly because, like sheep, they tended to 'go astray' (Isa. 53:6) and repeatedly needed to be found (i.e., saved) and subsequently shepherded within the fold of the ministry of God's Word and Spirit.

Now this 'ninety-nine' in the parable have often been held to be the soundly converted body of believers — the true Christians, safe and secure in the bosom of the church. Thus the well-known evangelical hymn begins, 'There were ninety and nine that safely lay in the shelter of the fold...' On the face of it, this does appear to be the most straightforward reading of the text.

There is, however, an important point to note in Jesus' own application of the parable. He then describes the same 'ninety-nine' as **'ninety-nine righteous persons who do not need to repent'** (15:7). Now it is possible to explain this to mean that the ninety-nine were truly believing people who did not need to repent in the sense of having to return dramatically from a period of going seriously astray. This is possible, and there are commentators who feel that this is the best way to interpret the text.[1] But there are examples elsewhere in which Jesus spoke in a similar way about the self-satisfied people within the Old Testament church. In John 9:39 he described the Pharisees as 'those who see', when his point was that they were really blind. In Luke 5:31; Mark 2:17 and Matthew 9:13, he called them those who were 'healthy' and who did not need a doctor, when he obviously meant that they were blind to their own desperate need.

Furthermore, in these passages he immediately went on to say, 'I have not come to call the righteous, but sinners to repentance.' What was his point? It was first to explain why he reached out to the people they had written off — the 'tax collectors' and 'sinners'. But it was also a way of saying that 'There is none righteous, no not one,' and that it is a problem that there were so many people who *felt*, subjectively, inwardly and even sincerely, that they were in good spiritual and moral shape and had no need of Jesus Christ and his gospel of saving grace. Jesus came to save sinners. And sinners ought to feel their condemnation and lostness. That is the point.

In this light, it seems altogether likely that Jesus was being ironic and was suggesting that the 'ninety-nine righteous persons who do not need to repent' were representative of the Pharisees and the self-righteous folk who do not think they have any need of repentance. The ninety-nine in the fold constitute the Old Testament church — a spiritual environment in which easy assumptions about being right

with God were made, proclaimed and believed day in and day out
— much the same, we might note, as is done in the lifeless churches
of our own day and age. We cannot be dogmatic about this
interpretation, but it is consonant with one of the major themes in
Jesus' ministry and it speaks pointedly to the actual state of the
Jewish ecclesiastics to whom he was ministering at the time.[2]

The one lost sheep — sinners saved by grace

If this is so, then the lost sheep represents, not simply a notorious
sinner who is dramatically converted, but all of the people who are
actually saved by the Lord Jesus Christ. The lost sheep is the elect
of God, chosen from the foundation of the world to be holy and
blameless in his sight (Eph. 1:4). This sheep represents those who
are yet to come to saving faith and those who have already been
converted and truly know the Lord. These are the people for whom
the Lord has a purpose of salvation. These are the ones with whom
the Holy Spirit is dealing. They have come to feel their lostness and
destitution and blindness. This is the great difference experientially
between the one and the ninety-nine: the one who is up in the
mountains feels constant need and can do nothing about it, while the
ninety-nine are comfortable in *their feeling* of being 'home and dry'.

It is at this point that we should again take careful note of the
context in which Jesus told the parable. He had become noted for his
ministry to 'tax collectors' and 'sinners' (15:1-2). The former were
the agents of the Roman government and were viewed by the Jews
as lackeys and traitors. The latter category — the so-called 'sinners'
— were just common people who were rough and uneducated and
paid very little attention to the law as expounded by the Pharisees.
To the Pharisees, these were inferior classes of people — not the sort
of people they wanted in 'their church' — and they were therefore
very critical of Jesus for associating with them. They took occasion
from this to seek to discredit Jesus' ministry — the idea being that
anyone who associated with such 'riff-raff' could hardly claim to be
a great teacher, far less the promised Messiah.

Jesus' answer made the very opposite point. The fact that he
ministered to such folk was exactly what should be done. It was
actually evidence of his office and calling as the Messiah, the great
Shepherd of the sheep, the Saviour of lost people!

The lost coin (15:8-9)

This parable always brings back a scene from my childhood. In the early 1950s, money was scarce in our house and a ten-shilling note had many times the purchasing power of its modern highly inflated descendant, the fifty-pence piece. My mum had just got a fire going, and as I was watching the flames dance up around the coals, I suddenly spotted a ten-shilling note away in the back, unburned but surely soon to be consumed. 'There's a ten bob note in the fire!' I shouted. And before I could even think what to do, my mum's arm flashed through the flames and rescued the errant note, singed a little but still spendable. How that money got into the fireplace, no one could figure out, but it is certain it only got out in one piece because of my mother's quick mind and determined action.

The parable — a coin lost and found

Suppose, asks Jesus, **'a woman has ten silver coins...'** (15:8). These would be drachmas, each representing a day's pay for a labourer in those days. They probably were 'part of her dowry', which she wore 'as ornamental decorations on her headdress'.[3] They may well have constituted most, if not all, of her personal wealth. All we are told is that she **'loses one'** of the coins somewhere in her house. We are not told why. It doesn't matter. Like ten-shilling notes somehow fluttering into fireplaces, such things happen and are for ever mysteries. The point is that this was a major loss, materially and probably sentimentally. What would you do in her situation? Would you not **'light a lamp, sweep the house and search carefully'** until you found it? And having found it, might you not call your friends and say, **'Rejoice with me; I have found my lost coin'**? (15:9).

The meaning of the parable — a love for the lost

This parable is so simple that some commentators seem to have felt a compulsion to make up the difference with a mass of speculative pseudo-exegetical filler. Thus the woman's lamp, as she searches for the coin, is the gospel, while the broom with which she sweeps out her house is the law![4] Even Matthew Henry has the coin lost in the dirt floor as an emblem of the sinner's soul overwhelmed with the love of the world.[5] Such speculations need to be steadfastly resisted. This is a parable, not an allegory like *Pilgrim's Progress*. The best interpretation is also the leanest — that is to say, the simplest explanation that gives proper weight to all the leading features of the story, language and context — and it is surely just that the woman's zeal to find her lost coin, and her rejoicing once she has recovered it, is a picture of the love the Lord has for those whom he is seeking, finding and saving through the gospel message, and therefore also a picture of the love that ought to animate his followers in their witness in the world of lost people.

Joy in heaven (15:7,10)

The capstone to both parables is the rejoicing of the shepherd and the woman over the recovery, respectively, of the lost sheep and the lost coin, and the astounding revelation from Jesus that this is emblematic of **'rejoicing in heaven'** over the salvation of lost people.

More rejoicing over one repentant sinner (15:7)

There is **'more'** rejoicing in heaven, says Jesus, over **'one sinner who repents than over ninety-nine righteous persons who do not need to repent'**. We have already suggested that this is an ironic statement, in which the Lord, after the pattern of Matthew 9:13, Luke 5:31 and John 9:39, was actually begging the question as to how 'righteous' the ninety-nine really were. No one is righteous, in fact (Ps. 14:3; Rom. 3:10). If this is so, then when he says there is more rejoicing over one repentant sinner, he does not mean to imply there is any rejoicing over ninety-nine 'righteous people'. He is merely carrying through the irony in the contrast. It would be like a mother who says to her child at homework time, when he protests that he is tidying up his room, 'I'd be more pleased if you did your homework.' The weight of the pleasure is on the task to be done, the excuse of doing some other good being in effect an avoidance of the true responsibility. When Archbishop Trench claims that *more* joy over a true believer implies there is *some* joy in heaven over what he calls 'legal righteousness', he forces himself into a plain contradiction of God's known attitude to the best works of lost people.

Jesus' point is that, whatever the unconverted moralists may think of their standing with God, the rejoicing in heaven is going to be over those who are saved by grace, and not over those who dream that their tidy lives will commend them to God. Herman Hanko makes the point crystal clear: 'The Pharisees were righteous in their own eyes. They had no need of Christ or of repentance, for they had no sin. There was no need to rejoice over their rescue, for they needed no rescue. But over a lost one there is rejoicing. Such a one may be a lowly and despised sinner... He may even be scorned and derided — or worse, ignored by self-righteous people... But Christ found him and brought him home. See, he is on his knees weeping. But the angels are singing beyond the skies.'[6]

God rejoices (15:10)

Not only is there rejoicing in heaven, but God himself is joining in the rejoicing! This is the import of the rejoicing **'in the presence of the angels of God over one sinner who repents'** (15:10). No doubt the angels and the redeemed in glory rejoice, but it is God who leads the chorus! Here is a window on heaven to lift up our hearts. When we think of God in heaven, we tend more often to think of the Judge upon his throne, his brow knitted with disapproving wrath over the activities of his sinful creatures. But Jesus here reminds us that there is always joy in heaven! God rejoices in his works (Ps. 104:31). God says of his New Covenant people, 'I will rejoice in doing them good and will assuredly plant them in this land with all my heart and soul' (Jer. 32:41). Heaven is a place of joy and holy mirth! God rejoices! He rejoices over even **'one sinner who repents'**. His joy answers to his love. His love seeks the lost. His joy attends their deliverance. Furthermore that love and joy are *particular* in their focus. God rejoices one by one, and name by name, over the ingathering of his people, whom he chose from before the foundation of the world.

The lost are to be sought. The needy are to be reached. This is God's will. This is why he sent his only begotten Son into the world. This is why he will rejoice when they are converted to Christ. It is therefore a mark of kingdom life in those who have already come to know the Lord that they love the lost enough to seek them out with the gospel message of salvation and rejoice when they come to Christ, as they themselves had done in earlier days. There ought to be as much joy in the church as there is in heaven over one sinner come to repentance.

15.
Welcoming the found

The parable of the prodigal son
(Luke 15:11-32)

'Bring the fattened calf and kill it. Let's have a feast and celebrate. For this son of mine was dead and is alive again; he was lost and is found' (Luke 15:23-24).

The story of the prodigal son has been called 'the pearl and crown of all the parables'.[1] It has also been called 'the gospel within the gospel' because it so vividly portrays something of the essence of the gospel of Jesus Christ. Lenski says that 'It has no equal in all literature.'[2] This is admittedly an overstatement, but a beautiful one none the less, for although the parable says nothing of the atonement that had to be made for sin, it does most touchingly portray both the desolation felt by the lost sinner and the matchless love of God as he welcomes the repentant to himself.

This parable is very similar to those that precede it. It forms a triad with the parables of the lost sheep and the lost coin and it is not surprising to find a gradient of rising intensity of lostness from the sheep (1 in 100), to the coin (1 in 10) and finally to the son (1 in 2). The Lord's presentation of the profound pathos of human lostness, and the joyous jubilation when the lost are found, comes to a mighty crescendo in the return of the prodigal son.

This story of the prodigal must be understood in the same context as the other parables of 'lostness'. Severe criticism had been levelled at Jesus by the Pharisees for his hob-nobbing with tax collectors and 'sinners' (15:1-2). Our Lord had not thought it beneath him, as they did, to have dealings with the flotsam and jetsam of society. Consequently, these parables were designed to emphasize that the seeking and saving of the lost, the unrighteous, the rejected, the despised, the poor and the miserable is of the essence of the Messiah's mission. Jesus sets aside the conventional attitudes of these 'church leaders' of the time as so much spiritual snobbery and hard-hearted self-righteousness, unworthy of the God who called them to serve him in proclaiming redemption among the people.

This parable differs from the other two in certain respects. It is more elaborate in the way it treats the twin themes of the human condition and the love of God. More significantly, it changes the focus from the love that seeks the lost to the love that *receives* the lost. In this way, Jesus rounds out the comprehensive scope of salvation; it is seeking, but it is also receiving. In this we have a point of perennial relevance for the church. Many Christians and many churches can be enthusiastic about spreading the gospel and winning the lost, but are highly selective in practice as to the kind of people with whom they want to build their churches. Especially in the USA, the 'church growth' theorists have developed sociological criteria for planting churches and therefore promote evangelism in white-flight suburbs populated by young upwardly mobile professionals. There is little or no emphasis on seeking the old, the sick, the needy, the mentally retarded, the widowed and the people of other races and social classes, except in terms of diaconal ministry from already thriving 'yuppie' congregations. The parable of the prodigal does not present God as an ecclesiastical CEO seeking to expand his corporation with the best and the brightest, but as a Father who grieves over the lostness of his wayward children and rejoices to receive them back, in all their weakness and helplessness. The Lord embraces all who come to him in repentance and faith. This parable teaches us how to receive the returning sinner, who has been found by the grace of God.

The parable is a study in attitudes and how they translate into actions. The three main characters — the prodigal, the elder brother and the father — in quite different ways show us how we ought to love lost people and love our God.

The prodigal's adventure (15:11-16)

The younger of a wealthy man's two sons asked his father one day for his **'share of the estate'** and his father **'divided his property**

between them' (15:11-12). This meant that the younger son was paid a cash sum in settlement of his share of the inheritance and in lieu of the value of the property and livestock, which would remain intact and continue to be managed by the father and the older son.[3] This kind of arrangement is not unknown today. I know a son of a Pennsylvania farmer who was given the 'college fund' his father had been saving up for his education, in a lump sum, so he could leave home and forge a new life on the West Coast.

The young man was neither the first nor the last to want to make his own way in the world. His father probably had no illusions about his motivation and must have let him go with that heavy heart and sense of foreboding that has been shared by millions of parents across the years, as they watch their children head off to an uncertain future. That future soon went very sour for the young man. He duly went to a **'distant country and there squandered his wealth in wild living'** (15:13). A famine arose, he had no money left and in his need he went to work for a citizen of that country, **'who sent him to his fields to feed pigs'**. Even then, he did not have enough to sustain himself, for **'He longed to fill his stomach with the pods that the pigs were eating, but no one gave him anything'** (15:16). His humiliation was complete. His life was in ruins. Here was a Jewish boy in a Gentile country, his money all gone, tending ceremonially unclean animals (Lev. 11:7) and desperate enough to want to eat pig swill! So much for independence and freedom! He was at the end of himself!

The meaning of this story is perfectly plain. It is a picture of what happens when someone turns away from God. 'Note,' comments Matthew Henry, 'if God leave us ever so little to ourselves, it will not be long ere we depart from him. When the bridle of restraining grace is taken off we are soon gone.'[4] And the consequences are grim. The same writer searchingly analyses the condition of those who are lost and without God in the world in terms of nine characteristics.[5] Each of these could be developed as a sermon in a series on the nature of the human predicament, but we can only list them here. The 'sinful state,' says Matthew Henry, is:

1. A 'state of *departure* and *distance* from God... The world is the *far country* in which they take up residence, and are as at home.'

2. A '*spending* state', that is, one in which 'wilful sinners

waste their patrimony; for they misemploy their thoughts and all the powers of their souls, misspend their time and all their opportunities, do not only bury, but embezzle, the talents they are entrusted to trade with for their Master's honour; and the gifts of Providence, which were intended to enable them to serve God and to do good with, are made the food and fuel of their lusts'.

3. A *'wanting* state' — one of spiritual famine. 'Wilful waste brings woeful want.' Just look around you.

4. A *'servile* state... They that commit sin are the *servants of sin* (John 8:34).'

5. A 'state of *perpetual dissatisfaction*'. More is always needed. Like the rock group, the Rolling Stones, their cry is always, '[I Can't Get No] Satisfaction.' Not to live God's way is to labour for 'what does not satisfy' (Isa. 55:2).

6. A 'state which *cannot expect relief from any creature*'. The world's cures are worse than the illnesses. Just look at the fruit of the secular-humanist state's efforts to put right what ails her godless citizens. It is no wonder that 49% of Britons say they would leave Britain if given the opportunity.[6] But the grass is no greener on the other side of the hill! '"There is no peace," says my God, "for the wicked"' (Isa. 57:21).

7. A 'state of *death*'. The father said his son was dead (15:24,32). Without new life in Christ we are spiritually dead (Eph. 2:1).

8. A *'lost* state . . . lost to his father's house; they had no joy of him'. It is all so much waste when lives are self-destructing and have no direction but downwards.

9. A 'state of *madness* and *frenzy*' (see Eccl. 9:3). 'Sinners, like those that are mad, destroy themselves with *foolish lusts*, and yet at the same time deceive themselves with foolish *hopes*; and they are, of all diseased persons, most enemies to their own cure.'

The world is full of people who need the Lord because they share the spiritual state of which the prodigal son is the illustration and the emblem. Until and unless we come to Christ, our snouts are buried in the pig's trough eating the bitter fruits of our lost condition. This, says Jesus with uncompromising honesty, is the need of men and women in a nutshell.

The prodigal's return (15:17-21)

The lost son one day **'came to his senses'**. Like the friend of my youth who drove off a Scottish Highland road under the influence of alcohol and awoke from his stupor with a deep conviction of his danger, his sin and his need of a Saviour, the young man suddenly saw himself as he really was and admitted he was finished if he kept on in the way he was going. He was brought to a heart-conviction of sin and to a genuine repentance for that sin.

Notice, too, that whereas the lost sheep and the lost coin were found by the exertions, respectively, of a self-sacrificial shepherd and a quietly diligent woman — both figurative of the evangelistic thrust of the gospel, the prodigal son was 'found' in the operations of his conscience as he reflected on his circumstances and the irresponsibility that produced them. The meaning is that God brought him to his senses — not independently of his past experience and upbringing, to be sure, but in isolation from any immediate evangelistic witness of the Lord's people.

This is not at all unusual. I remember a man who was converted to Christ in a similar way. He had been brought up in a Christian home but had for years given himself to a godless way of life. Every Sunday afternoon he would meet his pals in a hotel bar to booze the hours away. One day *en route* to his rendezvous, he was stopped in his tracks by a sudden and overwhelming conviction that he was lost and was wasting his life in rebellion against God. He turned on his heels and walked into town to a church of the denomination of his youth. Soon after he came to a profession of saving faith in Jesus Christ.

One also thinks of Brownlow North, a great-grandson of the eighteenth-century British prime minister Lord North. He was playing cards one evening, when he fell ill and was gripped by the sense that he was going to die. 'My first thought then was,' he later wrote, 'Now, what will my forty-four years of following the devices of my own heart profit me? In a few minutes I shall be in hell, and what good will all these things do me, for which I have sold my soul?' Out of this awakening, he not only became a Christian but went on to become one of the great preachers of the 1859 Revival in Scotland and Ireland.[7]

He realized how far he had fallen (15:17)

You can choose to wallow in your miseries and never learn from your afflictions. Plenty of people either sink into a slough of despondency or just go on being determined to live the same way regardless. So, it is a blessing when personal disaster results in candid self-examination and something of a true self-knowledge. Nothing will ever change in anyone's life until that point is reached. Everything else is a species of what psychologists call 'denial' — the unwillingness to face the real facts about one's condition and circumstances.

It took a very hard swallowing of his pride for the prodigal to admit to himself that he had wrecked his life and squandered all his advantages. This awareness hit him — as it always does anyone in a similar pickle — at the most practical level. **'How many of my father's hired men have food to spare, and here I am starving to death!'** He, who once had everything, had now come to the end of his resources. He had hit rock bottom! This kind of awareness is a prerequisite for any progress. It does not guarantee progress by itself, but in the Lord's hands it prepares the way for a new start.

He confessed his sin against God and man (15:18)

The proof that the young man *truly* understood his predicament is that he turned to God in confession of sin. **'I will set out and go back to my father and say to him: Father, I have sinned against heaven and against you.'** The order is the same as David's in Psalm 51:4: 'Against you, you only, have I sinned and done what is evil in your sight...' The bottom line is that all sin is against God. He had sinned against his father, to be sure, but to admit no more than that would be to miss the point that 'sin' is defined by God and sinners are accountable to him for everything they have done in the flesh. People can admit wronging other people and never be truly convicted of sin. Facing God's judgement seat is something else again, because it is an acknowledgement that God's *absolute* standard of right and wrong is fundamental and inescapable.

Wronging others in a world without God is just a relativist experience — at best a mistake and an infringement of social harmony. True conviction of sin has eternity in view and understands that God has both a right to be offended and a right to call us to account.

He decided to cast himself on his father's mercy (15:19)

Co-ordinate with true conviction of sin is the determination to seek mercy from the one who is able to show it. The prodigal resolved to tell his father, **'I am no longer worthy to be called your son; make me like one of your hired men.'** The significance of this petition is that it is an acknowledgement that the young man has *no claim* upon his father. He accepts that his father *owes him nothing*! His inheritance is gone, so he asks only for employment as a servant. He casts himself upon his father's free grace, knowing that his father would be in the right to reject him.

This is not the whole story, however, for there is an underlying *hope* in the young man's appeal that his father will be merciful. It is a desperate, but not a *despairing*, appeal. The character of the father inspired a certain hope.

And so it is when someone comes to God for salvation. The penitent comes without any merit, without any claim on God, and with a readiness to accept his just anger — but he comes because he has a rising awareness that he is a God of grace. Like the prodigal, he knows for sure that there is no grace in any other and he goes to the one source of real mercy in the universe.

He acted on his new faith (15:20-21)

The prodigal did not merely hatch a pious-sounding plan. He *acted* on his new conviction. Real faith acts. It does not stop with words. The matter-of-fact description of what he did — **'So he got up and went to his father'** — enshrines a profound act of personal faith. He moved his feet in the direction of his convictions.

He was not disappointed. While he was still **'a long way off'**, his father intercepted him and **'threw his arms around him and kissed him'**. His faith was answered with a father's love, with forgiveness of sin and reconciliation as a son. It is a wonderful picture of the grace of God in the gospel of Jesus Christ. Those who come, like the prodigal, in the exercise of an open-faced, open-hearted trust in the mercies of the Lord will find him full of grace. Those who come to him will in no way be cast out.

The father's joy (15:22-24)

Over-arching the whole scene is the earnest love of the father in his willingness to receive his lost, but now repentant, son. He rejoices in his return, clothes him in the robes of restored honour, kills **'the fattened calf'** and celebrates with a feast for the whole household.

It is clear that *the father had never stopped loving his son.* 'Out of sight' had not meant 'out of mind'. He must have been watching for him, to be able to run out and bring him in. He was ready to receive him every day. His daily prayer was for his return. When this is applied in terms of the love of God, it is, as with the 'lost sheep' and the 'lost coin', an expression of his eternal love and sovereign grace for those whom he is determined to save from their sins. It is 'not that we loved God', says John in his first letter, 'but that he loved us and sent his Son as an atoning sacrifice [i.e., propitiation] for our sins' (1 John 4:10). God's loving eye is upon the most backslidden of his people and the most resolutely rebellious of his elect.

It is also clear that, in the last analysis, it was the love of the father that drew the prodigal to return. In these days of so-called 'dysfunctional' families — a secular euphemism for godless, sin-blighted homes — the experience of a loveless or abusive father or mother, or the absence of any home to go to, provides no motive to think of returning. The prodigal was blessed with a good home and a father who loved him. When he 'came to his senses' in the 'distant country', he remembered that love and it awakened hope in his soul.

So, when we proclaim the character of the God of the Bible and preach his Son, Jesus Christ, as the Saviour of sinners, we lift up a hope which every repentant sinner can embrace — that the Lord will not turn away any who come to him in faith, trusting in Christ for salvation. We need to know that wherever we have been, however deeply engulfed in sin we have become, the Lord will take us to himself when we cast ourselves on him. And he rejoices in the presence of the angels over every one who so repents!

The older brother's protest (15:25-31)

The immediate reaction of the older brother to the return of his wastrel sibling was less than enthusiastic. When he learned the cause of the celebration, he **'became angry and refused to go in'**. He refused to welcome his lost brother back home (15:28). When his father pleaded with him, he poured out his objections in no uncertain terms.

The anatomy of a bad attitude

First, he felt he was being cheated of his *proper recognition*: **'All these years I've been slaving for you...'** (15:29). His first thought was not generous, but accusing. He had borne the burden and the heat of the day all along, yet no one had put on any celebration for him! How easily we resent the attention paid to others! Our sense of 'fairness' is never keener than when someone else is receiving some special recognition. The self-centred response is to ask, 'Why him and not me?' or 'Why him and not my husband, or my son?' The happy experiences of others often crack the façade of niceness and reveal a deeper layer of bitterness and self-centred resentment. Some years ago, a young man of unquestionable gifts for the eldership was elected to serve as an elder in the church of which he had been a member for not much more than a year. One day shortly afterwards, a woman who was closely related to two men who had been long-standing members, but were passed over in the election, asked the minister, in a wounded tone, 'Why is it that it's the last man in the door that gets elected an elder?' A sober consideration of the facts always recedes before the imperatives of hurt pride. The truth is that the older brother had not been cheated of anything. He just thought himself to be more worthy of recognition than his younger brother. He therefore reproached his father for never giving him so much as a **'young goat'** so that he could celebrate with his friends (15:29).

Secondly, he indulged a *self-righteous attitude* towards his brother. He had **'never disobeyed [his father's] orders'** (15:29). We have no reason to doubt the veracity of this claim. He had been the loyal one, while the other brother gallivanted around the world. But such is the nature of sin in the human heart that our steadfast faithfulness can easily be turned into the badge of an overweening *amour-propre*, when it is, after all, only what we ought to do (cf. Rom. 12:1).

Thirdly, he betrayed a *lack of love* towards his brother by writing him off as an unforgivable incorrigible. This is first signalled in the

way he denominated him **'this son of yours'**, rather than 'my
brother'. To this he added a scathing résumé of the younger man's
backslidings: he had **'squandered [his father's] property with
prostitutes'** (15:30). No doubt prostitutes did figure in the prodigal's 'wild living' (15:13), but it showed an unforgiving spirit in the
elder brother to state the problem as he did. He put the worst possible
construction on the younger brother's backsliding by not only
twisting the truth (he had squandered his own property, not his
father's) but by implying that he ought not to be received back into
the family (as if he could never change his ways). It is as if he did
not want his brother to repent. It is as if it would have suited him
better if the lad had remained lost in sin and destitution. Whatever
grace might have been in the elder brother's heart was crowded out
by his 'holier than thou' attitude!

Finally, he showed a decided *disrespect* for his father, when he
rebuked him for killing 'the fattened calf' to celebrate the lad's
return. He did not even attempt to understand his father's actions. He
merely treated him as if he were soft in the head to rejoice in his son's
return.

The character of the older brother

The older brother has long been the principal 'whipping boy' of the
New Testament. Most commentators see him as a self-righteous
Pharisee and apply to him the trenchant denunciations of our Lord
as recorded in Matthew 23. He is cast as the archetype of the
hypocritical and unconverted church member — the 'nominal
Christian' who outwardly pays lip-service to the law of God, but
inwardly has an unchanged heart that knows nothing of the power
of God. The Reformed expositor John R. de Witt, for example,
speaks of 'the ultimately graceless condition of the elder brother',[8]
and the Lutheran R. C. H. Lenski views him as 'the picture of work-
righteous Pharisees'.[9] He is not a believer, caught in a moment of
weakness, but an unbeliever wallowing in his self-righteousness.

This interpretation is less than fully satisfying, however, when
certain aspects of the text are given their proper weight. The father
says to the older brother, **'My son, ... you are always with me, and
everything I have is yours'** (15:31). This is, of course, a rebuke of
his sinful attitude. But while these words can be said by the Lord to
a genuine Christian believer who has fallen into something of the
spirit of self-righteous Pharisaism, they cannot be said to an

unconverted hypocrite in a 'graceless condition', even if he is a church member who has an outward show of Christian piety and morality. The older brother is in constant and firm fellowship with his father — 'always with me' — and his inheritance is securely his: 'Everything I have is yours.' This is a call for the brother both to be what he really is — his father's son and his brother's brother — and not to give himself to an ungracious attitude. The older brother, then, is a picture of sin in the life of the believer.[10] Not surprisingly, in their zeal to prove that the older brother was an unbeliever, the commentators either have to argue that the father's words do not really mean what they plainly express, or else have to ignore them altogether.[11]

Is it not more consistent with what the father actually says to understand the older brother, real faults and all, as a true believer and make application from it to the attitudes of believers to new converts from the world? It is certainly more dramatic to have this apply to a class of notoriously self-righteous 'Pharisees' whom we all abhor and with whom we would not wish to be associated. This, however, can too easily become an 'us' and 'them' line of approach, which lets 'us' apply the parable to other people and sidestep its relevance to ourselves.

It seems to me that the father's words to the older brother are all the more pointed because they constitute, primarily, a call to *believers* to receive the lost into the fellowship of Christ's body with something of the same love and forbearance with which the Lord himself redeemed every sinner he draws to himself. How easy it is to be like the older brother and be unforgiving towards repentant and returning backsliders — especially those whom we conceive to have wronged us personally in some way! Like the older brother, we need to learn the graces of humility and a forgiving spirit in the arena where they most matter and are alone truly put to the test — in receiving those who have sinned against us in some way. The prodigal had wasted his inheritance and put his father's family to shame. It not only cost him his pride to repent and return; it cost his family something of their pride to receive him with glad hearts.

Conclusion: 'He was lost and is found' (15:32)

The concluding point of application is in the father's final words to the older brother: **'We had to celebrate and be glad, because this brother of yours was dead and is alive again; he was lost and is**

found.' Here we return to what occasioned the triad of 'lostness' parables — the Jewish church leaders' criticism of Jesus, that he welcomed 'sinners' and ate with them. They just did not love the lost. They wanted a nice church with their kind of people. There was no joy in their hearts over any 'sinners' that repented. Over against this, the parable shows us that joy over lives that are transformed by the grace of God is a spontaneous necessity of Christian experience. *Not* to rejoice, as Lenski so aptly puts it, 'would be monstrous, for it [that joy] means that spiritual death has been turned into everlasting life'.[12]

It is surely significant that, just as the book of Jonah leaves us with a rebuked prophet and no inkling of how he responded to that rebuke, so this parable leaves us with the unanswered question as to what the older brother did about his father's warm insistence on the necessity of celebrating the prodigal's return. This abrupt ending in effect puts that same question to the hearer. How did the older brother respond? Did he change his mind and embrace his brother? We are not told. But what we do have is the same challenge addressed to our own souls. Any self-righteousness in our hearts is flushed out into the open. We cannot escape it. Do *we* love the lost? Do we joyously welcome new converts into the family of our fellowship? Are we with the Lord and his angels as they rejoice in heaven? Or do we pick and choose as to the Christians we are willing to embrace?

16.
Commitment

The parable of the shrewd manager
(Luke 16:1-15)

'No servant can serve two masters... You cannot serve both God and Mammon' (Luke 16:13).

You will recall that Jesus came under severe criticism from the Jewish church leaders for associating with the lower elements of society, the 'tax collectors and "sinners"' (Luke 15:1-2). The Lord took occasion from this to teach his hearers that the essence of his ministry and his kingdom is the seeking and saving of the lost and the despised. He developed this theme in his parables of the lost sheep, the lost coin and, most gloriously of all, that of the lost son, who after wasting his substance in a life of dissolution, came to repentance and returned to his father's house, to be received with love and rejoicing. Here was a picture of the sovereign love of God drawing lost people to himself and a foretaste of the coming victory of the risen Christ as he would save his people from their sins. The gospel of Jesus Christ is for 'prodigals' — for lost and helpless sheep — and is, simply, the fact that he died, bearing in his death the just wrath of God against sin, and rose again to secure the salvation of all who would come to faith in him as their Saviour and Lord.

In the sixteenth chapter of Luke, Jesus begins to develop something of the implications of his gospel for his disciples. The Christian salvation is totalitarian in the sense that it is redemption for the purpose of being devoted to God with all of one's heart, mind and strength. The story of the prodigal son had illustrated, however, that among the sons of the father — the covenant people of God — there is a perennial problem of divided loyalty and backsliding from

God's will. On the one side stand the pure and holy claims of the law of God, and from the other side there sounds the siren call of the world, the flesh and the devil. It is to address this tension in the lives of his people that Jesus told them the parable of the shrewd manager.

The shrewd manager (16:1-8)

The parable unfolds in three parts: we are told of his problem (16:1-2); of his solution to the problem (16:3-7); and, finally, of his commendation by his former master (16:8).

The manager's problem (16:1-2)

The manager of a certain rich man's properties was **'accused of wasting his [employer's] possessions'** in some way and was given notice of his dismissal. He had been unfaithful in his stewardship. This sets the scene for the parable. Jesus wanted his disciples to realize that they were stewards of the gifts of God. The life of God's kingdom is a stewardship from God and it is therefore very important that we grasp the essential principles of biblical stewardship.

First of all, the human task on earth is a *God-given* stewardship. We have nothing that we have not been given, Paul tells us (1 Cor. 4:7). 'The earth is the Lord's, and everything in it,' says the psalmist (Ps. 24:1). In absolute terms, we have nothing we can call our own. We are creatures. God made us and everything is his. Therefore the eternal response of the believer will be:

> 'You are worthy, our Lord and God,
>   to receive glory and honour and power,
> for you created all things,
>   and by your will they were created
>   and have their being'
>
> (Rev. 4:1).

It is man's calling, as the image-bearer of God, to exercise a responsible stewardship over his creation.

Secondly, our stewardship is a *spiritually directed* task rooted in the redemption purchased by Christ for his world. Consequently, it looks forward to perfect fulfilment in the 'new heavens and the new earth', which will come into being at the consummation of his kingdom, upon his return as Judge of the living and the dead. In the meantime, 'It is required that those who have been given a trust must prove faithful' (1 Cor. 4:2).

Thirdly, our stewardship involves a wholehearted service to Jesus Christ. Life is to be *Christ-centred* — not a 'religious' compartment in an otherwise secular existence. Our stewardship is simply making obedience to God's Word the principal and constant business of every day's life.

With these principles in mind, we can more clearly understand the implications of the parable.

The manager's stratagem (16:3-7)

The manager was in trouble, but he soon proved himself to be as clever as he was crooked, in the way in which he extricated himself from his predicament. Realizing that his job was about to be lost, he devised a scheme to ensure his future well-being. While he still had the power to do it, he reduced the obligations of his master's debtors by giving massive discounts. In this way, he put all the debtors into a kind of moral debt to himself. They owed him favours that he could call in at some future date. On the other hand, even if he had given away some of his master's assets, he had at least settled the accounts and realized a great deal of cash in the process. He would have reasoned that his master would be pleased at least to get some return on his business and would certainly make no effort to overturn his actions, simply because to do so would lead to angry customers and loss of business.

It was outrageous and self-serving for the manager to do this, but it was exceedingly shrewd. One modern commentator thinks he was seeking 'approval by being honest and charitable to his master's debtors'.[1] To this it has to be said that the notion that he was 'honest' is simply unsupportable! And if he was 'charitable', it was to himself — and with his master's money! He was what the Americans call 'a shyster'. His only principle was 'looking after number one'! Such is the perverted wisdom of this world — the kind of cleverness we admire, while at the same time deploring its results.

The manager's commendation (16:8)

It is in this same sense, surely, that the master **'commended the dishonest manager'**. He did so because, in his dishonest way, the manager **'had acted shrewdly'**. Perhaps the rich man kicked himself just a little for not firing the fellow sooner, but, on the other hand, he might well have been a little relieved to have cut his losses. In any event, he could recognize genius when he saw it, however evil it might have been. He could see that this was a man who knew how to live by his wits and knew the value of other people's money.

The final statement of the parable itself sets the story in 'the right light for the hearers'.[2] **'For the people of this world,'** says Jesus, **'are more shrewd in dealing with their own kind than are the people of the light.'** 'This is the world, isn't it?' Jesus is saying. 'It is a simple fact,' observed Lenski, 'in matters of their own generation wordlings are decidedly shrewder than Christians.'[3] There is a characteristic cleverness and a down-to-earth realism in the way that the world of the unconverted works. The 'people of the light' often suffer by comparison because of their tendency to be trusting and even naïve in the way they deal with people. This is the way things are in the world. This is to be expected because the 'people' (literally, 'sons') bear a relationship to 'the world' (literally, 'the age'). Their heart is in the things of the present age. They are attuned to the works of darkness. It is their natural environment. The 'people [sons] of the light,' just because they have embraced 'the light [that] shines in the darkness' (John 1:5), find themselves at odds with the world and its worldliness.

God and Mammon (16:9-15)

Having told the story, Jesus immediately interpreted and applied it to his hearers. He developed this along three lines: first, the proper place of worldly wealth(16:9); secondly, an exposition of faithful and the false stewardship of God's gifts (16:10-12); and thirdly, a statement of the antithesis between God and the world (16:13-15).

The use of worldly wealth (16:9)

The essential lesson of the story of the shrewd manager lies in the contrast between his conduct as a son of 'this world' and that of the disciples of Jesus as the sons of 'the light'. **'I tell you,'** says Jesus, **'use worldly wealth to gain friends for yourselves, so that when it is gone, you will be welcomed into eternal dwellings.'** The crooked manager used money to buy what he thought was most important at that juncture in his life, namely, financial security in the face of unemployment. He used worldly wealth for a very practical worldly end.

The Christian ought to learn from this to the extent that he uses his worldly wealth for spiritual and eternal ends. This in effect reiterates what Jesus had taught his disciples about earthly and heavenly treasures in the 'Sermon on the Mount': 'Do not store up for yourselves treasures on earth, where moth and rust destroy, and where thieves break in and steal. But store up for yourselves treasures in heaven, where moth and rust do not destroy, and where thieves do not break in and steal. For where your treasure is, there your heart will be also' (Matt. 6:19-21).

The steward worked for worldly security, but it would inevitably soon be 'gone'. You, believer, must labour to 'make your calling and election sure' (2 Peter 1:10). He laboured for the 'food that spoils' — you, for that which 'endures to eternal life' (John 6:27). There is, incidentally, no suggestion here that anyone can buy his way into heaven. There is no meritorious winning of salvation in Jesus' teaching. To 'gain friends for yourselves' refers to the fruit of saving faith — the kind of practical godliness of which Jesus speaks in connection with a later parable: 'The King will reply, "I tell you the truth, whatever you did for one of the least of these brothers of mine, you did for me"' (Matt. 25:40). It is living for Christ every day, in the prospect of being welcomed into 'eternal dwellings' — i.e., heaven — by him and his Father. Unlike the shrewd manager, the citizens of God's kingdom live in the light of eternity. They are to live with as holy a devotion for the Lord's will as that of the steward was unholy in its addiction to the ways of the world.

Encouragements to faithful stewardship (16:10-12)

To drive this lesson home even more pointedly and encourage the disciples to be faithful stewards of God's gifts, Jesus presented a three-part argument.

First, he laid out a simple axiom about basic commitments: **'Whoever can be trusted with very little can also be trusted with**

much, and whoever is dishonest with very little will also be dishonest with much' (16:10). Everybody intuitively makes these connections. Someone who cannot balance his chequebook is not likely to make a good Chancellor of the Exchequer. During the 1992 presidential campaign in the United States of America, the fact of Bill Clinton's openly acknowledged adultery with one Gennifer Flowers raised the question in public debate as to how a man who has cheated on his wife could be trusted with the government of a great nation. There is no mystery in what Jesus is saying. We see people's basic character in the way they handle themselves in the little things of life — when, so to speak, no one is looking. That is why employers are interested in a prospective employee's past performance. This is why advancement generally depends on a proven track record. By their 'fruits' you will know what people are like inside, what their priorities are and what they think is really valuable in life.

Building on this, Jesus then says, **'So if you have not been trustworthy in handling worldly wealth, who will trust you with true riches?'** (16:11). Jesus is now talking about kingdom life — what it means to be a follower of God. His thrust is as follows: if you live your life with respect to the things this world affords in the same way as the shrewd manager in the parable, you reveal your character as a rebel against God. You can go to church all you like and talk up a storm about your spirituality, but it will cut no ice with God. In your heart, you are living for yourself, and your 'ethics', such as they are, are a sham to cover your greed and dishonesty. No one in that spiritual state is going to be trusted with the **'true riches'** of God's kingdom. If 'things' and 'this life' are the be-all and end-all of life for us, what makes us think we are fit for the glory yet to be revealed? Blithe assumptions about 'going to heaven when we die' are sentimental fantasies. The question then is: what is our actual relationship to God, to his Son and to the real issues of time and eternity?

Finally, Jesus twists the screw a little tighter by asking, **'If you have not been trustworthy with someone else's property, who will give you property of your own?'** (16:12). Were it *our own* property that we frittered away through poor management, we might always argue that it was ours to waste. Jesus removes this excuse by emphasizing that what we have is not our own at all! It belongs to another. God has placed us here and endowed us with our being and our responsibility to serve him as his image-bearers. The gospel of the kingdom is proclaimed to us, that we might follow the King, Jesus the promised Messiah. In the gospel, we are promised an inheritance that will never fade away. We are promised the right to be called the children of God. We are shown the sure prospect of everlasting life in the reconciled fellowship of heaven. How, then, asks Jesus, will this become our own possession if in the meantime we are flagrantly denying the Lord in our use of his present gifts? The argument is unanswerable. God will never reward our rejection of his Son and dismissal of his will for our lives with the joy of his salvation in the unending bliss of his heavenly glory. His unstated conclusion is, of course, that we waste no time in giving ourselves to the Lord, by following him in faith and obedience, to the end that we might receive the fulness of his covenant promise in Jesus Christ.

The antithesis and its application (16:13-15)

The great reason for all this is the antithesis between God and the world in its lostness. **'No servant can serve two masters... You cannot serve both God and [Mammon]'**[4] (16:13). Divided loyalties are impossible. The unbeliever is actually single-minded in his devotion to his materialist god — which is why he is so successful in a world of money-worshippers. Too often, however, Christians are actually double-minded, because they love Jesus Christ, but linger with worldliness. Jesus is telling us to be single-minded in the pursuit of personal holiness towards God, because ultimately we can have but one master — either God or Mammon.

The **'Pharisees, who loved money,'** did not miss the Lord's meaning. They were on the other side of this antithesis, although they wanted both to have their cake and eat it. They armed themselves against the truth by **'sneering at Jesus'** (16:14). They found his teaching contemptible, as the cultured despisers of the gospel always have done and always will do.

Jesus' reply was a withering epitaph for materialism in all its forms: **'You are the ones who justify yourselves in the eyes of men, but God knows your hearts. What is highly valued among men is detestable in God's sight'** (16:15). Here, he drives the principle of the antithesis to their hearts and consciences. They can deceive men into thinking they are fine, upstanding and even godly people — but God knows their hearts. Truth to tell, they knew enough about themselves, even under the scar tissue of hardened consciences and the layers of mental self-deception built up over years of hypocritical rationalization of their sins, to recognize that Jesus was exposing some raw nerves. They realized, as do all the unconverted, that their backs were to the wall before the searchlights of plain, unvarnished truth, and that they must surrender or continue with redoubled fervour to hold down the truth in unrighteousness. And so the lesson of the shrewd, unprincipled manager comes down to cases with inescapable clarity. The worldly church leaders *are* like the crooked manager. The world of unbelievers is squandering its assets in the pursuit of Mammon. And the way of joy is the way of new life in God's kingdom, through faith in the Son of God.

17.
Heeding the Word

The parable of the rich man and Lazarus
(Luke 16:19-31)

'If they do not listen to Moses and the Prophets, they will not be convinced even if someone rises from the dead' (Luke 16:31).

Jesus' declaration that no one can serve both God and Mammon did not sit very well with the Pharisees. The reason was, of course, that they 'loved money' (Luke 16:13-14). So, for all their talk about God and their outward attention to the finest details of rabbinic rules and regulations, they were inwardly devoted to themselves and their twin gods of wealth and prestige.

They did not use their wealth 'to gain friends' with a view to being 'welcomed into eternal dwellings' (16:9). They did not let it serve the purpose of honouring God and so turn it to the goal of 'laying up treasures in heaven'. They treated it as their god, 'the mammon of unrighteousness'. They were, in the end, trusting in their false god and their false legalist religion, when they really needed to be trusting in the living God in the exercise of a living faith and repentance.

To drive home the imminence of their danger and the corresponding urgency of repentance, Jesus told the story of the rich man and Lazarus. In this parable, he lays on us two great truths. One is the perfect justice and absolute finality of God's judgement of sinners. The other is the sole sufficiency of God's revealed Word to call sinners to repentance and new life. It must be remembered that this is set in the context of all Jesus had just taught about the love of God as he seeks and saves the lost — the parables of the lost sheep, the lost coin and the prodigal son in Luke 15 — as well as his teaching about commitment to God as over against this world's goods in the parable of the shrewd steward (Luke 16:1-13).

As with other parables, we need to bear in mind that this is a story and not a history. Parables are based on real events and actual experiences, but are interlaced with literary devices and figurative language, in order to present their message with a heightened drama and vividness. This is God-breathed fiction teaching us God's infallible truth. This is pointedly illustrated in this parable, in the conversation between the rich man, in hell, and Abraham, in heaven. In fact, there is no seeing into heaven from hell. Hell is utter separation from the presence of God. There are no conversations across the chasm that separates the redeemed and the damned. Furthermore, until the return of Christ, those who have died are in what is called the 'intermediate state'. Their disembodied souls await the general resurrection of the Day of Judgement, when the dead will be reunited with their bodies — glorified bodies in the case of the elect — and thus equipped for the final state of God's consummated eternal kingdom of glory.

We must therefore approach the text reverently and carefully, so as to distinguish the literary device from the message it is designed to convey.

The story itself is very straightforward. There are two main parts. The first concerns the two men in this life (16:19-22), while the second pictures them in eternity (16:22-31).

'Filthy rich' and 'dirt poor' (16:19-22)

The two men lived very contrasting lives in this world. The rich man was immensely wealthy and missed no opportunity to enjoy it. He **'dressed in purple and fine linen and lived in luxury every day'** (16:19). He was, so to speak, 'filthy rich' — and he loved it.

Lazarus, in contrast, was 'dirt poor'. His name is the Latinized version of the Hebrew 'Eleazar', which means, 'God helps.' He begged for his living, he was constantly ill and he was so hungry that he was **'longing to eat what fell from the rich man's table'**. But he didn't even get the scraps that would have been thrown to the rich man's pet dogs. All he got was the attention of the pariah dogs — the scavengers of the streets of the Levant — they **'came and licked his sores'** (16:20-21).

Here is a timeless picture of the inequities of a fallen world. On the one hand, we see the wealth of the voluptuary and, on the other, the misery of the destitute. For the world in general, these disparities will remain until the Second Coming of Christ. For Lazarus and the rich man, these circumstances continued until both men died. At death, however, Lazarus was taken to heaven by the angels, to **'Abraham's side'** ('bosom,' AV), while the rich man **'died and was buried'**, only to open his eyes **'in hell'** (16:22-23). All this sets the scene for what follows in 16:23-31, but let us notice two vital points before we move on to Jesus' main themes.

Riches per se *did not condemn the rich man*

The sin of the rich man was not that he was rich. His problem was that he failed the test that the presence of the poor beggar afforded him. The presence of the poor reveals the character of the rich. The necessities of the 'have nots' bring out the best and the worst in those who 'have'.

Note also that both men in the story are professed believers in God. The rich man claims to be a child of God — in 16:24 he addresses the patriarch as 'Father Abraham'. The calling of those who 'have' is, before God, to give to those who have need (Eph. 4:28). Lazarus was a test of the rich man's faith. He was a test of the presence or absence of a living faith — a faith that works — in that rich man's heart. And that test was failed, because the rich man was apparently unmoved by the plight of Lazarus. Lazarus was on his doorstep and the rich man did nothing for him.

Stated this simply, we might be tempted to think of the rich man as a vicious, cynical pagan, living in licentious opulence, like some of the latter-day Roman emperors. The likelihood is, however, that he was just an outwardly decent synagogue-going fellow, who happened to have expensive tastes and the income to indulge them. For all we know, he might have started in humble circumstances and become used to a higher 'standard of living' as his business prospered. People become used to luxury and easily welcome it as a necessity for themselves. Our so-called 'consumer society' has made yesterday's luxuries into today's basic staples. That is the inevitable trend of productivity, and it is something for which to be thankful. For example, as I write these words on my PC and make my corrections electronically, I think back to what a trial it was to

write my earlier books on a mechanical typewriter! And not long
before that, I had to learn to write with pen, ink and inkwell!
'Luxury' is relative.

What is not is the attitude we have to the need around us, when
we find ourselves in the position to do something to help. The rich
man did not care about Lazarus. He let him rot at his own gate! This
heartlessness, however, is not the exclusive preserve of the very
rich. It is common in ordinary people and it betrays not only an
attitude towards others in their misery, but to God himself, who
requires us to be compassionate with our whole heart and to offer
practical help with all our strength.

Poverty per se *did not save the poor man*

We ought also to note that this parable does not teach that Lazarus
was saved because he was poor. Social activists and liberation
theologians love to use the Bible in this way. God, however, is not
a Marxist. Economics are not determinative of redemption. It is true
that God is sovereignly pleased to choose (i.e., elect) the 'weak
things' of the world to shame the 'strong'. He is merciful and full of
compassion (Ps. 78:38; 86:15; 111:4; 112:4; 145:8). But salvation
is always and exclusively 'by grace' and 'through faith'. It is 'not
from yourselves, it is the gift of God — not by works, so that no one
can boast' (Eph. 2:8). Poverty is not a virtue, any more than self-
generated good works are really good. Neither our circumstances in
life nor our so-called 'good works' commend us to God as deserving
to be saved.

Indeed, those circumstances that dog our lives — illness,
accidents, unfair treatment, career setbacks, natural disasters,
personal handicaps and the like — are the common experience of
human beings in a fallen world. They are not distributed on some
simple scale of 'This deserves that.' 'All share a common destiny
— the righteous and the wicked, the good and the bad, the clean and
the unclean... As it is with the good man, so with the sinner' (Eccl.
9:2).

Lazarus, as a believer, would have been the first to confess this.
With Ezra, he would have admitted that he had suffered less than his
sins deserved (Ezra 9:13). He certainly would not have shrugged it
all off with some glib modern pietism like 'Praise the Lord anyway!'
He would not have absolved those who treated him shabbily. But
neither would he have treated his miseries as ground for his

salvation. Lazarus was saved by grace through faith both in his physical poverty and *from* spiritual poverty. God was his riches, when he otherwise had none.

It is worth pointing out that God's grace for sinners is also supposed to be ministered through the way they care for one another in response to their real needs. It falls to the rich to have a care for the helpless poor. The rich man did not love God, and therefore Lazarus was left to live and die a pauper at his gate. This is the condemnation of so many of those who 'have' — they care not a whit for the plight of people who 'have not', and even less for the claims of God.

God had his hidden treasures of faith, hope and love for the believing Lazarus. He has gospel contentment for the poor that trust him. And these blessings come to their fulfilment, as they did for Lazarus, in a reconciled eternity with the Lord (cf. 1 Peter 1:4-5).

Three cries from hell (16:23-31)

The second part of the parable recounts three exchanges between the rich man, in hell, and Abraham, in heaven. The rich man makes two requests and one statement, all of which further reveal his spiritual state. In each case, Abraham replies with the most searching responses. This conversation is imaginary, but its teaching is very real. What the rich man says is expressive of the mind-set of the lost, while what Abraham says is a word from God about the way in which God deals with people in time and eternity. The purpose is that any who have ears to hear might change their ways now and escape the just judgement of God. Incidentally, this is the only instance in Scripture of prayer to a saint and it can hardly be construed as anything but an implicit condemnation of the practice. Jesus commands believers to pray to their 'Father in heaven' (Matt. 6:9). Scripture teaches that only Jesus and the Holy Spirit are heavenly intercessors for God's people (Rom. 8:26-27,34; Heb. 7:25). It is unbelief that leads people to try climbing to heaven by other routes of their own invention.

'Have pity on me' (16:23-26)

The rich man was in torment. **'He looked up and saw Abraham far away, with Lazarus by his side.'** This moved him to cry out,

'Father Abraham, have pity on me and send Lazarus to dip the tip of his finger in water and cool my tongue...' (16:23-24).

The essential thing to note is how utterly self-serving this prayer was. There is no true prayer in hell. There is no true prayer in unbelievers 'saying' their prayers in this world either. The rich man was suitably respectful in addressing Abraham as 'Father', but that was mere form. There was no reflection on *why* he was in hell and no repentance for his former manner of life. All he wanted was an end to his punishment. He was not contrite, merely sore. And Lazarus? Well, he could be the water-boy to serve his immediate need! In life and in eternity, Lazarus was no more than scenery for the rich man's life-commitment to his own comfort. Especially in hell, the lost will not see past themselves, and the memories of their former life only serve to intensify their uncomprehending agonies. God is not more in their thoughts in a lost eternity than he was in their life on earth.

Abraham's answer is instructive. He made two points, each one answering to a component of the rich man's request.

First, the rich man needed to realize that there was a reason why he was in agony in the fires of hell. **'Son,'** said Abraham, **'remember that in your lifetime you received your good things, while Lazarus received bad things...'** In these facts lay the explanation for the new circumstances, under which Lazarus was **'comforted'** in heaven, while the rich man was **'in agony'** in hell (16:25). Note that this does not teach a crude doctrine of reciprocity by which the rich on earth become poor in eternity and the poor on earth rich.[1] The point here is that the rich man's 'good things' *were* the things of this world, and that world was gone for ever! Lazarus did not receive 'comfort' because his hard life had merited it, but because the saving grace of God had delivered him for ever from the 'bad things' that afflicted him during his lifetime. The rich man's god had been his 'good things' and his god had failed him. He had made his bed and now he had to lie in it. There will be many people in hell who are as uncomprehending of their lot as that rich man. They are no more repentant in eternity than they were in time. They still believe they are good folk who never deserved to be treated this way by God.

Abraham's second point explains the irreversible nature of his lost condition. There is no relief in hell. The **'great chasm has been fixed'** and there is no movement across it in either direction. 'The state of damned sinners,' comments Matthew Henry, 'is fixed by an irreversible and unalterable sentence. A stone is rolled to the door of the pit, which cannot be rolled back.'[2] There is no 'second chance' to turn to God after the end of this life. The door is locked and the key is thrown away — for ever. The unrepentant are sealed for ever as the reprobate lost. They die as they lived, neither wanting God to be their God, nor admitting their sinful rebellion against him. The lost in hell would not repent, even were they to have the opportunity. Such is the bondage of the reprobate will to sin and its consequences.

'Let him warn them' (16:27-29)

Seeing the uselessness of trying to get comfort for himself, the rich man's thoughts turned to his **'five brothers'**. If Lazarus could not bring cold water to hell, perhaps he could take a message to earth, to save these brothers from future torment? Why, we might ask, this latter-day interest in his brothers' welfare? Was it love for their souls? 'It is clear that it was not love,' says Brownlow North, 'for there can be no love in hell; especially there can be no love to the souls of men; but the Rich Man had learned in hell, what had never probably occurred to him on earth, ... that amongst the many things with which God had then entrusted him, had been the souls of his tenants, his dependants, his household, and especially of his younger brethren.'[3] He knew what example he had shown them. He knew how he had encouraged them in the same kind of life that had put him in perdition. He knew that 'His brothers' blood was on his head, and that so sure as he and his five brothers were shut up together for eternity, he would through eternity be shut up with five more torturers and tormenters.'[4] He prayed to spare himself more torment. Think of it: fathers with the sons they trained for hell; mothers with daughters they encouraged in sin; teachers with the pupils they taught to despise God and his truth; and unbelieving preachers with the congregations they deluded with their false gospels and unsound doctrine — all reunited in a lost eternity! Brownlow North, pleading with unconverted ministers that they repent, remarked, 'I do not believe there exists a more miserable being, even amongst the lost themselves, than a lost minister shut up in hell with his congregation.'[5]

Abraham's answer shows that 'There is no request granted in hell.'[6] **'They have Moses and the prophets; let them listen to them.'** Let them heed the Word of God! God had already made available a full and sufficient testimony to the way of salvation. It was not as though the brothers, as Jews, had never heard God's Word. The same principle still applies. The Bible is still the world's most purchased book, but do people listen to it? It gathers dust in a million homes and is explained away in ten thousand pulpits. No, the condemnation of the lost is not that they had insufficient opportunity to be reconciled to God, but that they would not listen to the unmistakable thunderings and entreaties of his Word as it is revealed in Scripture. The Scriptures proclaim Jesus as the way to everlasting life, while apostate clerics and their blind victims consign God's Word to the darkness and in its place preach sociology and self-image psychology.

'They will repent' (16:30-32)

The rich man was not finished. **'"No, Father Abraham," he said, "but if someone from the dead goes to them, they will repent."'** For him, as for so many, the Bible is not enough. God is wrong. We need more than a book and a bunch of words, even if God did give them to us. We need miracles and signs and wonders. 'A wicked and adulterous generation asks for a miraculous sign,' said Jesus (Matt. 12:39; 16:4). 'Jews demand miraculous signs and Greeks look for wisdom,' wrote Paul (1 Cor. 1:22). But living faith is 'sure of what we hope for and certain of what we do not see' (Heb. 11:1). The rich man's hope, that a resurrected Lazarus would do the trick and save his brothers, was still missing the point. Had he, even in hell, come to believe that all that God had said through the Scriptures was true, he would have acknowledged that his scheme was unbelief itself. Even in hell, he did not take God's Word for what it proclaimed itself to be. And even the evidence of his being in hell, under the wrath of God, did not convince him. Indeed, seeing Lazarus with Abraham, neither dead nor covered with sores, did not convince him about the truth of God's Word!

Abraham's reply was not only the last word to the rich man, but is the last word to unbelief in every generation: **'If they do not listen to Moses and the Prophets, they will not be convinced even if someone rises from the dead.'** Had the rich man believed his Bible, he would have known this already. King Saul saw a Samuel brought back from the dead, and it did not change him! And the New Testament confirms all this for us. A different Lazarus was to be raised from the dead by Jesus, and all the Pharisees wanted to do was make him dead all over again! Eutychus, who fell from the window during Paul's long sermon in Ephesus, was raised to hear many more sermons, but unbelief went on its way, unpersuaded by the miracle. And then there is *the* resurrection — that of Jesus himself. This was the 'sign of Jonah', which was to be the only sign given to the Jews (Matt. 12:39-41). Even that has not persuaded the world to embrace the Saviour! Indeed, even some bishops of the Church of England do not believe it ever took place, except in the existentialist fantasies of his followers. When Jesus comes again on the Great Day, it will be too late to listen to 'Moses and the Prophets', even for those who see with their own eyes that he is the Judge of the living and the dead. So powerful will be their unbelief that all they will summon from their souls is the prayer that the mountains fall upon them to hide them from the wrath of the Lamb (Rev. 6:16). And like the rich man in the parable, they will still be fighting God in hell itself, eternally unwilling to listen to the Word!

Summing up...

The parable of the rich man and Lazarus illumines several doctrines that are at the very heart of the Christian faith.

First is *the finality of death and the justice of God's judgements*. It is not that death is a great leveller. It is true, in a sense, that death blends the sceptre with the spade. All that really means is that death ends earthly life. Death, then is really only a leveller if this life is all there is. The fact of divine judgement means, however, that death is the great *divide*, for it is at that moment that the saved pass into glory and the lost into hell. Scripture teaches that 'Man is destined to die once, and after that to face judgement' (Heb. 9:27). The fact that 'The beggar died' and 'The rich man also died' reminds us that we too will soon die ... and then appear before God's judgement seat (Rom. 14:10).

Second is *the full sufficiency of the gospel of Christ for the salvation of lost men and women*. 'Faith comes from hearing the message, and the message is heard through the word of Christ' (Rom.10:17). For all who need a Saviour, this simply means that we, like the rich man's brothers, must listen to the Word of God. For those who would witness for Christ, and especially for his ministers, who preach the gospel, this requires the most careful attention to the Word and the disavowal of all methods and teachings not clearly set forth in Scripture. The Word of God is the saving word about Christ.

Finally, the parable impresses upon us the urgent claim that *Jesus Christ is the only Saviour of sinners, such as we all are by nature.* 'Salvation is found in no one else, for there is no other name under heaven given to men by which we must be saved' (Acts 4:12). In the last analysis, the parable is about your need and mine to heed the Word of God and respond in terms of faith in Christ. Whom are you trusting for life and salvation? Who guides you day by day? Where are you going? What is the meaning of your life? Who is your God? Who is your Saviour? This is the vital question, posed by the parable of the rich man and Lazarus. What is your relationship to Jesus Christ?

18.
Dutiful service

The parable of the obedient servant
(Luke 17:7-10)

'So you also, when you have done everything you were told to do, should say, "We are unworthy servants; we have only done our duty"' (Luke 17:10).

When I was a Boy Scout, I vividly remember having to promise 'to do my duty to God and the Queen'. As a boy soldier in my school's Combined Cadet Force, this same theme of 'doing one's duty' was dinned into me every Friday afternoon, as we square-bashed round the playground, or learned to handle a .303 Lee Enfield rifle and contemplated the dread prospect of being part of Britain's 'thin red line' in World War III. Youthful romanticism aside, this discipline was a useful experience because it emphasized personal responsibility and commitment. It emphasized duty, putting yourself on the line for other people, for your country, and for what it purportedly represented. Duty means the giving of ourselves, because of particular principles that govern our lives and convince us that this is simply what we ought to do.

Today we hear far more about 'rights' than we do about 'duty'. Human rights, civil rights, legal rights, consumer rights, animal rights — 'I want my rights' is the universal cry. People are taught to think first of what others owe them and are encouraged to sue for damages on the most slender of pretexts.

There is admittedly a close relationship between 'rights' and 'duties'. My rights with respect to you define your duties towards me — and vice versa. If, for example, the civil government has a duty to protect its citizens, then each citizen has a right to that protection. The government has a right to expect the citizenry to obey the law, while citizens ought to feel it a duty to be law-abiding. These relationships can only work when both sides conscientiously observe their proper roles and responsibilities. If no one feels any duty, then all will inevitably infringe on the rights of others.

In our era of one-sided attention to 'rights', then, it is hardly surprising that selfishness is the leading motive in public and private life. Whatever can be got away with becomes the moral standard of the moment. The missing element is any sense of an absolute standard of right and wrong, the only possible source of which is, of course, the claims of God upon our life and service as revealed in his Word, the Bible. Whenever our thinking ignores or moves away from our duty to God, as he has defined it, to what we determine to be our rights, we have tacitly established ourselves, and not the Lord, as the central focus of our life. When we begin with the Lord and obey his Word, we go on to service and contentment in him. When we begin with self, we are condemned to self-service and the discontentment that flows from never having everything quite the way we want it. Jesus' parable of the obedient servant sets our lives in the context of our duty to serve the living and true God.

The servant's service (18:7-9)

The parable itself

The story pictures a farmer who had a **'servant'** working for him. It falls into three phases.

First of all, *the servant was a 'slave'* (17:7, Greek, *doulos*). He was not a hired hand in our modern conventional sense. His payment was his keep, and while he had some definite rights, the fact remained that he was 'owned' by his master.

The law of God made certain provisions for such economic servitude. It allowed a man to choose to become a slave, presumably for the security it offered (Exod. 21:5-7). It also allowed for the sale of a man to pay off his debts (Deut. 15:12). Similarly, a thief could be forced to work off the restitution of his theft (Exod. 22:3). When the debts were paid, such slaves went free. We should note that the enslavement of Africans by the Arabs and Europeans in recent centuries was not at all the same kind of slavery. African slavery was blatant man-stealing, and as such is condemned by God's law as a capital crime, requiring nothing less than the death penalty (Deut. 24:7; cf. Exod. 21:16).

This sets up the basic relationship in Jesus' story. There is an extremely tight bond of servitude between the farmer and the servant — far tighter than any acceptable employer-employee relationship today. This is the key to understanding the parable.

Secondly, *the servant was at his master's beck and call* (17:7-8). Given such an arrangement, asks Jesus, would you tell the fellow, when he came in from the field, **'Come along now and sit down to eat?'** In other words, would you have your servant sit at your table and eat a meal that you had prepared? The answer Jesus expects is the obvious one. The man is the servant and you are the master. His work includes preparing and serving the evening meal. Only **'after that'** might he **'eat and drink'**. Jesus' point is very simple. You do not normally give a servant the special honour of sitting at your table just because he has done what he was supposed to do. Doing your duty is not the same thing as doing a favour.

Thirdly, it follows that *no special thanks were due to him* for doing his work (17:9). Jesus pressed home the point: **'Would he** [the farmer] **thank the servant because he did what he was told to do?'** This NIV rendering is rather harsh. It conveys the idea that the only times we need bother thanking anyone for doing something is when they have performed some unsolicited and extra-special kindness. Well, let it be said that good manners are always to be practised in all our dealings with other people. We ought to thank the waitress who serves the table, even though she is paid to do the job. In such contexts, our 'Thank you' is simply a recognition of a job well done. But in his story, Jesus has something different in mind than basic manners. The text would be better rendered, 'Does he count himself especially obligated to the servant?' There is no implication that the master was discourteous or unappreciative. It is rather a recognition that there was no call for a medal of honour or an appreciation dinner. No *special* thanks were due to him.

The meaning of the parable

In this everyday story from Bible times, we have yet another example of Jesus arguing from the lesser to the greater. The relationship between the farmer and his servant illustrates the relationship between God and people. It is altogether beside the point to use this parable to seek to determine such questions as Jesus' attitude to slavery, or to suggest that he is somehow giving employers *carte blanche* to exploit their workers. We have already seen that God's law is not silent on these subjects and, on that authority, we may certainly say that Jesus was not advocating either of these oppressive practices. Jesus had one end in view in his parable, and that was to give us a picture of the relationship we bear to our God.

Just as the servant is the property of his master, *so are we the property of our God*. He is our sovereign Lord. He controls and directs us. He tells us what to do and orders our lives according to his Word. We meanwhile have an obligation to obey him. Like the servant, we are not our own. We belong to God — lock, stock and barrel. Like the servant, we are duty bound to obey our orders. God has the right to require us to do his will. Indeed, in our relationship to God, we have fewer rights than the servant in Bible times. We have no inherent rights before God. We have no claims upon him by any *natural* right. Our obligation is absolute and unconditional. He is sovereign over our lives.

Doing our duty (17:10)

Our Lord applies his parable with searching clarity: **'So you also, when you have done everything you were told to do, should say, "We are unworthy servants, we have only done our duty."'**

Concentrate on the job

Jesus focuses on *our responsibility*. His language is emphatic: 'So you also...' tells the hearers that the ball is in their court. He summons us to a single-minded commitment to our heavenly Father. 'My eyes are ever on the Lord,' says the psalmist (Ps. 25:15).

Do everything you are told

The job is to be finished. You are to do **'everything you were told to do'**. There is to be no shirking the work. Don't look over your shoulder to see what other people are doing or not doing. Don't even think that the boss might be giving you too much to do. You know what to do, and the time allotted. It is your job and nobody else's, so do it diligently and with a single mind. 'Whatever you do, work at it with all your heart, as working for the Lord, not for men' (Col. 3:23). If this is true for the most ordinary tasks of our day-to-day work, how much more must it be true of the life of Christian discipleship as a whole? Life is discipleship. The blueprint for that life is the Word of God. The goal is the glory of God. The motivating force is the Holy Spirit applying the Word to propel us towards the goal. And the great motivation is the love of Christ as a Saviour and Lord:

> 'I have trusted in the Lord
>   without wavering,' says the psalmist,
> 'Test me, O Lord, and try me,
>   examine my heart and my mind;
> for your love is ever before me,
>   and I walk continually in your truth…
> My feet stand on level ground'

(Ps. 26:1-2,12).

Keep things in proper perspective

Having done the job, Jesus then tells us how we should evaluate it: **'We are unworthy servants; we have only done our duty.'**

This immediately raises a question. How can a servant be 'unworthy' after he has done everything he was told to do? The best answer is that the word rendered 'unworthy' in our version (the Greek, *achreioi*) conveys the idea that even when I have done all my tasks as I should, I have not really benefited my master in any appreciable way. The notion is a good deal more subtle than merely being deficient in some way. The Authorized Version renders this 'unprofitable' and that is somewhat nearer the mark. Even here, it needs to be explained that I am 'unprofitable', not because I am no good at what I am doing, but because my best efforts do not appear to profit my master very significantly.

It is obvious that this is only the humble and sincere expression of a faithful servant. The master, however, may well count the servant's work to be very profitable. He is, after all, in the position to make such a judgement about his business. The point is that, particularly in our relationship to God, we ought not to regard simply doing what is expected of us as if it were some fantastic favour that calls for glittering rewards and honours. Doing our duty to the Lord faithfully is no ground for pride, and no justification for a thirst for recognition. 'However much our faith is increased, and is able to do and actually does in the Lord's work,' writes R. C. H. Lenski, let no claims of merit enter your minds.'[1] This is the central point of the parable for Christian experience and attitudes.

Our reasonable service

Perhaps the most difficult point to grasp from this parable is the most inescapable implication of all — namely, that God does not owe us a thing. That is just another way of saying that our very best works have no necessary claim upon God and, furthermore, do not add to his essential glory. John Calvin correctly observes that 'All the services which we render to him are not worth a single straw.'[2] We have no meritorious claims upon the Lord, even when we do our duty as Christians. Like the servant in the story, we have no right to any special award for merit. Soldiers who look smart on parade and keep their weapons clean do not get the Victoria Cross for their pains. They may just escape being bawled out by the sergeant-major! Our best works do not *entitle* us to anything from God. They are only what we should have done. They always fall short of his perfect standard. And in so far as they are good at all, they are themselves the gifts and fruits of his grace, which he 'prepared in advance for us to do' (Eph. 2:10).

Perhaps you baulk at this and ask, 'Does God not promise rewards to our faithfulness?' Yes, we answer, rewards are promised — and delivered — in abundance. One of the most beautiful examples is where Jesus speaks about how his faithful disciples will wait expectantly and eagerly for the return of the Son of Man. Their reward will be that he will 'dress himself to serve, will have them recline at the table and will come and wait on them' (Luke 12:37). This is the grace of Jesus Christ in action. Rightly understood, all of the promises and rewards of God are as much grace as were the works to which they are added. The reward is promised to the exercise of faith, not to the unaided, autonomous production of meritorious works of our own. The apostle John says quite explicitly that the 'right' to become children of God, no less, flows from saving faith in Jesus Christ — that faith which is 'the gift of God' (John

1:12; Eph. 2:8-9). Practical godliness is the response of faith to the will of God.

It is a measure of God's goodness towards believers that he is pleased, sovereignly and graciously, to be our debtor. He is willing to receive our imperfect works of faith as that to which he not only sends forth his rewards and blessings, but from which he derives pleasure and glory. He makes our obedience his glory. There is joy in heaven when a sinner becomes a 'new creation' in Jesus Christ. God rejoices in the practical godliness of his image-bearers, who have been washed in the blood of the Lamb. This in turn powerfully reminds us that the practical focus of the Christian life is simply to do our duty as the bond-servants of our Father God, whose love sent his Son to save sinners like us from our sins. 'We owe him everything that lies in our power,' says John Calvin.[3] Because he has redeemed us, we can live for him. He enables us in such a way that we find his yoke to be easy and his burden to be light. He is no slave-driver, but the gentle Shepherd of his beloved sheep. We therefore are empowered by his grace to 'present [our] bodies a living sacrifice, holy, acceptable to God' — indeed, this is our 'reasonable service' (Rom. 12:1, AV).

> Go, labour on: spend and be spent,
> Thy joy to do the Father's will;
> It is the way the Master went;
> Should not the servant tread it still?
>
> (Horatius Bonar, 1808-89).

19.
Perseverance

The parable of the persistent widow and the unjust judge (Luke 18:1-8)

'Then Jesus told them a parable to show them that they should always pray and not give up' (Luke 18:1).

One day, Jesus was asked a question about the coming of the kingdom of God. When would it happen? How long are we to wait for that great day? The questioner obviously wanted to know the exact day — a common concern among Christians today. Jesus' answer was basically to say that this was the wrong question! The coming of the kingdom was not a matter of 'careful observation' — i. e., calculation and prediction. Neither is the kingdom something that can be identified in a particular place — no one can say, 'Here it is,' or 'There it is.' In other words, resist the temptation to set a date for the coming of the kingdom. Why? 'Because,' said Jesus, 'the kingdom of God is within you' (Luke 17:20-21). In the living faith of those who love God, the kingdom of God is *now*!

This did not mean, Jesus hastened to add, that there was not a day coming when the Son of Man would be revealed (17:30). Such a day would come, but when it did, it would be like the coming of the Flood and the destruction of Sodom — that is, totally unpredictable. 'No one knows about that day or hour ... but only the Father,' says Jesus. 'So you also must be ready, because the Son of Man will come at an hour when you do not expect him' (Matt. 24:36,44). Being ready for the Great Day of the Lord's coming again emphatically does not include speculating about the date! That should be the end of all date-setting! A date-setter is bound to be the inventor of a false

prophecy.[1] No! Being ready for the Great Day means living the life
of God's kingdom now, in a world in which he is sovereignly
disposing of events and working out his purpose towards that day,
known only to him, when Christ will return as the Judge of the living
and the dead, and the kingdom of God will be revealed in all its
fulness and glory.

The disciples had as yet very imperfect notions about what was
to happen to Jesus and the kingdom that he was proclaiming, in the
time leading up to the day of the Son of Man (Luke 17:30). They did
not realize that there would be many years — even many thousands
of years — before this Great Day, and that they would be called to
lives of praying, working and waiting for the Lord. There would be
many trials for the church — they would 'long to see one of the days
of the Son of Man', but would not see it (17:22). In other words,
Christ's return will never be soon enough for Christian people. They
will be impatient for him to return, bring his kingdom to its
consummation and clean up all the mess of a fallen world once and
for all. They will cry with the martyrs under the altar, 'How long,
Sovereign Lord, holy and true, until you judge the inhabitants of the
earth and avenge our blood?' (Rev. 6:10). Jesus knew that the time
before the Great Day would hold difficulties and disappointments
for his followers and that they would sometimes be tempted to give
up. He therefore told them the parable of the persistent widow **'to
show them that they should always pray and not give up'** (18:1).

The widow and the judge (18:1-5)

The story has two characters — a very determined woman and a
judge who didn't care. The widow had a problem. She had been done
an injustice by someone and sought redress of her grievance from
the judge. It is quite possible that she had been made destitute by the
crime and had come to the judge out of desperation. She was alone,
without a husband or resources, and had been viciously exploited in
her vulnerability. Only the judge could put this right.

The judge, however, was no help. He **'neither feared God nor
cared about men'** (18:2). He was an ungodly and uncaring man.
In his theology and his practice, he did not recognize that the civil
magistrate was instituted by God to be a minister for good and a
terror to evil. For him, being a judge was a job. He was in it for

number one, not for the good of people and society, and still less for the law of God. He was 'his own man' in the worst sense of the term. For whatever reason, he refused to hear the widow's case.

The widow, however, did not give up. She **'kept coming to him with the plea, "Grant me justice against my adversary"'** (18:3). She nagged and she nagged, and began to wear down his resistance. The judge cared enough about his comfortable life to want the woman off his back, so he decided to **'see that she gets justice'** (18:5). His attitude had not changed. He still had no time for God or for the opinions of men and women. He really could not have cared less about the rights and wrongs of the widow's case. He was a time-server and just wanted peace. So he ended up doing the right thing for the wrong reason. He granted her plea and she gained some relief in her distress.

Jesus' application (18:6-8)

When Jesus turns to the application of his parable, he turns not to the virtue of the widow, as we might have expected, but to the **'unjust judge'**, whose behaviour apart from the final decision was thoroughly reprehensible. **'And the Lord said, "Listen to what the unjust judge says"'** (18:6). How, you might well ask, can we *listen* to such a wicked man? What kind of a lesson can his behaviour possibly have for us?

A lesson about God

We must bear in mind that this parable, like that of the shrewd steward (Luke 16:1-13), teaches by means of a contrast. The bad actions of a bad man teach us something about the good actions of someone else — in this case, as we shall see — none other than God himself! It is essential to the message of the parable that the judge be an ungodly wretch — the more wicked the judge, the more forceful the lesson of the story.

The unjust judge is to be compared with God. Perhaps only the Son of God could ever have dared to do such a thing. Would it have entered the head of any godly person to use a bad man as an illustration of the character of God? But that is what Jesus does! When you think about it, the reason is obvious enough. If this wicked judge will yield to the mere persistence of a widow he neither knows nor cares about, how much more will the holy God of Israel hear the persevering prayers of his believing people? Will not the Lord, who loves his people with an everlasting love, pour out his goodness upon them, when they cry to him in their troubles? Jesus says it: **'And will not God bring about justice for his chosen ones [Gk,** *eklecton* **('elect')], who cry out to him day and night? Will he keep putting them off? I tell you, he will see that they get justice, and quickly'** (18:7-8).

Matthew Henry has marvellously described the contrast between the widow's situation *vis-a-vis* the judge, and that of the relationship of Christians to the Lord in terms of no fewer than nine points,[2] which may be summed up as follows:

1. She was a *stranger* to the judge, whereas God knows his people.

2. She was *alone*, but God's praying people are many (Matt. 18:19).

3. She came to a judge who kept her *at a distance*. Our God tells us to come boldly and teaches us to cry, 'Abba, Father' (Heb. 4:16; Rom. 8:15).

4. She came to an *unjust* judge. We come to a righteous Father, concerned about those in distress (John 17:25).

5. She approached the judge *on her own account*. God already is engaged in his own cause, and we, in praying for ourselves, are asking him to plead his cause (Ps. 74:22).

6. She had *no friend* to speak for her. We have an advocate with the Father, Jesus Christ, the Righteous One (1 John 2:1).

7. She had *no encouragement* from the judge. We have the promise of God that he will hear and answer our prayers.

8. She could only go to the judge *at certain times*. We can cry 'day and night' to the Lord.

9. She knew her nagging would *provoke* the judge. We know that the prayer of the upright is God's delight (Prov. 15:8).

God's loving eye is upon his elect people. He has a plan and purpose of grace for every one of them. No one will pluck them out of his hand. They are the apple of his eye.

A *lesson about perseverance*

The persistent widow is to be compared with God's believing people, not just as individuals, but as a body. She represents the church. She is 'a picture of the church at prayer'.[3] The church is 'the bride of Christ'. But the Bridegroom has ascended to glory and, without his *bodily* presence, she remains in the world to serve him and to wait for that glorious reunion of the last Great Day when Christ returns.

It is true that there is a *real*, spiritual presence of Jesus Christ with his church on earth. He has promised to be with his people always, even to the end of the world (Matt. 28:20). Where two or three are gathered in his name, he has promised to be in the midst (Matt. 18:20). Jesus has sent the Holy Spirit to be the church's Comforter (John 14:16-27). Yet the church is, in a sense, like a widow. The widow in the parable had her consolations too — the memories of her husband and the things they had shared — the hope of meeting again one day in glory. But still, he was gone and she was left. The widow also had her 'adversary', whoever that was. So have God's people on earth an adversary, the devil, who goes around like a roaring lion seeking whom he may devour (1 Peter 5:8). The true church, like the widow, is vulnerable, exploitable, open to persecution and lives in a world that is not tremendously hospitable to the gospel message. Hence the church, like the widow, frequently finds herself crying out to the Lord, 'Grant me justice against my adversary' (18:3).

The widow, then, affords a lesson about perseverance in prayer and in the Christian life, and with it a longing for the return of Christ. 'The saints do not always long earnestly for the return of Christ,' writes Herman Hanko. 'This is because they do not live always in the clear consciousness of their widowhood.' Too often, the same writer observes, 'The Church becomes spiritually lethargic and doctrinally sleepy. The Church no longer seeks the return of her husband, but seeks instead a lover in the world.'[4]

Incentives to persevere

From the thrust of Jesus' parable, we can draw out a number of profound certainties that provide us with the strongest incentives to be praying people.

First is the certainty that *our prayers will be answered*, as we faithfully and persistently go to the throne of grace for grace to help in our time of need. 'Then they cried out to the Lord in their trouble', says the psalmist, 'and he delivered them from their distress' (Ps. 107:6). God will not, like the judge, 'keep putting them off'.

A second certainty is that *the justice of God will be carried out in the earth,* 'and quickly'. Compared with our sinful impatience, God seems slow in working out his purposes, but the truth is that he has determined the perfect moment to deliver us from affliction and to answer our deepest and holiest desires. 'With the Lord,' says the apostle Peter, 'a day is like a thousand years, and a thousand years are like a day. The Lord is not slow in keeping his promise, as some understand slowness. He is patient with you, not wanting anyone to perish, but everyone to come to repentance' (2 Peter 3:8-9). Divine justice is only 'deferred' — in truth, only apparently deferred — to fulfil his purpose of grace for those he is calling to himself.

This leads us to a third certainty, namely that *God's purpose of salvation will be fulfilled.* This is the obverse of God's certain justice.

> 'From heaven you pronounced judgement,
>   and the land feared and was quiet—
> when you, O God rose up to judge,
>   to save all the afflicted of the land'
>
> (Ps. 76:9).

The purpose of his kingdom and the centuries through which it grows and develops is to redeem a people out of lost humanity.

> 'You will arise and have compassion on Zion,
>   for it is time to show favour to her;
>   the appointed time has come...
> For the Lord will rebuild Zion
>   and appear in his glory'
>
> (Ps. 102:13).

Finally, we have here a promise that as believers continue to wait on the Lord with persevering prayer and practical obedience, *they will grow in grace.* Augustine (A. D. 354-430), commenting on Psalm 37:10, 'A little while and the wicked will be no more,' says,

'It was not for nothing that the apostle said, "Pray without ceasing" (1 Thess. 5:17). Can we indeed without ceasing, bend the knee, bow the body or lift up the hands, that he should say, "Pray without ceasing"? There is another internal prayer without intermission, and that is the longing of your heart. Whatever else you may be doing, if you long after the Sabbath of God, you do not cease to pray. If you do not wish to cease to pray, see that you do not cease to desire; your continual desire is your continual voice. You will be silent, if you leave off loving; for they were silent of whom it is written, "Because iniquity shall abound, the love of many shall wax cold." The coldness of love is the silence of the heart; the fervency of love is the cry of the heart.'

The Bible teaches a doctrine of the perseverance of the saints. True believers in Christ will never perish (John 3:16). They have eternal life right now and for ever (John 3:36; 5:24; 6:37). They will be kept by the power of God and never separated from the love of God (John 17:11-15; Rom. 8:35-39; 1 Thess. 5:23-4; Jude 24-25). For that reason, they will love and serve their Lord and Saviour, persevere in their faith, endure their temptations and afflictions and overcome the world (Heb. 12:28; 1 Cor. 1:7-9; 1 John 5:4).

A final exhortation

Jesus concludes with a sombre reminder that he will be returning one day: **'However, when the Son of Man comes, will he find faith on the earth?'** This brings the hearers back to the subject they had been discussing before he told them the parable of the widow and the judge. Yes, there is a great day coming when the Son of Man will appear and the work of his kingdom will be completed. The question is not, 'When will this day be?' or 'In what place will the kingdom be found?' The real question is, 'What will he find when that day dawns?' More pointedly still — for this is the practical implication of Jesus' question — 'How are you living *now*?' In what spiritual condition would he find you, were that day to be today? How are *you* living your life right now? Are you living in the light of the coming of the Son of Man? Or are you living for yourself? Is the life of God's kingdom *within you* today and every day? Are you living for the Lord? Do you pray every day, 'Your kingdom come,' and do you practise, 'Your will be done on earth'?

So when Jesus asks if he will find faith on the earth, he is not suggesting that there will be no faith when he comes. He is acknowledging that we do live in a fallen world that affords challenges to our faith, a world in which, sadly, the love of many will grow cold (Matt. 24:12). He is inviting us to examine ourselves in the light of that fact and be realistic as we set ourselves to live for him in a fallen world. Above all, he is pointing us to perseverance in our own faith. Yes, he will find faith on the earth. He will find a people who are praying without ceasing, who are overcoming the world and who will reign with him in glory.

Would you be part of that? Believe in the Lord Jesus Christ and you will be saved. Persevere to the last and you will receive a crown of life.

20.
The right attitude

The parable of the Pharisee and the tax collector
(Luke 18:9-14)

'I tell you that this man, rather than the other, went home justified before God' (Luke 18:14).

Jesus had been telling his disciples about the coming of the kingdom — that day of the Son of Man when all human history would come to its culmination and consummation (Luke 17:20-37). This event would, however, never come soon enough for Jesus' followers. Sinful impatience with God's timetable would tend to gnaw away at their spiritual vitality and confront them with the recurring temptation to lose heart and give up praying. Accordingly, in the parable of the persistent widow, Jesus emphasized the need for perseverance, so that 'they should always pray and not give up' (18:1).

The Lord then followed this up with a second parable which is closely connected with what he had just been saying about persistence in prayer. This parable of the Pharisee and the tax collector deals primarily with *attitudes* in prayer. It shows us what the heart of true prayer is, as opposed to the nature of false, self-righteous prayer. Jesus anticipated the possibility that many people might well 'pray and not give up' in an *outward* sense, while having a wrong attitude of heart towards the Lord. Such people would be deceiving themselves into thinking that they were persevering in the faith and pleasing God, when in fact they were spiritually as dead as the dodo. 'Let him who thinks that he is standing, take care lest he fall.'

Jesus wanted his followers to 'pray and not give up' in the *inward*, truly evangelical manner. He wanted them to engage in true prayer, not a ritual sham. He wanted them not to give up living a life of real faith, not to go through the motions of some empty form of godliness that denied its power (2 Tim. 3:5).

He told the parable to **'some who were confident of their own righteousness and looked down on everybody else'** (Luke 18:9). It is a mistake to assume that this means that Jesus was speaking to a group of Pharisees. In the absence of a specific identification, it is likely that this was just a group of his followers and hearers, which happened to be made up of people who were not impressed with Pharisees or tax collectors, but had likes and dislikes of their own. Send into almost any church today a young man who is a little different — perhaps unconventionally dressed, and with an ear-ring and a pony-tail — and watch the nice middle-class Christians instantly begin looking down on him! The Lord was not speaking to some other group that we all agree are not quite 'kosher'. He was not talking about 'them' as opposed to 'us'. He was speaking to you and to me! And he was pinpointing that secret spirit of the Pharisees that lurks in the dark corners of the soul.

Jesus had already warned his hearers to 'be on [their] guard against the yeast of the Pharisees and Sadducees'(Matt. 16:6), and he wanted them, to use Paul's later words, to 'get rid of the old yeast that [they might] be a new batch without yeast' (1 Cor. 5:7). It is possible to despise the Pharisees and yet still be one of them deep down. What is needed is a new heart altogether, transformed by the renewing power of God. This is what the gospel of the kingdom is all about. The 'blood of Christ, who through the eternal Spirit offered himself unblemished to God' will 'cleanse our consciences from acts that lead to death, so that we may serve the living God' (Heb. 9:14).

This is the general perspective of the parable. When we examine the story in its details, we will see that it speaks of two men, two prayers and two results.

Two men (18:10)

'Two men went up to the temple to pray, one a Pharisee and the other a tax collector.' We are already aware of these two classes in Jewish society. The Pharisees were a sect of legalistic orthodox Jews who prided themselves on their careful observance of the details of God's law as interpreted and elaborated by their rabbinic tradition. They saw themselves as the Hebrews of the Hebrews (cf. Phil. 3:5). The tax collectors were at the opposite end of the spectrum. They were regarded as the lackeys of imperial Rome and as people without scruples.

As we shall see, the Pharisee represents those who are concerned about respectability and external holiness, yet who neglect the question of inward spiritual uncleanness, while the tax collector represents those who are crushed by their own sins and cry out for deliverance to the only one who can save them. This contrast is heightened by the circumstance that, whereas a Pharisee would never miss the appointed times of prayer (cf. Acts 3:1), a tax collector would hardly, if ever, darken the door of the temple. The one prays merely because he always prays; the other cries to God because he is in desperate need and is repenting towards God for his sins.

Two prayers (18:11-13)

The Pharisee prayed about himself (18:11-12)

The Pharisees characteristically loved to pray standing in the synagogues and on the street corners 'to be seen by men' (Matt. 6:5). This man was no different. He **'stood up and prayed'**. The posture itself was not the problem. Standing is one of the Bible's prescribed postures for prayer.[1] The problem was the desire to be seen by others in performing what was an essentially private spiritual exercise. It is very likely that the Pharisee went boldly forward to the Holy Place and stood by himself. He put space between himself and the other, in his eyes lesser, worshippers. He was a man apart. He was of the spiritual élite of Israel and wanted everybody to know it. Notice three things about his praying.

First, he **'prayed about himself'**. What this means is that, in effect, he prayed *to* himself. He called on the name of God, but everything he said was in the nature of self-address. This is not difficult to do. It illustrates something profoundly important about real prayer. Prayer only takes place when a believer comes out of himself and enters the presence of the Lord. Perhaps you have begun to pray and soon come to feel that you have ended up talking to yourself. Millions of people, I believe, just talk to themselves and wish as hard as they can, and really think that is genuine prayer communication with God. Real prayer, as defined by God himself, is an entrance into the holiest by the blood of Christ. It is coming to the throne of God through a personal faith in our Mediator, Jesus Christ. It is a conscious act of faith in the power of the Holy Spirit as he lives and motivates the believer's innermost being. The focus of biblical prayer is always the holiness of God and the praise of his name. It is in this context that the desires of our hearts are to be expressed and his promises in the Word claimed on the basis of Christ's finished work of atonement for sin.

The format of the Lord's Prayer encapsulates that sense of deeply personal God-centredness. Mnemonics can be trite, but the word ACTS has helpfully captured the spiritual order and tone of prayer for many a young Christian — there is first Adoration, then Confession, followed by Thanksgiving and, finally, Supplication.

To this spirituality of prayer the Pharisee was oblivious. He was talking to himself and preening himself before his inferiors. What follows in the parable confirms this vividly.

Secondly, he *compared himself to others:* **'God, I thank you that I am not like other men...'** His eye is not on God. It is on other men. He does not, however, compare himself with the great saints of old, like Moses, or Job, or Samuel, or Elijah. No! He compares himself with **'robbers, evildoers, adulterers,'** and even with another worshipper that day in the temple — **'this tax collector'**. He has no sense of guilt. He expresses no need for forgiveness and avoids all reflection on God's real standards for personal holiness. He has no sins to confess. All he can see is how good a fellow he is. He has, after all, never done any of the terrible things that these gross sinners do. To be sure, he gives a nod towards the Lord. But his gratitude to God is so obviously hollow that it is hardly necessary to dismiss it as a form of words. This is a prayer that proves the man had not entered the presence of a holy God. He lived in the world of his smug self-righteousness, and prayed to the altar of his own pride.

Finally, he *reviewed his recent achievements* as a keeper of the law: **'I fast twice a week and give a tenth of all I get.'** One might be excused for responding, in the American idiom, with a slightly mocking 'Whoop-de-doo! Well done me! What a good boy I am!' God only commanded one fast a *year* — on *Yom Kippur*, the Day of Atonement. The Pharisee had improved on that by over one hundred times! God commanded a tithe on income, but he tithed on everything he received — like you tithing on your birthday presents. In all this self-congratulation, he entirely missed the point of God's law. He forgot the 'more important matters of the law — justice, mercy and faithfulness' (Matt. 23:23). He failed to see that God is not interested in mechanical observances, even of things that ought to be done. He failed to see the depravity of his own heart. He failed to see that his 'improvements' on God's standards were a stench in God's nostrils and that his very best good works were no better that filthy rags (Isa. 64:6). He did not see that without faith it is impossible to please God (Heb. 11:6) and that whatever is not of faith — motivated by confiding faith in Christ as Saviour — is sin (Rom.14:23).

The Pharisee did not see that our best works do not commend us to God, but are only our duty and, in any case, are only acceptable to him as they flow out of the exercise of faith in his Son. The sure mark of self-righteousness is the use of 'good deeds' to make God our debtor. We see it in everyday life. People feel that if they are good Boy Scouts and do a good deed every day, then God owes them something. When something bad happens, you will hear someone say, 'Why did God let this happen? He was an honest fellow all his life!'

The tax collector stood at a distance (18:13)

The tax collector was overwhelmed with grief for his sins. He **'stood at a distance'**. He was just there, somewhere, not in a prominent position and wholly unselfconscious about what he was doing. He was not there to be seen by others. He was there to meet with God.

So keenly does he grasp the meaning of coming into the presence of a holy God that he loses himself completely in the experience of crying out to him. **'He would not even look up to heaven, but beat his breast and said, "God, have mercy on me, a sinner!"'** If he had come with any composed prayer in his mind, it dissolved in the anguish of his convicted soul. The world around him vanished from his view, as he ascended in prayer to the throne of grace.

The prayer of the heart always gets to the heart of prayer. The word rendered 'have mercy' is not the commonly used Scripture word for mercy. The Greek *hilastheti* means 'be propitious' — that is, 'Turn away from your anger and look upon me with grace.' Propitiation is the appeasement of God's wrath, as distinct from that mercy which is compassion for someone in their distress. This man realizes that his sin has offended God and that God has a right to be angry with him. It is the exact opposite of the Pharisee's assumption that God must be pleased with him, because he has done so many good things. The tax collector is under profound conviction of sin. He realizes that the human condition is a state of total depravity — not an utter depravity, but a total depravity in which everything we do is fatally tainted by sin in some way or other. He is not thinking of one set of sins as being worse than others. He is simply convinced he is a sinner and needs a Saviour! He is at an end of himself and all attempts to justify himself before God.

Furthermore, the tax collector did not compare himself to any-body else. He simply cried, **'God have mercy on me, a sinner.'** The text actually says *'the* sinner' (Gk, *to hamartolo*). In his own mind, at the moment of his prayer, he needed grace more than anyone else in the world. He was *the* sinner! How often people have said, 'I'm no worse than the next man,' as if this is an achievement of some kind. It is, of course, just a protest that my personal standard is all right with me and ought to be all right with anyone, God included. Any additional bursts of good work on my part are only 'icing on the cake'. The tax collector indulged in no such delusions of self-justification. He knew he needed the sovereign grace of God to save him and reconcile him to God. He cast himself, without excuse, without reservations, and without conditions upon the Lord!

> Not the labour of my hands
> Can fulfil thy law's demands
> Could my zeal no respite know,
> Could my tears for ever flow,
> All for sin could not atone:
> Thou must save, and thou alone.

Consequently, the right approach to God is to come saying,

> Nothing in my hand I bring,
> Simply to thy cross I cling;
> Naked, come to thee for dress;
> Helpless, look to thee for grace;
> Foul, I to the fountain fly;
> Wash me, Saviour, or I die.[2]

Two results (18:14)

The tax collector was accepted by God. That is the true psychology of conversion. People are asked by some modern evangelists to 'accept Jesus', or to 'receive Jesus into [their] hearts'. The emphasis is all on man's decision. God's acceptance is assumed as a necessary condition of gospel truth, but he otherwise stands helplessly waiting for man to open the door to his new life. I once heard a famous preacher say, 'God has voted for you; Satan has voted against you; you have the deciding vote.' This kind of man-centredness — the crass, modern face of the old Arminian error — has no support from Scripture. The tax collector didn't think he had 'the deciding vote'. He knew his theology — and his heart — better. When conviction of sin gripped him, he just fled as fast as he could to God's mercy and pleaded for it, making no facile assumptions about God's attitude. His reason, had he been able to think it through with the cold dispassionate aridity of the average writer in a theological journal, would have been that a mere decision to turn to God is not the same thing as a pronouncement of redemption from a God who had every right to put him in hell for his sins. He did not see his appeal for mercy as equivalent to receiving mercy. He applied out of the cauldron of his guilt and fear, trusting that God would answer in grace and bring a new reconciliation between them into his experience. 'He asks for mercy, and that is all he dares to ask,' says Simon Kistemaker. 'He prays and waits for God to answer.'[3]

This is precisely what happened. **'I tell you,'** says Jesus, **'that this man, rather than the other, went home justified before God.'** The Pharisee no doubt felt impregnably justified as he went home. The tax collector would still have felt humble, penitent and undeserving of God's forgiveness, even if the Lord had given him peace in his heart and joy in his Redeemer. Feelings are not the point here. The point is that, whatever their feelings respectively, the one was still lost and the other was now saved.

There is, however, every reason to believe that the tax collector went home knowing he was a new man in the sight of God and that it was all of God's sovereign grace.

The tax collector had 'a broken spirit' and a 'contrite heart' — the attitude that God 'will not despise' (Ps. 51:17). It was no accident that his prayer began with the first words of the fifty-first psalm: 'Have mercy on me, O God...' He had accurately assessed himself

in terms of the biblical perspective on man's rebellion against God.
'Never are you higher in God's esteem,' wrote Charles Simeon of
Cambridge, 'than when you are lowest in your own. Fear not but that
they who trust in God's mercy shall find mercy at his hands. Let that
faithful saying of the Apostle's sink deep into your hearts, "Christ
Jesus came into the world to save sinners; of whom I am chief" (1 Tim.
1:15). Look truly to the Saviour, and you may "go down to your
house justified". To every believing penitent he speaks as he did to
that repenting sinner — "Thy sins are forgiven... Thy faith hath
saved thee; go in peace" (Luke 7:48,50).'4

Jesus closes with a reiteration of the principle he had enunciated
in connection with the parable of the best seats: **'For everyone who
exalts himself will be humbled, and he who humbles himself will
be exalted'** (cf. Luke 14:11). 'See also,' says Matthew Henry, 'the
power of God's grace in bringing good out of evil; the publican had
been a great sinner, and out of the greatness of his sin was brought
the greatness of his repentance; *out of the eater came forth meat*
[Judg. 14:14]. See, on the contrary, the power of Satan's malice in
bringing evil out of good. It was good that the Pharisee was no
extortioner, not unjust; but the devil made him proud of this, to his
ruin.'5

Thomas Manton, one of the greatest of seventeenth-century
English preachers, beautifully and searchingly applies the message
of Jesus' parable: 'Consider your misery by reason of sin. The
Redeemer hath no work to do in stupid and senseless souls. They
that know not their misery regard not their remedy. The offers of the
gospel are always made to the sensible [i.e., the self-aware], the
broken-hearted, the weary, the thirsty, the heavy-laden. Many are
welcome to Christ that know not themselves penitent believers; but
never any welcome that knew not themselves condemned sinners
(Luke 18:13,14).'6

Part III:
The consummation of the kingdom

**The parables of Jesus' ministry
in the week before the crucifixion
(Matthew 20-25; Luke 19)**

21.
The last and the first

The parable of the workers in the vineyard
(Matt. 19:27 - 20:16)

'So the last will be first, and the first will be last' (Matt. 20:16).

Only Jesus knew it at the time, but his ministry had entered its final days. He was about to go up to Jerusalem to meet his death at the hands of the 'chief priests and the teachers of the law' (Matt. 20:18). In a week's time he would bear the wrath of God against sin in his own body as he died on the cross, and in ten days he would rise from the dead for the justification of his people. It was in anticipation of this, the great climax of his earthly ministry, that Jesus began to direct his followers' thoughts to the consummation, or completion, of the kingdom of God and the related themes of death and judgement to come. He does so by means of a series of nine parables on the 'last things'.[1]

The first of these, the parable the workers in the vineyard, was occasioned by our Lord's famous encounter with the 'rich young man'. This fellow had come to him with the question about what he had to do to inherit eternal life. Jesus told him to sell all his possessions and give them to the poor, thereby exposing the young man's real problem: he worshipped wealth rather than God. Consequently, 'He went away sad, because he had great wealth' (19:22).

'What will there be for us?' (19:27)

This prompted Peter to ask a question. He and the other disciples had never been wealthy, but they had left everything to follow Jesus.

'We have left everything to follow you! What then will there be
for us?' (19:27). He was asking, in other words, 'We see what
happens to those who do *not* give up everything to follow you. But
what happens to those who *do*?' Jesus' answer is arguably the most
amazing and unexpected reply in all of his recorded ministry: **'I tell
you the truth, at the renewal of all things, when the Son of Man
sits on his glorious throne, you who have followed me will also
sit on twelve thrones, judging the twelve tribes of Israel. And
everyone who has left houses or brothers or sisters or father or
mother or children or fields for my sake will receive a hundred
times as much and will inherit eternal life'** (19:28-29).

The Lord then adds an almost cryptic caution: **'But many who
are first will be last, and many who are last will be first'** (19:30).
In the first instance, this harked back to the case of the rich young
man. He was 'first' in his own eyes and in the eyes of many others.
He was well off, he was respectable, he was a moral fellow, even
religious, but he did not love God unconditionally. He loved himself
and his wealth, as of first and consuming importance. He had room
for God as long as he did not get in the way.

But it also responded to Peter's original question. Peter had said
that he had given up everything for Jesus, and asked what was going
to be in it for him. He sacrificed everything for the Lord. He was a
leader of leaders in Jesus' advancing movement. Jesus saw Peter
drifting into pride, and thinking of himself as 'first', perhaps even
imagining that the sacrifice was in the past and the rewards were just
around the corner. 'Look, Peter,' Jesus was saying, 'watch your
thinking and guard your heart, because many who seem to be "first"
may turn out to be "last". Beware of congratulating yourself for your
self-sacrifice and don't fall into the trap of thirsting after rewards as
if you have merited them by your good deeds.' It was to expound this
theme and lead Peter to a deeper understanding of his destiny as a
believer that Jesus then told the parable of the workers in the
vineyard.

The workers in the vineyard (20:1-15)

The hiring of the workers (20:1-7)

The story first describes the hiring of the workers. **'The kingdom
of heaven is like a landowner who went out early in the morning**

to hire men to work in his vineyard' (20:1). He went out several
times during the day to hire more men, but there are two basic
groups. This was probably because the vintage had come and the
grapes had to be picked with the utmost despatch so as not to let any
pass their peak.

The first group was hired at the beginning of the day and they had
made a definite agreement with the landowner for a particular rate
of payment: **'He agreed to pay them a denarius for the day...'**
(20:2). This was the standard daily wage for a labourer in those days.

The second group consisted of all those who had been hired later
in the day, whether at the third (9 a.m.), sixth (12 noon), ninth (3
p.m.) or eleventh (5 p.m.) hours. They needed work of any kind and
did not negotiate a definite pay scale; they accepted their employer's
commitment to pay them **'whatever is right'** (20:3-7).

The paying of the workers (20:8-15)

The end of the working day would have come at the twelfth hour —
around 6 p.m. Accordingly, the foreman was told to pay the men
their wages (Deut. 24:14-15). A number of points stand out in this
process.

The men were paid, **'beginning with the last ones hired and
going on to the first'**, i.e., in *the reverse order of their hiring* (20:8).
This was designed, one assumes, to ensure that the men who were
hired first would be there to witness the way in which the others were
dealt with. Anyone who has 'clocked out' on pay-day knows that
nobody waits around until everybody has been paid! It is also the
case that people are not usually paid in this order. We need to
remember that this is a *story*, and neither a documentary about
employer-employee relations, nor a prophetic picture of the se-
quence in which God judges people on the Day of Judgement. The
order of payment is a literary device to bring out clearly the main
point of the story, which is about the free grace of God and the
necessity of receiving it with a glad heart.

All the workers, including those who worked for only an hour,
were paid *a full day's wages*, **'a denarius'** (20:9). The employer
fully honoured his contract with the men he had hired first, but
generously gave full pay to those who came later and with whom he
had no contract.

The men who had worked all day did not, however, appreciate
this generosity. They were *annoyed* to be paid only the agreed wage

and expected more money, when their turn came to be paid. **"These men who were hired last worked only one hour," they said, "and you have made them equal to us who have borne the burden of the work and the heat of the day"'** (20:10-12). Surely the employer was unfair to them?

In response, their employer pointed out that he had been *generous* and not unfair (20:13-15). He had paid the earlier workers what had been agreed upon. He had, to be sure, paid the later workers more than they could have expected. He could have kept much of that money, but he did not. **'Don't I have the right'**, he asked, **'to do what I want with my own money?'** They really had nothing to complain about. Indeed, had not their true attitude been revealed when the landowner asked, **'Are you envious because I am generous?'** (20:15). His generosity exposed their lack of generosity.

The meaning of the parable

It is very easy to *over-interpret* this parable. One way of doing this has been to read some spiritual meaning into every character and action in the story. Thus one commentator sees the foreman as representing Jesus, even though he is little more than a stage prop in the drama, evidently included for literary colour and no more.[2] Others have seen the later workers as the Gentiles, and the original workers as the Jews.[3] Irenaeus, one of the so-called 'Fathers' of the early church (second century A.D.) viewed the periods of the parable's day as periods of world history from Adam to the Day of Judgement.[4] The best reading is, however, the simplest — always allowing for the immediate context in which Jesus spoke and people listened. We must resist the temptation to find meanings in every detail.

Another way to misinterpret this parable is to use it to address the fields of economic theory and labour relations. While the parable is clearly set in the economics of first-century Palestine, it is not designed to defend *laissez-faire* capitalism or promote union-busting. The owner of the vineyard certainly had the right to do what he did, but we must bear in mind that Jesus was not trying to establish that right. He was simply using the story to illustrate a point about the kingdom of God and its rewards.

The key to the parable is in the simple fact that the vineyard owner paid all of his workers a denarius. All received a full day's

pay, whether or not they worked for a full day. That denarius refers
in a general way to the free grace of God in bringing people to the
kingdom of heaven. There is an inequality in being first as opposed
to being last, but God's saving grace is equally grace in the
experience of everyone who, through faith in Jesus Christ, becomes
a child of God. God's grace is free. It is not merited. Grace is grace!
No-one deserves it more or needs it less. It is unmerited favour from
God, applied to all who trust in Jesus as their Saviour.

The last and the first (20:16)

Jesus' final word of application is that **'The last will be first, and
the first will be last.'** Here, Jesus reverses the order of his original
statement to Peter in 19:30. This, I think, indicates a subtle shift of
emphasis from the negative to the positive — from a caution about
the conceit of wanting to be 'first' to the affirmation that God's grace
will be received by all who trust themselves to him, however humble
they may be in their own and others' eyes.

Cautions for those who would be 'first'

He rebukes *envy* in the workers who were 'first'. They felt swindled,
even though they had received a good day's pay for a good day's
work. 'Are you envious because I am generous?' their employer had
asked. The Greek reads literally, 'Is your *eye* evil because I am
good?' Why were they looking resentfully over other people's
shoulders to see how they were doing? Why were they envious at
all? Because they wanted to be the greatest and felt themselves
worthy of greater recognition. Applied to the Christian life, this
explains why some Christians are so protective of their place and
influence in the church. They really believe nothing will work
properly without them. And if they don't get their little place in the
sun, they become resentful. I do not know any pastor who has never
had to deal with such people in congregations he has served. This is
why it takes real grace in Christians for churches to enjoy happy
fellowship and experience growth. Receiving newcomers, who will
always have different backgrounds, experiences and outlooks,
however soundly converted to Christ they may be, means dying to
the desire to be 'first', the determination to do things only one way

and the unhallowed thirst to maintain a dominant role in the direction of the expanding fellowship. It means opening one's heart in self-effacing love. It means embracing certain differences and changes. It means esteeming others more highly than oneself (Phil. 2:3).

He also rebukes the *self-centred attitude* of the whole-day workers. They were so full of how much they deserved greater rewards. They would not see past themselves and their accomplishments. Personal merit was the focus of their protest — their efforts were worth more than those of the later workers. Translated into the terms of faith and the kingdom of God, this represents the problem of a graceless attitude to the things of God's grace — the paradox of sin in the Christian life. It is like saying, 'Yes! Salvation is by God's grace alone, but I've paid my dues!' There may be orthodoxy in the heart and mind, but the flesh is clinging to some good works as if they were badges of merit exalting the one who does them over certain other people.

The right attitude is, of course, to rejoice in the privilege of being a child of God, and present ourselves as 'living sacrifices' because it is our 'reasonable service' to our Redeemer (Rom. 12:1, AV). Our newness of life is *all* a result of his free grace and *nothing* of our own self-generated good works. The Lord sustains us every day. He will gather us with his elect in the Great Day at the end of the age. He has given us, so to speak, our 'denarius'. Will we then complain that he saves other sinners at 'the eleventh hour'? The very idea is monstrous and an utter contradiction of the spirit of the gospel. Rather we ought to rejoice with the Lord and his angels over any sinner who has come to repentance and faith!

Ultimately, the attitude of the workers was a *rejection of their covenant* with the vineyard owner. They were, in effect, indicting him for his grace towards the other workers and accusing him of thereby proving he had made a false covenant with them — a covenant that somehow cheated them of their just reward. As a picture of our relationship to God, it speaks about a turning away from faith in God as a loving, trustworthy and sovereign Father. Is God to be charged as unfair? Caught up in the vagaries of our uncertain lives, we sometimes wonder. The psalmist Asaph confessed that his 'feet had almost slipped', when he 'envied the arrogant and 'saw the prosperity of the wicked' (Ps. 73:2-3). David wondered if the Lord had forgotten him (Ps. 13:1). Habakkuk complained bitterly that God was not looking out for his people (Hab. 1:2-4). We are sometimes tempted to indulge in similar sentiments. But over against that stands the fact that God is all of grace. He does all things well. And even if we do not, and cannot, understand many of the mysteries of his providence, the fact remains that his perfect love does cast out fear in trusting, believing hearts. We can rest upon his perfect righteousness and absolute goodness.

Encouragements for those who are 'last'

It is better, then, to be the 'last' who are first, than the 'first' who are last. When Jesus says, **'The last shall be first,'** he is encouraging a certain *attitude of heart*. Do not fear that you will miss out on the blessings of God, by being humble and quiet-spirited in your Christian life. The world thrives on competition and fosters the attitude that if you don't push yourself, no one else will and you ought not to be surprised if you make nothing of yourself. The world's way is always along the line of thrusting self-promotion. The world does not belong to the 'wallflowers'. The kingdom of God — both living the kingdom life here, and entering the heavenly kingdom hereafter — is radically different. Humility and obedience, not pride and self-advertisement, are the marks of gospel grace and the harbingers of divine rewards. Human 'lastness' is the antecedent to God-given 'firstness'. God resists the proud, but gives grace to the humble. He who loses his life for the sake of Jesus and the gospel will gain it. Dying, we live, said the apostle Paul of the hardships of faithful ministry. The apparent paradox of the Christian life is that true exaltation is alone the fruit of a surrender to evangelical humility before God and man. 'Humble yourselves therefore under the mighty hand of God, that *he* may exalt you *in due time*' (1 Peter 5:6, AV, my emphasis).

Even more fundamental than the matter of our attitude of heart is the truth that Jesus' statement — 'The last shall be first and the first shall be last' — is about the attitude of *God* towards the salvation of sinners. The reversal of 'first' and 'last' is not about the *order* in which the redeemed will be admitted to heaven. It is about the free, generous and even-handed grace with which God embraces those who come to him in faith through the mediation of his Son. To be saved by his grace is to be saved *just as much as every believer* and to be saved by the *same grace* that saves every believer. God is good. He does not turn away people because they come to faith after other people. You will perhaps recall that the Christians in Thessalonika two thousand years ago were worried about what happened to those who died before the coming again of Jesus Christ. Did they somehow miss out on the glories of heaven? No, said Paul, 'According to the Lord's own word, we tell you that we who are still alive, who are left till the coming of the Lord, will certainly not precede those who have fallen asleep. For the Lord himself will come down from heaven, with a loud command, with the voice of the archangel and with the trumpet call of God, and the dead in Christ will rise first. After that, we who are still alive and are left will be caught up together with them in the clouds to meet the Lord in the air. And so we will be with the Lord for ever. Therefore encourage each other with these words' (1 Thess. 4:15-18).

Those who might have been expected to be last — the dead, whose bodies lay in the ground or in the sea — actually rise first. But notice that the essence of the matter is not the order, *per se*, of the ingathering of the dead and the living, but the simultaneity of their reception into the completed glory of Christ's heavenly kingdom. Caught up *together*, they will be for ever *with* the Lord! The encouragement with which the apostle enjoined the Thessalonians to encourage one another was not so much the fact that the dead would rise first, but that, having risen, they and the living would be united in heavenly fellowship with their Saviour. The 'last' and the 'first' merge in the common experience of the saving grace of God in Jesus Christ his Son.

22.
Living for the Lord

The parable of the ten minas
(Luke 19:11-27)

'I tell you that to everyone who has, more will be given, but as for the one who has nothing, even what he has will be taken away...' (Luke 19:26).

Jesus was in Jericho on his way to Jerusalem for the Passover and his death on the cross. At that time there was a general feeling among the Jews that **'the kingdom of God was going to appear at once'** and no doubt the disciples were caught up in it to some extent (19:11). His disciples were beginning to realize that something momentous was about to take place. They had already heard Jesus predict his death and resurrection, but they did not really understand him (Luke 18:31-34). 'Jesus may die,' they may have reasoned, 'but he will immediately return and rule in glory here in Jerusalem.'

The Lord discerned that there was an 'end of the world', or 'coming of the kingdom', fever among the people. He was also well aware of the fact that when people become obsessed with a 'date-setting' approach to prophecy, and particularly with an *imminent* fulfilment of that prophecy, they tend to neglect their immediate tasks. Then, when the fulfilment does not come on the date set, they are liable to become very discouraged, even to the point of falling away from their faith. The parable of the ten minas speaks to this point. In it, Jesus says, 'Wait a minute! Let's keep our eyes on the job we are to do right now, and in the meantime wait patiently for the consummation of God's kingdom.' He was instructing his followers what they were to do while they were waiting for his return.

It was not accidental that the immediate occasion for the telling of the parable was Jesus' encounter with the tax collector Zacchæus. This notorious character was amazingly converted and, against the usual chorus of self-righteous objections that he associated with tax collectors and sinners, Jesus told the people the purpose of his ministry: 'For the Son of Man came to seek and to save what was lost' (Luke 19:1-10). Jesus had come to bring new life to lost people — to 'save his people from their sins' (Matt. 1:21). His followers — with a notable exception in Mary of Bethany (Mark 14:8-9; John 12:7-8) — saw this in exclusively triumphalistic terms and had no grasp of the necessity of Christ's death on the cross, resurrection from the tomb and ascension into heaven, far less the slightest conception of the future ministry of the church of the New Testament for millennia to come, until at last Jesus would return to deliver up his completed kingdom to his God and Father (1 Cor. 15:24). Jesus, accordingly, determined to prepare them for the reality that they would soon be facing.

One king and ten minas (19:12-25)

When Herod the Great died in 4 B.C. — the actual year of the birth of Jesus — his son Archelæus travelled to Rome to claim his father's throne from the Emperor Augustus. At the same time, a deputation from the Jewish people was sent to plead with the emperor not to give the kingdom to Archelæus. This kind of thing was not uncommon in the Roman Empire, for tributary kings and claimants to vacant thrones were obliged to go to Rome to deal with their overlord, the Roman Emperor.

This event, and others similar to it, provided the model for Jesus' parable of the ten minas. Jesus used the story of an earthly kingdom — the history of which was well known to his hearers — to make a point about the heavenly kingdom, of which he was himself the King. In Jesus' parable, a **'man of noble birth went to a distant country to have himself appointed king and then to return'** (19:12). Notice how the story unfolds.

The story itself

Before he left, the nobleman **'called ten of his servants and gave them ten minas'**. He made it clear that he expected them to put this money to work while he was away and make a profit by the time he got back. Each man received one mina (= 100 drachmas) — the equivalent of three months' wages for an ordinary worker (19:12-13).

The citizens, meanwhile, did not want the nobleman to be their king and attempted to prevent his accession to the throne. They sent a delegation after him to say, **'We don't want this man to be our king'** (19:14). In the background, there is an underlying opposition to this potential king.

In due course, this nobleman returned as king. The first thing he did was to call his ten servants to account for their stewardship (19:15-26). First, we hear about the faithful servants, who had succeeded in producing various levels of return on the original investment capital. These were appropriately rewarded — the servant who made ten minas was given the rule over ten cities; the one who had made five received five cities for his domain.

Another servant had, however, made no profit on his mina. He returned it with the explanation: **'I have kept it laid away in a piece of cloth.'** Instead of putting the money to work, he had hidden it in a napkin! He then had the audacity to excuse himself on the ground that he **'was afraid'** of his master, because he was **'a hard man'**, who would **'take out what [he] did not put in and ... reap what [he] did not sow'** (19:20-21). In the annals of lame excuses, this takes the prize, for he could at least have lent it to the bank. The NIV's **'on deposit'** is a paraphrastic rendering of the Greek *trapezan*, meaning 'table', in this case the moneylender's 'bench' — hence our word 'bank' (19:23).

The king duly acted on his reputation as a hard man. He confiscated the servant's mina and gave it to the man who had ten. Venture capital chases productivity and profit. It is the death of any economy when money is left in a drawer doing nothing. Therefore, the do-nothing people will lose every time. Nothing ventured means nothing gained ... and a great deal lost.

The second thing the king did was to mete out his justice to his various subjects. His *modus operandi* was set out in response to the protest of the unproductive servant at his solitary mina being given to the man with ten minas. The king enunciated the principle that **'To everyone who has, more will be given, but as for the one who has nothing, even what he has will be taken away,'** and went on to decree the execution of his enemies (19:26-27). There are three basic categories in the king's programme for his new subjects.

The first consisted of those diligent servants who were faithful to the charge they had been given, They were rewarded with gifts and honour: 'To everyone who has, more will be given.'

The second grouping was comprised of those who simply did not do their jobs properly: 'Even what he has will be taken away.'

The final category was made up of declared enemies **'who did not want [him] to be king over them'**. They were judged and put to death in the king's presence.

The focus of the parable

Jesus clearly told this story to illustrate what was to happen in his life and ministry, in particular his departure to claim his kingdom and his return to put all things under his feet with everlasting finality and to judge the living and the dead. He used the story of Archelæus to teach something about the kingdom of God and the King of that kingdom. No one would have thought that Jesus was likening himself to the wicked Archelæus, or in any way condoning the manner in which the ethnarch had treated his subjects a generation before.[1] This was simply a vivid and unforgettable way of fixing in the minds of the hearers the context in which they could later understand his imminent crucifixion and resurrection and his second coming at the end of the age.

What is of particular practical moment for us is what is meant by the money — the ten minas — given to the servants. Each servant received the same amount. This surely represents the gospel of Christ's kingdom. The servants — the followers of God's anointed King — had all heard the good news. All of them had professed to be followers of the king. All claimed to know him and love him. All had the task and calling of serving him faithfully — of showing forth the love of their Lord and, if God granted it, of bearing fruit for him, some tenfold, others fivefold, and so on. The central focus of the parable, then, is on *living for the King who is coming again* — for 'Jesus Christ, who is the faithful witness, the firstborn from the dead, and the ruler of the kings of the earth' (Rev. 1:5). The theme is living for the Lord, in the present manifestation of his kingdom upon earth and in prospect of the completion of the kingdom in the Great Day when he comes to judge the living and the dead. That judgement begins at the 'house of God' — the church — as he sifts his faithful servants from the unfaithful. It ends with the condemnation of those who persist in unrepentant opposition to the claims of the gospel and the kingly rule of the Lord. And in all this, the urgency of living each day as his people is placed squarely before our hearts and consciences.

Jesus, then, is referring to *spiritual life* in a spiritual kingdom. His kingdom 'is not of this world' (John 18:36). It is neither 'worldly' in the ethical sense, nor 'earthly' as to its origin and essence. It does not consist in political power. It is not made up of so-called 'Christian nations', even though the nations ought to serve Christ as ministers of good and terrors to evil (Rom.13:1-5). Rather, it is a 'holy nation' of believers in Jesus Christ drawn from every country on the face of the globe. The cross is the heart of it; saving faith in Christ is the mark of citizenship; Christ, risen and victorious, is its King and Head; and the church is the visible manifestation of the kingdom on earth while the world lasts.

Jesus means us to realize that our lives are to focus on *obedience* to God's will day by day. Someone once said that the Christian should live each day as if it were his last, and there is no doubt a sense in which this is true. But it is perhaps a greater truth that every Christian should plan a life of continuing obedience, in the assumption that Christ will not return tomorrow. Let the events of Christ's second coming interpret the prophecies and the promises; our present calling is to live each day for him in a positive manner — expecting blessing for as many days and years as he shall give us.

Jesus also reminds us that faithfulness to the king receives a *kingly reward*. Practical obedience multiplies joy in the heart of the believer. In contrast, disobedience always casts a shadow across the soul. It is a law of God's kingdom that those who love the Lord will enjoy more of his love and mercy in their lives, while those who pay him outward lip-service, but inwardly remain unmotivated to live according to his Word will lose what little 'light' and blessing they have known. The 'reward' of the hypocrite is the taking away of those things for which, deep down, he had no time in any case. But, says Paul, 'The man who plants and the man who waters have one purpose, and each will be rewarded according to his own labour' (1 Cor. 3:8). Like Moses, we ought to be 'looking ahead to [our] reward', and regard 'disgrace for the sake of Christ as of greater value than the treasures of Egypt' (Heb. 11:26). 'Let us stand ready,' said Charles Simeon, 'to give up our account with joy. So shall we have confidence before him, and not be ashamed at his coming [1 John 2:28].'[2]

'Occupy till I come' (19:13, AV)

There is work to do before the Lord returns! This is the perspective of the parable for every day's discipleship. Just as a football team works the ball up the field, always retaining possession and always with an eye on the other side's goal, so God's people live for him with their eyes on his goal for them. The Authorized Version's **'Occupy till I come'** catches something of the expectancy with which Christians give up their days to Jesus. The fact that he is coming provides the dominating motive. The Saviour who is the subject of our faith and the depository of all our hopes is coming.

Our rendezvous with destiny

Even now we are *en route* to a rendezvous with the crowning triumph of our Redeemer. Sometimes we wish that Jesus would return right now. We echo the prayer of the apostle John: 'Amen. Come, Lord Jesus' (Rev. 22:20). We understand the cry of the martyrs when they call to the Lord, 'How long, Sovereign Lord, holy and true, until you judge the inhabitants of the earth and avenge our blood?' (Rev. 6:9). Why, we ask, should this world of sadness and misery, of oppression and hardship, of disease and death, go on century after century? The answer is that Jesus has a plan of redemption to work out throughout these many generations. He is building his kingdom as he seeks and saves lost men and women in every generation. As long as there is a generation to be born, from which he plans to raise up people to praise and magnify the Lord, then the world will last, the gospel will be preached and believers will still have the Lord's commission to 'occupy, till I come'. Only when the last elect sinner is saved from the last generation of humanity will the voice of the archangel and the trumpet of God signal the coming of the Lord and the end of the age (1 Thess. 4:16).

Every Christian is part of this great work of God

How is his purpose of gathering in lost people to his kingdom to be accomplished? Surely through the preaching of the gospel and the witness of the church in every succeeding generation! By you and me, Christian friend! This is what Jesus' disciples should have known — that there was work to be finished before the Lord would return. When the last sermon has been preached, when the last 'reason for the hope that is in you' has been given in personal evangelism, when the last language has been translated and its speakers given a Bible in their own tongue, when the last unreached people has been reached for Christ, the last martyr put to death; and the last sinner converted to Christ — then the waiting will be over. Jesus will return and human history will come to its completion in the consummation of our Lord's kingdom and glory.

Do you need an incentive to be about the Lord's business? 'To everyone who has, more will be given...' There is a crown of life for all who are faithful till he comes.

> O all the earth, sing to the Lord
> And make a joyful sound.
> Lift up your voice aloud to him;
> Sing psalms! Let joy resound!
>
> Because he comes, he surely comes,
> The judge of earth to be!
> With justice he will judge the world,
> All men with equity.[3]

23.
Christ our cornerstone

The parables of the sons and wicked tenants
(Matt. 21:23-46)

'The stone which the builders rejected, the same is become the head of the corner' (21:42, AV; Ps. 118:22).

When Jesus was teaching in the temple courts on the Tuesday before his crucifixion, he was approached by **'the chief priests and the elders of the people'** with the challenge: **'By what authority are you doing these things? ... And who gave you this authority?'** (21:23). Just the day before, he had ejected the moneylenders from the temple and the crowds had received him as a prophet (21:12-16). Although these might seem to be the normal questions to ask in such a context, they were in fact dishonest. All that Jesus had done, not only since his triumphal entry to Jerusalem but throughout his three-year public ministry, argued strongly that he had acted with God-given authority. The Jewish leaders knew as well as the next man how to draw obvious conclusions, so ignorance was not their motive for asking. They wanted to trip Jesus up somehow — hence their deceptively naïve approach.

Jesus knew very well what they were up to, so he answered them in a very subtle way. He asked them where John the Baptizer had got his authority. **'John's baptism,'** he asked, **'where did it come from? Was it from heaven, or from men?'** If they answered him, he would answer them. When they discussed it among themselves, they realized that they couldn't give an answer. Why? Because, if they said John's authority came from God, they would condemn their own unbelief. On the other hand, if they said it was just **'from men'** they would incur the anger of the people, who all believed that

John was a prophet from God. They were hoist with their own petard! They could not answer without exposing themselves as the hypocrites they were. So they took the safer, but humiliating, way out: they said lamely, **'We don't know'** (21:25-27).

That gave the Lord all he needed to deliver his *coup de grâce.* **'Then he said, "Neither will I tell you by what authority I am doing these things"'** (21:27). That was just his way of saying, 'You are a bunch of liars. You do know the answer. You know John came from God. You also know he pointed to me as the promised Messiah. You know very well that my authority is from God, but you just won't admit it either, because that would be to condemn your own unbelieving hearts. And you won't come out and deny me, because you are afraid of the people who think I am a prophet. That's the real truth, isn't it? You know it is!' So much for these great church leaders and erstwhile defenders of the faith!

One can imagine that many people, and perhaps especially the disciples, were puzzled by the negative attitude of the Jewish leadership towards Jesus and his ministry. If it was clear to them that John had been called by God to his ministry, and that Jesus was the one for whom John had prepared the way (see Mal. 4), then why was there such virulent opposition to Jesus from the very people who ought to welcome him most enthusiastically? To explain this situation, Jesus then told the parables of the two sons and the tenants.

The two sons — a fact of disobedience to God's will
(21:28-32)

The parable of the two sons continues to keep the case of John the Baptizer in view. The story is straightforward. A man had two sons. One rebelled against his authority, but later **'He changed his mind and went.'** In contrast, when the other son was asked to work in the vineyard, he immediately said he would, **'but he did not go'.** **'Which of the two'**, asked Jesus, **'did what his father wanted?'** They knew the answer was obvious. **'"The first," they answered'** (21:29-31).

Jesus pulled no punches in applying this to his hearers: **'I tell you the truth, the tax collectors and the prostitutes are entering the kingdom of God ahead of you.'** Why was this so? For two reasons, says Jesus. In the first place, when John had come preaching repentance, they did not believe him, **'but the tax collectors and prostitutes did'**. Whereas people from the dregs of society believed John's message, those from the upper echelons of respectable society rejected him — and, indeed, made him a martyr. In the second place, these very people who claimed to know, love and obey the living God *still* did not repent and believe him, **'even after [they] saw this'** — that is, even after they saw the lives of these 'sinners' transformed by their new-found faith! (21:31-32).

This surely teaches us the fundamental truth, as John Calvin puts it, that 'Faith does not consist merely in a person giving subscription to true doctrine, but also includes something greater and deeper: the hearer is to deny himself and commit his whole life to God.'[1] More than that even, it explains why it is, as Jesus said on an earlier occasion, that 'the men of Nineveh' and 'the Queen of the South' (i.e., the Queen of Sheba) would 'rise at the judgement with this generation and condemn it' (Matt. 12:39-42). The gospel was being proclaimed; people were coming to faith; but there were still plenty who hardened their hearts against the Lord. The Son of God, says John, 'was in the world, and though the world was made through him, the world did not recognize him. He came to that which was his own, but his own did not receive him. Yet to all who received him, to those who believed in his name, he gave the right to become children of God — children born not of natural descent, nor of human decision or a husband's will, but born of God' (John 1:10-13).

The tenants — the nature of hatred towards Christ (21:33-41)

The parable of the wicked tenants explains the nature of the disobedience described in the story of the two sons and so shows us something of the true enormity of Israel's sin. The relevance of this to the church today is obvious.

A very bad situation (21:33-39)

A landowner planted a vineyard and rented it to some farmers while he went away on a journey. Around the harvest-time, he sent his **'servants'** to collect **'his fruit'**, i.e., rent paid in kind. But the tenants '**beat one, killed another and stoned a third**'. Another batch of servants were given the same treatment. Finally, he sent his '**son**' to them, reasoning, '**They will respect my son.**' The tenants, however, saw this as a golden opportunity to take permanent possession of the vineyard. '**This is the heir,**' they said to one another. '**Come, let's kill him and take his inheritance.**' So they killed him.

The story offers a picture of the failure of the Old Testament church down the centuries. God had been good to them. He had given them his covenant promises. For example, through Abraham they would be a great nation and the means of blessing to all the nations (Gen. 18:18-19; Gal. 3:8,14). He gave his law through Moses at Sinai (Exod. 20). At 'many times and in various ways', God spoke to them through the prophets (Heb. 1:1). Israel had the Word of God. Paul would later testify, 'Theirs is the adoption as sons; theirs the divine glory, the covenants, the receiving of the law, the temple worship and the promises. Theirs are the patriarchs, and from them is traced the human ancestry of Christ, who is God over all, for ever praised! Amen' (Rom. 9:4-5). Notwithstanding all these advantages, they fell away from God and killed the prophets and stoned those who were sent to them (Matt. 23:37). Then in the fulness of the time, God's Son and Heir came into this vineyard and what did they do, but lay wicked hands on him and put him to death, even the death of the cross? (Phil. 2:8). He came to his own and his own received him not (John 1:11). They crucified the Lord of glory (1 Cor. 2:8).

What would you do? (21:40-41)

Jesus then posed the obvious question: '**When the owner of the vineyard comes, what will he do to those tenants?**' His hearers duly served up the obvious answer: '**He will bring those wretches to a wretched end ... and he will rent the vineyard to other tenants, who will give him his share of the crop at the harvest time.**' It is impossible, as Kistemaker has pointed out,[2] that Jesus' hearers would not have noticed a reference here to the 'Song of the Vineyard' in Isaiah's prophecy,

> 'I will sing for the one I love
>   a song about his vineyard;
>   My loved one had a vineyard

on a fertile hillside.
He dug it up and cleared it of stones
    and planted it with the choicest vines.
He built a watchtower in it
    and cut out a winepress as well.
Then he looked for a crop of good grapes,
    but it yielded only bad fruit'

(Isa. 5:1-2).

Nor would they have forgotten the conclusion of the song, or missed the point that Jesus was making about Israel's attitude to the message and the messengers of the kingdom of God:

'The vineyard of the Lord Almighty
    is the house of Israel,
and the men of Judah
    are the garden of his delight.
And he looked for justice, but saw bloodshed;
    for righteousness, but heard cries of distress'

(Isa. 5:7).

Retributive justice is inevitable for a world that rejects God. Not to receive Christ and the gospel of saving grace will one day be answered with a sentence of everlasting death from the very lips of the Son of God. He who is the 'Lamb of God', who died for those who believe, will be the 'Lion of the tribe of Judah' who sits in righteous judgement upon those who will not believe (Rev. 5:5-6).

The stone the builders rejected (21:42-46)

Jesus did not leave them to draw their own conclusions. He made the application of the two parables crystal clear. He made three main points.

God's plan predicted the rejection of his Son (21:42)

The disciples needed to understand that what was happening to Jesus — rejection by the Pharisees and Sadducees, and his impending death — accorded with the already declared will and purpose of

God. Jesus quoted from Psalm 118: **'The stone the builders rejected, the same is become the head of the corner'** (21:42, AV; Ps. 118:22). He changes the figure from a vineyard to a building and from farmers to builders. The builders are the Jewish leaders; the stone they reject is Jesus. The disciples had to see that this was not some spanner thrown in God's works, but rather was the Lord's doing, to be **'marvellous in [their] eyes'**. Jesus was preparing them for his death. He sought to remove the offence of his death by showing that it was absolutely central to God's plan for his kingdom. The discouragement they felt over his predictions of death — not to mention the despair that gripped them after he actually died — ought to have been tempered with this great consolatory truth.

Later, when Christ was enthroned in triumph, having risen from the dead and ascended to heaven as the mediatorial King, it would become clear to them that no one could ever say, 'I helped to put him there.' He gained the victory alone, according to the sovereign purpose of God, and did so in a manner that confounded every worldly expectation as to how God's kingdom would be established. The 'builders' threw away the very 'stone' that God made the 'head of the corner' — the cornerstone, from which is determined the placing of every other stone in the building. Jesus was the starting-point for the completed building of God's spiritual temple (1 Peter 2:4-10).

God's kingdom requires living faithfulness from us (21:43)

It follows that the kingdom of God will be **'given to a people who will produce its fruit'**. Those of the Old Testament people of God who reject the Messiah — the 'natural branches' of the covenant family tree—would be cut off, while new branches would be grafted on and would flourish in practical faithfulness to the Lord. This would issue in the extension of the gospel to the other nations of the world — the so-called Gentiles. It would be 'first for the Jew, then for the Gentile' (Rom. 1:16; cf. 2:9-10). The same principle applies at the individual level for the Gentiles, for, as Paul says in Romans 11:21, 'If God did not spare the natural branches [apostate Jews], he will not spare you either [apostate Gentiles].'

There could hardly be a more searching warning about the perils of rejecting or stifling the gospel of Jesus Christ. And yet there is certainly an implicit consolation here, because it contains the promise that the Lord will always have his faithful people in this world and will be with them by his Holy Spirit to lead and guide them in the paths of his righteousness (Ps. 23:3). As the lip-servers and hypocrites let him down and show themselves for what they really are, the Lord draws others to saving faith and practical discipleship. This is also why some churches die. They cease both to believe the Bible and to preach the true gospel of Christ. Consequently, the mantle of proclaiming the message of new and everlasting life in Christ is passed to others, who will go on in the strength of the Lord.

God's King will judge his enemies (21:44-46)

The rejected 'cornerstone' not only builds his kingdom. He judges the living and the dead. **'He who falls on this stone will be broken to pieces, but he on whom it falls will be crushed'** (21:44). Jesus thereby reveals himself as the fulfilment of God's word to Israel through the prophet Isaiah:

> 'See, I lay a stone in Zion,
>   a tested stone,
> a precious cornerstone for a sure foundation;
>   the one who trusts will never be dismayed'
>
> (Isa. 28:16).

> 'And he will be a sanctuary;
>   but for both houses of Israel he will be
> a stone that causes men to stumble
>   and a rock that makes them fall'
>
> (Isa. 8:14).

The apostle Peter confirms this in 1 Peter 2:4-8, in a passage in which he quotes Isaiah 28:16; Psalm 118:22 and Isaiah 8:14 together to show that Jesus is *the* 'living Stone', precious to believers and a stumbling-block to unbelievers (See also the 'Rock' of Isa. 51:1; Deut. 32:4,15,18,30-31; Zech. 3:9; cf. Rev. 5:6).

The once-rejected Jesus will visit the ultimate rejection upon those who rejected him. This judgement comes one by one to those who oppose him to the last. 'The singulars [in verse 44],' remarks Lenski, 'speak of the individual persons, for the guilt of unbelief and hostility is always personal.'³ To stumble over Christ, to baulk at the claims of the gospel, is to 'be broken to pieces'. That is to say, it is not Christ who is damaged, but you. *Not* to respond receptively to Jesus is to harden one's heart and shrink from the light of truth, and thus to deepen the spiritual problem of personal unbelief. But to have Christ fall upon oneself *is* the final judgement and means being 'crushed'. The Greek word *'likmesei'* carries the idea of being ground to a fine dust. This is the wrath to come, from which we are called to flee (Matt. 3:7). 'Judgement can be pictured with no greater severity,' observes R. C. H. Lenski.⁴

The Pharisees and the chief priests did not mistake Jesus' meaning, but decided to stumble at his words and hazard the portents of his wrath, They tried to find a way of arresting him, but were prevented by their fear of the people, who believed him to be a prophet (21:45-46). As usual, people on their way to a lost eternity are more afraid of those who can kill the body than of the God who can put both body and soul in hell (Matt. 10:28). They ought rather to have received Christ as the true cornerstone of the kingdom God was building. The parables called every hearer to follow Christ. Although the core of the apostolic church was to be Jewish, the Jewish nation as a whole rejected Christ, an occurrence which drew forth from Jesus his heavy-hearted lament over Jerusalem (Matt. 23:37-39). In due time, the gospel was spread across the Gentile world. Paul would say to Greek converts in Ephesus, 'Consequently, you are no longer foreigners and aliens, but fellow citizens with God's people and members of God's household, built on the foundation of the apostles and prophets, with Christ Jesus himself as the chief cornerstone. In him the whole building is joined together and rises to become a holy temple in the Lord. And in him you too are being built together to become a dwelling in which God lives by his Spirit' (Eph. 2:19-22). When we come to Christ in faith, he is the fixed point from which our life is for ever after measured. He is *our* cornerstone, and we then know *who* we are, *why* we are, *where* we are and *whose* we are.

24.
Many are called but few are chosen

The parable of the wedding banquet
(Matt. 22:1-14)

'For many are called but few are chosen' (Matt. 22:14, AV).

The parable of the wedding banquet is somewhat similar to Luke's parable of the Great Supper[1] (Luke 14:15-24). The two ought not to be confused. The parable recorded in Luke anticipated the 'filling of God's house', namely, the completion of the kingdom of God. This parable, told in the last days before the crucifixion, was very obviously given in prospect of our Lord's imminent death. In it, Jesus follows through on his earlier theme by focusing it more specifically and, in this way, emphasizing that the time had come to press the claims of his message of the kingdom with the utmost urgency.

Consequently, the parable has something of the flavour of a last great summons to follow Jesus, before eternal darkness envelops the careless and indifferent. We are brought to the edge of eternity and made to look alternately down into the abyss of hell and upward to the glory of heaven. The parable presents us with the great divide — and the great decision. Jeremiah's words of long before rise up to grip our souls, 'Behold I set before you the way of life and the way of death' (Jer. 21:8), while Joshua's challenge impels us to choose now and to choose for ever: 'Choose you this day whom you shall serve' (Josh. 24:15). If you are to be at the wedding banquet of the Son of heaven's King, then you must accept his invitation without delay, for your time is short and your response is a matter of life and death, for both time and eternity!

The parable and its perspective (22:1-13)

The story tells of a king who **'prepared a wedding banquet for his son'** and sent his servants to tell those he had invited that the time had come, **'but they refused to come'** (22:2-3). Nothing daunted, the king sent more servants out to reissue the invitations. They still paid no attention, however. One went off to his field, another to his business, and the rest **'seized his servants, ill-treated them and killed them'**. The upshot of this was that the king **'sent his army and destroyed those murderers and burned their city'**. This was one king that was not to be trifled with! (22:6-7).

The basic perspective of the parable is not difficult to discern. The king is God the Father. The king's son is the Lord Jesus Christ. The wedding banquet is the union of Christ with his bride, the church. Those first invited are the old covenant people, the Jews. Their general rejection of the king's summons — and, by implication, of the king's son — incurred the king's wrath to such an extent that he unleashed his army upon them to bring them to justice. This is no doubt a picture of the ending of the Jewish theocracy and the cessation of temple worship, and therefore has its fulfilment in the Roman destruction of Jerusalem in A. D. 70. Although the fact was masked by the perennial normality of daily life in Palestine, the old order was on its last legs, while the new — not to be confused with the 'new world order' fantasies of politicians in the aftermath of the collapse of Communism — was dawning. Jesus Christ is alone the hinge of history. The era between his first and final advents *is* the new (covenant) world order, the age in which the gospel is preached and the elect gathered from the four winds, all culminating in the great and terrible day of the Lord — great for those who love him; terrible for the unrepentant, reprobate lost.

It is this eschatological climax of history, of which the passing of the old covenant was but a foretaste, that forces upon every generation the urgent necessity of fleeing the wrath to come and embracing new life in Christ as offered in the gospel.

Invited guests (22:8-10)

The call that went out to those who did not deserve to be invited represents the extension of the gospel to the other nations of the world. The filling up of the guest list in this manner indicates the purpose of God to save people out of the world and effect the complete triumph of the gospel of his kingdom over all opposition. **'Go to the street corners'**— where the layabouts have always hung out — **'and invite ... anyone you can find.'** The call is promiscuous, entirely unselective. There is no targeting of the suburbs and a well-scrubbed middle class, as with the 'church-growth movement' theorists of our day. Just call sinners — especially those that look like sinners, the loitering lost and needy ne'er-do-wells. And that was what happened, with the result that the wedding hall was filled with people, including both **'good and bad'** — in other words, sinners of all shapes and sizes, and every type and stamp.

Improperly dressed (22:11-13)

That done, there remains an unresolved problem. Do these sinners, good and bad, just find themselves in heaven, in the state of salvation, *as they are*— still good and bad. Does God like us just the way we are? The final sentences of the parable give the answer. The king came in to meet the guests and spotted a man **'without wedding clothes'**. The assumption must be that the guests were provided with the appropriate robes by the king's officials, but somehow this man got in without being screened and thereby acquiring the proper dress. The king asked how he had got there without wedding clothes. No answer was the loud reply! **'The man was speechless.'** He had no right to be there and he knew it. The king accordingly had him removed **'into the darkness, where there will be weeping and gnashing of teeth'**.

It was the possession of wedding clothes that validated the guests' presence at the feast. These were the clothes that made the men, so to speak. They were the emblems of acceptance with the king, the symbols of a radical transformation in both personal character and relationship to the father of the king's son. The 'good and the bad' become new people on account of the 'robe of righteousness' given them by the sovereign grace of the king (cf. Isa. 61:10). The man who was improperly dressed to the outward view was also inwardly unrenewed. He is the person who sneaks into Christ's sheepfold 'by some other way' — namely, a hypocritical show of external religion — rather than entering 'by the gate' of saving faith (John 10:1). We cannot take our sins to heaven. Nothing that defiles will ever enter, 'but only those whose names are written

in the Lamb's book of life' (Rev. 21:27). A sham acceptance of
Christ will not do. The Lord's eye penetrates the naked conscience
of the hypocritical professor and renders him speechlessly defence-
less. The articulate assurance which makes such folk the scourge of
sincerely simple Christians in this life is stripped away for ever
before the relentless interrogation from the judgement seat.

So breathtaking is this moment that parabolic fiction gives way
to sober fact, as Jesus opens hell to receive its own. The eternal
darkness swallows the reprobate, to the unrelieved accompaniment
of the agonies of the damned. Not a pretty picture, perhaps, but only
words compared to the real thing. And yet there is grace here for
those who care to listen. Better to hear Jesus now and repent, than
to hear him later and go down to the pit!

The outward call of the gospel: 'Many are called' (22:14)

Jesus sums up the parable with a pregnant word of application, best
rendered in the Authorized Version: **'For many are called, but few
are chosen.'** As a proof text for the doctrine of election in general
and that of effectual calling in particular, this is rightly beloved by
all who love the doctrines of grace. It *is* impregnably Calvinistic.
Yet, it must be said that Jesus' primary purpose was not the mere
establishment of a doctrinal proposition about God's sovereignty,
true as it undoubtedly is. His immediate goal was to lay his finger
on the consciences of his hearers, that they might be gripped by the
necessity of not stopping with the call as they have heard it, but
would go on to make their calling and election sure.

Behind, in towering majesty, stands the absolute sovereignty of
God's grace. But before, with earnest importunity, is the appeal to
the sinner to come to Christ that he might have life — to be one of
the chosen, rather than the merely called. The parable impels us to
the decision point and its purpose is not to write the epitaph for those
who will not believe in Jesus, but to inscribe the cup of salvation for
those who will.

The meaning of the wedding feast

We need to remember what the wedding feast signifies. *Ultimately*,
Jesus was talking about that final and everlasting feast — the

marriage supper of the Lamb described in Revelation 19. Heaven itself is likened to a feast in which all the redeemed of the Lord fellowship together with their Saviour. The sharing of the meal is a picture of spiritual union and communion with Jesus Christ in heaven, just as the Lord's Supper speaks of that communion with Christ that believers enjoy now, in the prospect of his second coming (1 Cor.11:26). Isaiah, speaking of Zion as a figure of the heavenly Jerusalem, declares,

> 'On this mountain the Lord Almighty will prepare
>   a feast of rich food for all peoples,
> a banquet of aged wine—
>   the best of meats and the finest of wines'
>
> (Isa. 25:6).

This is the feast of the glory yet to be revealed — in the great day when Jesus gathers all his people together and his kingdom is consummated for ever.

The wedding feast also has a contemporary reference, for it speaks of the present union of believers with Christ by faith. There is a sense, however incomplete and provisional, in which the feast is *now* experienced by believers. This is what Paul means when he says that since Christ 'our Passover has been sacrificed for us,' we must 'keep the feast' (1 Cor. 5:7, AV). The 'feast' is our new life, lived by faith in him. The same theme is found in Revelation 3:20, where Jesus says to wavering Christians, 'Here I am! I stand at the door and knock. If anyone hears my voice and opens the door, I will come in and eat with him, and he with me.' We are being called to a feast — to living union with Christ by faith and a life of daily practical godliness — and that feast points to the final feast, that is the glory of heaven.

Called to faith in Christ

It is to *Christ*, then, that people are called in the evangelization of the world. The king in the parable sent his servants to **'tell them to come'** to his son's wedding feast, but they 'refused to come' (22:3). What does this tell us about the gospel of Christ?

First, it emphasizes that it is a *call* to believe. A king's invitation is a summons! The language used today in proclaiming the gospel is more like that of salesmanship than the imperative of command. The gospel is 'presented' and people are invited to 'accept', 'ask' or even 'allow' Jesus 'into their hearts'. This is virtually a reversal of the biblical psychology of conversion, because the movement is all from Jesus to man, and indeed within man himself. Man, with his free will, alone and unaided, is in centre stage, while Jesus waits — as the pathetic pre-Raphaelite icon in William Holman Hunt's painting of Revelation 3:20[2] — a helpless spectator of otherwise autonomous human decision-making. In contrast, the direction of the movement in the biblical call to faith is from man to the Lord. He calls us to himself with a voice of winsome authority. The question that then confronts the challenged sinner is not so much whether he will 'accept' Jesus, but whether Jesus will accept him. Do I desire acceptance with God and salvation from my sins? Then, says Jesus, 'Hear and your soul shall live!' The focus is on God's free grace in Jesus Christ the only Mediator. Yes, all who come to him, he will in no way cast out! The call is not one of plaintive impotence, however, but of majestic authority.

Secondly, the parable shows us that a mere *external* call will not bring people to salvation. The gospel call is a command — a divine summons — but human hearts and minds are by nature at enmity with God. They pretend to autonomy from God and they resist the overtures of God's grace. This is why 'Many are called, but few are chosen.' The number coming to saving faith is not co-extensive with the gospel call to salvation in Christ. Some of the ways in which people respond negatively to the gospel are illustrated by the characters in Jesus' parable. Some simply 'refuse to come' (22:3). They give the gospel no second thought. They are totally unmoved and thoroughly indifferent. They neither need it nor want it. They are not interested, thank you very much! Jesus means nothing to them. There are others who are more interested in **'field'** and **'business'**— that is, for them the decisive concerns in life are 'things' and 'prosperity' (22:5). God is a far-off king and Jesus is perhaps a name, but it all cuts no ice with them. They are otherwise engaged. Then there are those who are militantly opposed to the gospel and who persecute its messengers (22:6). When they hear God's call, they are deeply offended and are strongly disposed to blot out this testimony for Christ.

Surely this explains the experience of the church with people's various *responses* to the preaching of the gospel? 'Many *are* called.' Vast numbers have heard the gospel message one way or another.

They have been called to repentance towards God and faith in the Lord Jesus Christ. They know something of the revealed will of God for the way they are living day by day. They have had some warning of God's wrath against sinners in their sins and have been told of his love in sending his only begotten Son into the world to be the Saviour of sinners such as they are. They have perhaps been entreated very earnestly to believe in Jesus and embrace him as their own Saviour. Nevertheless, how many have walked away from Christ and will have nothing to do with the things of God? Without a doubt, many *are* called but remain in their unbelief, cheerfully unpersuaded of the claims of Christ. Large numbers of people remain unconverted, not because they never heard the gospel, but because, having heard the call, they chose to go their own way.

'Few are chosen' (22:14)

It follows that until and unless the Lord makes the gospel call *inwardly effectual* by an act of his grace, in which the Holy Spirit applies the message of the Word to the heart with irresistible force (effectual calling), simultaneously renewing the heart and giving birth to a new nature (regeneration), no one will come to true repentance and faith but all will continue to reject the gospel. Just as water flows downhill, so the unrenewed human will follows the prevailing tendency of its condition, which is 'enmity with God' (Rom. 8:7, AV). All around them, the disciples saw evidence of their fellow-Jews' rejection of Jesus. And now, they were listening to Jesus talking about his rejection of the Jews. In a few hours they would hear him pronounce his fearful judgement upon the Pharisees (Matt. 23). It was becoming clearer to them that the original guests for the wedding feast were not coming. He had called, but they had not come. What did this mean? Was the Lord's purpose being thwarted? Was he not powerful enough to bring these people to himself? The answer to this was, that, in the last analysis, 'Few are chosen.'

How are 'the chosen' called?

Only in **'the chosen'** is the gospel call made *effectual* by the Holy Spirit. This is not something we can see or hear. God works secretly and sovereignly within human hearts as he makes the outward call effectual and renews old, spiritually dead natures, so as to bring the sinner to repentance and faith.[3] No one comes to Christ unless the Father draws him, and that process of attraction, captivation and spiritual arrest is a work of God's sovereign grace (John 6:44). It is in this internal call that the power of God effects the great change which issues in the self-conscious commitment of true conversion to Christ. The outward call leaves the hearers of the gospel message without any excuse for their disbelief of it. The inward, effectual call seats sinners, saved, at the wedding supper of the Lord Jesus Christ.

Who are 'the chosen'?

The people who rejected the original invitation are described by the king as those who **'did not deserve to come'** (22:8). This does not imply that the people who were invited later *did* deserve to come. The few who are chosen have no inherent worthiness. They could not *merit* their admission to the feast. They were there by free and sovereign *grace*: the servants had been charged to bring in anyone they could find (22:9). The guests were gathered, as we say, from 'all over the place'.

Here is a wonderful picture of the *mystery of God's grace* in the gospel. The 'chosen' are the same as 'anyone' his servants can find — and who, as a result, come to saving faith. In this seeming paradox, God's overarching purpose, settled fast in the heavens since before the foundation of the world, touches and transforms the lives of lost and careless sinners, who then, under the renewing influence of his Spirit, hear the Word with gladness for the first time and trust Jesus as their Saviour, repentantly, confidingly and happily. They are not saved 'against their will', in the conventional sense of that term. No one is dragged screaming into heaven, still convinced of his unbelief. Their will is transformed by the powerful grace of God in such a way as to bring them freely to embrace Christ. The compulsion of grace is a Spirit-driven change involving the radical and supernatural regeneration of human nature itself. This is not to say that sinners do not, as did Saul of Tarsus, 'kick against the goads' of convicting truth and find themselves in a sense both drawn to and repelled by the claims of Jesus Christ. When, however, the resistible grace of the outward call of the gospel gives way to the invincible grace of the effectual call, it is with humbled persuasion that we come to the Lord and with surprising joy throw ourselves willingly upon his mercy.

We have already noted that the 'chosen' are drawn from 'the good and the bad' — that is, *they were called without reference to their actual state* as we might define it. We are always quick to categorize people according to our personal ethical likes and dislikes and render our judgement as to their relative merit. We look out on the world and see people on a scale from goodness to badness. That is not how God sees it. He looks on the children of men and sees no one good. We are all like sheep and have gone astray. 'There is no one righteous,' says the Lord — adding, in case we missed it the first time, 'not even one' (Rom. 3:10). We look on the outward side. God sees our real spiritual condition. And every single one of us was in need of a Saviour.

A final implication is that Jesus was here teaching that no amount of rejecting the gospel could thwart the purpose of God to save a people for himself. *God will accomplish his will perfectly.* Even the wrath of man will be made to praise him. If Christians sometimes feel frustrated that the gospel of Christ does not advance as we hope it would, then reflect on the torment of the devil and his friends, who have to see every new Christian as a spiritual phoenix rising from the ashes of their best efforts to keep lost people lost. The gospel is *never* really in retreat — even if churches decline and professing Christians fall away; the reality is that every passing day sees real and irreversible additions to the true body of Christ. The number of the elect is being filled up and none of them can be plucked out of the Lord's hand. The apparent ebb and flow of church history masks the essential truth that Christ's kingdom only makes gains, because while sinners are saved, the saved are never subsequently lost.

Do you have the 'wedding clothes'?

The final question posed by the parable arises from the ejection of the man who, having been called to the feast and having gained admission, was ejected for not being dressed in the proper 'wedding clothes'. And it is, 'Do you have the wedding clothes?' We have seen already that these represent what Isaiah calls 'a robe of righteousness' and the 'garments of salvation' (Isa. 61:10). 'Salvation is righteousness,' comments Edward J. Young, 'for in the salvation of man, the righteousness of God is revealed; salvation is a state of being right with God. In the cloak of this righteousness God has clothed the exultant believer.'[4] So the question is, 'Are you saved? Are you a believer? Do you know Christ Jesus as your Saviour and Lord?'

In his letters the apostle Paul frequently speaks of us clothing ourselves with the Lord Jesus Christ (Rom.13:14; Gal. 3:27). With similar imagery he links Christ and his righteousness with our personal faith and practical obedience to show what it means to be a Christian. We are to put on 'the new self, created to be like God in true righteousness and holiness', and 'the full armour of God' (Eph. 4:24; 6:11; 1 Thess. 5:8). 'Therefore, as God's chosen people, holy and dearly beloved,' exhorts Paul, 'clothe yourselves with compassion, kindness, humility, gentleness and patience. Bear with each other and forgive whatever grievances you may have against one another. Forgive as the Lord forgave you. And over all these virtues put on love, which binds them all together in perfect unity' (Col. 3:12-14).

Are you living for Jesus Christ? Are the 'garments of salvation' the wardrobe of your heart and soul and mind? Then you can exult from the depth of your being:

> Jesus, thy blood and righteousness
> My beauty are, my glorious dress.

25.
Watching for Christ's return

The parable of the ten virgins
(Matthew 25:1-13)

'Therefore keep watch, because you do not know the day or the hour' (Matt. 25:13).

We live in a culture obsessed with the idea of 'security'. All our wars have allegedly been fought to provide security for our nation. At home, people expect the government to provide cradle-to-the-grave social security. There are to be no more worries about the future, individually or collectively. We want to feel secure and, more than that, we expect this as a *right*. Such at any rate is the promise of the social welfarism of the West — the promise without which no politician can expect to be elected in Europe or North America.

At its most ordinary level, security is simply being prepared for the foreseeable future course of our life. Like good Boy Scouts we are to 'Be prepared' — whether for school, job, marriage, family, illness, calamity, retirement or death. Rightly implemented, this is all a good and necessary part of being a responsible person. We ought to watch out for our future needs and contingencies in a wise and careful way. The tragedy is that more often than not, people make plans for the future without reference to God — his revealed realities and his preceptive will — with the result that an empty and wholly illusory security is built upon the false assumption that both he and his purposes are irrelevant to our well-being, both for time and eternity.

The idea of being prepared to meet God is actually thought of as bizarre, if not even mildly fanatical. The related concepts of watching enthusiastically for the return of Christ at the end of the age and meanwhile committing each phase of our life to the lordship of Christ and the leading of the Holy Spirit are likewise frequently looked upon with some bemusement. That is why the 'prophet of doom' is such a figure of easy ridicule in our society. You will often see him march across cartoons with a sandwich-board bearing the message: 'Prepare to meet your God.' To modern man, he is no sober herald of reality to come, but a religious maniac with an impossible eschatological agenda. Jesus will not, however, be so lightly denied. He was vitally concerned that his hearers be prepared for the eternity they would all soon enter. And to that end, he told the parable of the wise and foolish virgins.

Why watch for Christ's return? (25:1-5)

The aim of the parable of the ten virgins is to call hearers and readers to proper preparation to meet the Lord. It calls us to live each day in the light of eternity. It encourages us to live in the expectant anticipation of the return of Jesus Christ and so be ever ready for our death, should it come first. The parable certainly has the primary focus of the completion of Christ's kingdom at the end of the present world, but equally certainly has its practical application in our living lives of vibrant personal godliness while we wait for that great day. Far from being 'pie in the sky by and by', such a view of life is the most practical and God-honouring lifestyle in the world.

Paul had this in mind when he said, 'For to me, to live is Christ and to die is gain' (Phil. 1:21). In their daily lives, Christians bring eternity into time. They look towards, and live out of, heaven while still in this world. And because they are thus 'heavenly minded' they are uniquely equipped to be of the most 'earthly use'.

The first five verses of the parable paint a picture of the basic circumstances that will exist at the time of the Second Coming of Jesus Christ and offer three reasons for us to be ready to meet with him on that day. Jesus illustrates this from the typical form of a wedding among the Jews of that time. The bride and the wedding party waited for the bridegroom to appear. When they were told of his approach, the attendants would go out to meet him and together would return to the house for the wedding and the feast. In the parable, there are **'ten virgins'** — unmarried girls serving as bridesmaids. These girls represent the visible professing church in the world. 'Ten' carries with it the idea of completeness and indicates that the whole visible church is in view. That they are 'virgins' simply says that they all shared the same relationship to the groom — this representing that Christians share a common profession of faith, at least outwardly. The bridesmaids were all waiting for the bridegroom. Christians are all waiting for the Lord Jesus — or so their profession of faith implies.

Later it will turn out that some of them were not, deep down in their hearts, really waiting for the bridegroom. But at this point there was nothing evident in their lives to contradict their commitment or sustain even a suspicion that they might be insincere. From all outward appearance, they were prepared for the advent of the bridegroom. The point of the parable is at once to demonstrate the necessity of our preparation for Christ's coming and to confront our consciences with any neglect we may have indulged in with relation to that matter and warn us of the eternal consequences of disbelieving the gospel of Jesus Christ.

We must be wise (25:2-4)

Five of the bridemaids were **'foolish'** and five were **'wise'**. They all knew the groom was coming, but some of them acted as if he were not. **'The foolish ones took their lamps but did not take any oil with them.'** They took the picnic basket, but left out the sandwiches! This is a word to those professing Christians who live in practice as if the Lord were never coming. Indeed, many who think of themselves as Christians seem to live as if they will never have to die and give an account of their actions! Jesus calls us to take stock of the realities of God's Word and world.

The 'oil' is the symbol of preparedness, of spiritual vigilance. In Scripture, oil often represents the Holy Spirit (Exod. 30:22-33; Zech. 4:2,12; Acts 10:38; Heb. 1:9; 1 John 2:20,27). It seems clear that the 'lamps' represent the *outward* aspects of a profession of Christian faith, while the oil depicts the *inward* and *spiritual* reality of a living faith. We should notice that even the foolish virgins had some oil. There is a kind of work of the Holy Spirit in some people, which is, sadly, only temporary.

The foolish girls represent those who have 'tasted the heavenly gift [and] shared in the Holy Spirit', but fall back. They never were truly converted to Christ, even if they appeared for a while to be committed Christians. In contrast, **'The wise ... took oil in jars along with their lamps.'** They were prepared. Just as a good scout takes extra batteries for his torch when he goes off to summer camp, so the Christian gives special attention to living his life in the light of eternity.

We must be patient (25:5)

Only the triune God knows exactly when Jesus will return. According to his plan, Jesus will 'come quickly' and right on time. God knew that from the time-bound perspective of short human lives, this would never seem to be quick enough. As with the ten brides-maids, **'The bridegroom was a long time in coming,'** so it is for generations of Christians. They would always be tempted to feel that the Lord was delaying his return. You see this reflected in clichés such as '... if the Lord tarries'. Behind the hope that he will not 'tarry', lies a not unfounded suspicion that he may! This feeling is born of centuries, and now millennia, of waiting for the great event. Small wonder that the edge rubs off our sense of urgency and anticipation.

In part at least, this explains why Christians tend either to think very little about the second advent of Christ and even ignore prophecy altogether, or, at the other extreme, become almost obsessed with prophecy and feed their enthusiasm with speculations about the signs of the times and an exact and always imminent date for the Great Day. The latter always tend to interpret apocalyptic prophecy as applying to their own generation, while the former push it all off into a far distant future.

What Jesus is teaching is a patient urgency — the kind of watchfulness that lives every day with unhurried diligence, but is ready whenever the call should come. The eye of the horse has two focal points on the retina — one to focus on the grass on which it is grazing, and one to focus on the horizon while in the act of feeding. It can simultaneously see clearly both what it is doing and what may be coming. The eyes of our understanding need a dual focus that will keep our present task and our future hope in proper perspective.

We must be alert (25:5)

The longer the bridegroom delayed his appearance, the wearier became the bridesmaids: **'They all became drowsy and fell**

asleep.' Like Eutychus, who quite literally 'dropped off' during an all-night sermon of the apostle Paul's (he was sitting in a third-storey window at the time), the girls — both the wise and the foolish — just couldn't keep their eyes open. This was no sin, as some have suggested, but is simply a function of human finitude and the natural limitations of our frailty. We have other things to do while we are waiting for the end of the world. Our present responsibilities, like the virgins' drowsiness, envelop us so insistently that we find it difficult in the extreme to keep our minds on more distant eventualities. Our human frailties can soon shade almost imperceptibly into sinful negligence. Jesus wants us to pay attention to his promised return, but he understands our weaknesses and gently urges us towards spiritual alertness. The thought is parallel to Paul's later encouragement 'never [to] tire of doing what is right' (2 Thess. 3:13). We must not sleep on the job.

A further reason for alertness arises from the temptation to doubt the promises of God. 'You must understand,' says Peter, 'that in the last days scoffers will come, scoffing and following their own evil desires. They will say, "Where is this 'coming' he promised? Ever since our fathers died, everything goes on as it has since the beginning of creation."' The apostle's answer is still relevant. These people forget that the world was once destroyed by water, and is reserved for future destruction by fire. We should also bear in mind that 'With the Lord a day is like a thousand years, and a thousand years are like a day. The Lord is not slow in keeping his promise, as some understand slowness. He is patient with you, not wanting anyone to perish, but everyone to come to repentance' (2 Peter 3:3-9). God is longsuffering. If he wanted hell filled up, the world would have long since gone up in smoke. But he plans to bring people to repentance and populate heaven with a multitude too large to count. So don't complain if he takes his time! Keep your faith with a good conscience and be ready when he comes.

The dangers of not keeping watch (25:6-12)

'At midnight the cry rang out: "Here's the bridegroom! Come out to meet him!"' That is to say, when people were nodding off and all expectancy of the bridegroom's arrival was sinking without trace in velvet sleepiness, he finally appeared! This 'midnight' is the same time as the 'night' in which the 'thief' will come to surprise the

wicked — a time 'you will not know', the Lord tells the church
(1 Thess. 5:2; 2 Peter 3:10; Rev. 3:3). Hence the vital necessity for
being so prepared that this day will not come as a judgement, but as
our final deliverance: 'Behold, I come like a thief!' declares the
Lord. 'Blessed is he who stays awake and keeps his clothes with
him, so that he may not go naked and be shamefully exposed' (Rev.
16:15).

'Our lamps are going out!' (25:7-9)

Awakened by the news of the bridegoom's approach, the bridesmaids **'trimmed their lamps'** and went out to meet him. It was not
long before **'The foolish ones said to the wise, "Give us some of
your oil; our lamps are going out."'** The wise ones, however,
quietly declined the requests and directed them to **'go to those who
sell oil and buy some for [them]selves'**. It is possible to read this
reply in a tone of voice that makes it seem an unkind and even harsh
rebuff. That would be prejudicial both to the wisdom and the attitude
of the girls who had taken care to be ready for that moment. Had they
acceded to this request, then it would be most likely that none of
them would have had any light in the lamps before too long. There
simply was not enough oil to be divided among the ten of them and
still have any procession at all. There was no alternative for the
foolish virgins but to try and find a supply elsewhere.

    In relating this tale, Jesus had some important lessons in mind.
Most obvious is the fact that there is only *one source* of the oil of
preparedness for coming face to face with Christ. God is that
exclusive supplier and each one of us must go to him. 'Preparedness
is not transferable from one person to another,' notes William
Hendriksen. No one can believe the gospel for you. No one can grow
in grace for you. Your mother's holiness will not save you. The
pronouncements of a priest or the church will not give you a new
heart. You must, as the apostle to the nations implores of us, "Be
reconciled to God"' (2 Cor. 5:20). If you are not prepared to meet
the church's Bridegroom, whether on your death or the Great Day
of his coming — whichever comes first — you will have absolutely
no excuse and no one to blame but yourself.

    The parable also teaches clearly that there is no 'second chance'
to be saved after this life is done. There is no Roman Catholic

purgatory, where people spend millions of years being made holy enough for heaven. There is no preaching of the gospel in hell — an error based on a combination of the misinterpretation of 1 Peter 3:18-20 and the 'descent into hell' clause in the so-called 'Apostles' Creed'.[1] 'Now'— as you read these words and whenever you hear the gospel — 'is the day of salvation' (2 Cor. 6:2; cf. Heb. 3:7,13,15). Repentance and faith must come now. Nothing will bring you to heaven if you go into the presence of the Judge with an unrenewed heart that has steadfastly shut Jesus out of your life. Life is a bit like a one-innings cricket match. You can spend a long time at the crease and be bowled many gospel overs, but when the stumps fall and the bails fly, you are out, for ever!

The door was shut (25:10-12)

The foolish bridesmaids went off to find more oil. There is no indication that they succeeded in finding any. Eventually, they returned to the wedding banquet, only to find that **'The bridegroom [had] arrived... And the door was shut.'** When they asked to be admitted, the master of the house replied, **'I tell you the truth, I don't know you.'** Kistemaker notes that this was the rabbinic language for expulsion — a misbehaving pupil would be excluded from classes with the words: 'I don't know you.'[2] (In my old school, the equivalent expression was, 'Take your books and go.' All cultures have their own conventions.)

Most people want to escape the consequences of their sins. But they go on sinning anyway. When they have been caught and convicted, they may make a show of wanting to change, but it is often no more than a last effort to avoid the axe. Many who never gave a tuppeny toss for Jesus in this life, will, as it were, turn up late with protestations of their innocence. Jesus will not be fooled. He can spot new lies as well as old. Just as he will send packing the false prophets and miracle-mongers — who are legion in our day, as in his — so he will unmask the twenty-fifth hour hypocrites who want heaven and their old ways: 'Then I will tell them plainly, "I never knew you. Away from me, you evildoers!"' (Matt. 7:23). There is no oil — no regenerating work of the Holy Spirit — beyond the grave or in a lost eternity.

'Therefore keep watch' (25:13)

The Lord closes the story with a simple word of application: **'Therefore keep watch, because you do not know the day or the hour.'** Our Lord's logic is as plain as day. We all know that when we expect a visitor to arrive at our home for dinner at a fixed time — say 5 p.m. — then we phase our preparations so as to be ready just a little ahead of time. Indeed, if anything, we tend to leave our preparations to the latest feasible moment. On the other hand, if our visitor is arriving 'some time' tomorrow, we will make our arrangements earlier and maybe even post a lookout to give advance warning. The paradox is that the more indefinite the event, the more necessary is the proper state of readiness. That is why, to employ a darker figure, the Fylingdales Early Warning Station was on constant alert throughout the Cold War and why the Royal Navy's nuclear submarines had their missiles ready to rain devastation on any attacker's hearth and home.

The appointed times of both the Lord's return and of our death are set in the immutable timetable of God's purpose. These dates are, however, hidden from us. *We* do not know what a day may bring forth. It is all the more imperative that we live in a continuous state of trust in our Saviour. Our confidence must be in him. The 'when' of these events is irrelevant, except as a stimulus to personal holiness and a wholehearted commitment to keeping in step with the Holy Spirit (Gal. 5:25).

We are called to look *to* Jesus as we live every day in practical discipleship to him. We are not to look *for* Jesus, in the sense of scouring the Scriptures for clues to the date of his coming or, having believed someone else's prediction of his coming, taking ourselves off to the mountains or the woods to hunker down until the Great Day comes. Date-setters are false prophets, however sincere and otherwise respectable. Our calling is to live each day in the joy of our heavenward calling — and for as long as we live or the world lasts. With the oil of Spirit-filled preparation in our hearts, we will watch with urgent expectancy and quiet obedience for the coming of the Lord from heaven.

'Amen. Come, Lord Jesus' (Rev. 22:20).

26.
Working for Christ's return

The parable of the talents (Matt. 25:14-30)

'For everyone who has will be given more, and he will have an abundance. Whoever does not have, even what he has will be taken from him' (Matt. 25:29).

At first glance, the parable of the talents in Matthew's Gospel looks very like the parable of the ten minas in Luke.[1] Both have the same basic outline, the same cast of characters and employ very similar language and points of application. It looks as if Jesus, like many a preacher since, was reaching into his 'barrel' and giving an old sermon another airing. A closer look will reveal that for all the similarities, this was no mere repetition. There is a subtle and significant difference in the way Jesus applies the same basic story.

The parable in Luke was addressed to both his disciples and the crowds. The Lord emphasized, on the one hand, the opposition of the generality of the Jews to their prophesied Messianic King and, on the other hand, the responsibility of his committed followers to be steadfastly faithful to the gospel of God's kingdom while they waited for their King to return.

The parable here in Matthew finds Jesus addressing his disciples privately (24:3). This time the focus is narrower. According to their various God-given abilities, they would be given tasks and responsibilities that they must faithfully implement as the day of the Lord's return approaches. The immediate context — the parable of the ten virgins — teaches that we must *watch* for Christ's return. The parable of the talents says that we must *work* with a view to his return. This parable poses certain basic questions for us. What are the 'talents' that we are to be exercising? How are these talents to be used? And what does this mean for us today?

What are the 'talents'? (25:14-15)

Whenever we hear the word 'talent', we immediately think of
someone's natural abilities. For us, a person's 'talents' are his
special gifts and capacities — those things in which he does well and
which mark him out from other people. In ancient times, however,
a 'talent' was a standard unit of measurement, applied to both weight
and money. The modern connection with personal characteristics or
gifts would never have entered the mind of a Jew or a Greek of the
first century A.D. The talents in the parable appear to have been
made of silver and, although no one really knows what they were
worth, they would probably have represented more than a year's
wages for a labourer, perhaps a considerably larger sum.[2] This was
not chicken-feed! So when the **'man going on a journey'** distributed eight talents' worth of money among his servants, he left them
with considerable responsibilities. His action represented a good
deal of trust in both their competence and their diligence.

'Talents' do not represent 'gifts'

Even though the word 'talent' in modern English comes from the
Greek *talanton* as used in this parable, we should not forget that
Jesus was not talking about talents as we think of them in our
everyday lives. It is often merely assumed that Jesus *must* be using
the money talents as illustrative of natural and spiritual gift-talents
and how they ought to be used in the service of the Lord. This is very
neat and seems to fit. Indeed, it has become so embedded in our
language that we almost take it for granted that this was Jesus'
meaning. Closer attention to the parable shows that this is not the
case — and for three reasons that emerge from the text itself.

First of all, in the parable, all the men receive some 'talents': **'To
one he gave five talents of money, to another two talents, and to
another one talent'** (25:15). Do these represent the 'gifts' that God
has given to men and women, or do they represent something else?
There is certainly a sense in which every human being has been
endowed with his or her own particular capabilities and interests
and, certainly, some folk are more 'gifted' than others. This is true
of so-called *natural* abilities, but what of *spiritual* gifts? Jesus'
parable clearly has spiritual things in view, yet both the faithful and
the unfaithful servants received talents. Jesus was talking about how

people live for God — and with respect to the things of God. But how can unconverted people, who have so far not trusted in Christ as their Saviour, be said to have received the gifts of the Holy Spirit? They cannot! The 'gifts' interpretation does not fit. The 'talents' must represent something else entirely.

Secondly, you will notice that the one talent given to the **'wicked, lazy servant'** was taken from him and given to the man who by that time had ten talents (25:28). Here too, the 'gifts' interpretation falls down. How can one man's 'gifts' be transferred to another? This is just inconceivable.

Thirdly, it is explicitly stated that the talents were distributed to the servants **'each according to his ability'** (25:15). What is each man's 'ability', if it is not his 'gifts' in the broad sense? The parable, then, distinguishes between the 'talents' given to each man and the perceived gifts with which each man was already endowed! The 'talents' simply cannot be 'gifts'. They must represent what we do with our abilities, rather than these abilities themselves.

'Talents' represent the responsibility to serve the Lord

What, then, do the 'talents' signify? The best explanation is that they represent the various responsibilities and opportunities that God gives his people for their labour in the kingdom of heaven upon earth. The men in the story were all servants of the master. They knew this very well. They were respectively given five-, two- and one-talent jobs to do, according to the master's assessment of their various abilities.

These differing responsibilities presupposed certain observable and God-given gifts in each person. In other words, God deals with those who profess to be his followers as those who have a definite place in his kingdom. He gives them responsibilities and expects them to discharge them faithfully. This is even true of those who *later* prove to have been hypocrites who never inwardly were truly committed to the Lord. The several sums of money in the parable are simply particular places of responsibility in the work of God's kingdom in the world.

This is very simple to apply to ourselves. Jesus is saying that every professing Christian has God-given responsibilities and opportunities, within the fellowship of his people and according to his or her abilities, to serve his cause and kingdom. William Perkins, a sixteenth-century English theologian, summed this up in one glorious sweep of his pen: 'Now if we compare work to work, there is a difference betwixt washing of dishes and preaching the Word of God; but as touching to please God, none at all.'[3]

The highest calling in the world is to do for the Lord Jesus Christ what you *can* do and what you have been *given* to do, and to do it with your whole heart. This is how to please God. If you wash dishes, you are not 'only' a dishwasher in God's eyes. You are in kingdom work and your dish-washing is for Christ! When one day a woman anointed Jesus with expensive perfume, she was rebuked for this by some of those who were there. They implied that if she had really wanted to do something useful in God's kingdom, she would have sold it and given the money to the poor. Jesus rebuked them and pointed out that 'She did what she could' (Mark 14:3-9). Serving the Lord was never locked up in preaching and helping the poor. Christ is served when Christians do what they can — what he has given them to do in the circumstances of their daily lives. That is the challenge of the parable. Are you doing what you *can* for the Lord?

How are these 'talents' to be used? (25:16-27)

The underlying assumption of the parable is that there is no shortage of work for Christians to be doing in God's kingdom. There are responsibilities and opportunities to serve God in the fellowship of his church and as believers acting as salt and light in the wider community. There are love to be shared, prayer to be made, muscles to be flexed, children to be taught, sick to be visited, old folk to be comforted and, not least, a world to be witnessed to with the message of Christ. No one believer can do all these — or is even supposed to do many of them — but God has a place for every Christian to be faithfully committed to the work of his kingdom. The parable of the talents demolishes the idea of the 'inactive' Christian. If you are a fringe church member, who does no more than attend church services and lets other people do the work, you are sinning grievously against the Lord and his people. You are, as we shall see, burying your responsibity to God ('talent') in the ground. You have not begun to grasp the privilege and joy it is to serve and love the Lord 'with *all* your heart and with *all* your soul and with *all* your strength' (Deut. 6:5, emphasis mine.) You need to recognize God's sovereignty in your life in a new way!

Good and faithful servants (25:16-23)

Two of the men went to work. They knew that they were supposed to be productive. The different levels of resources represent different tasks. It is not necessary to think that one job was more important or more prestigious than the other. Responsibilities simply matched capacities. Accordingly, faithfulness is the currency by which the value of Christian service is to be measured, as opposed to some scale of importance. 'From everyone who has been given much, much will be demanded' (Luke 12:48). It was a case of 'the right task for the right man at the right time'. The man with 'five-talent' responsibilities exercised 'five-talent' faithfulness and reaped a 'five-talent' return. Similarly, the man with 'two-talent' responsibilities effectively executed his charge. Having given account to their master, both received their reward: **'Well done, good and faithful servant! You have been faithful with a few things; I will put you in charge of many things. Come and share your master's happiness!'** (25:21,23).

The central principle is that we are to be steadfastly faithful in what God has given us to do — whatever that may be. There is far too much spectator Christianity in the modern church. In part, this is the fruit of what may be termed the cult of 'full-time Christian service'. The minister or the missionary is paid to do the job, and meanwhile the rest of us put our money in the collection plate and sit back to see how well he does the job. It almost seems as if some people think that discipleship to Christ is only for people who are paid to be disciples! The scriptural pattern, however, is that being a Christian *is* a 'full-time' responsibility. More than that, it is a joy and a pleasure. Discipleship means living for Christ with every fibre of your being and, in relation to the work of his kingdom, bending yourself to do what you can as part of God's team.

One of the stories I learned as a lad growing up in Scotland was that of the fourteenth-century Countess of Dunbar — called 'Black Agnes' on account of her dark complexion — who successfully held Dunbar castle against an invading English army under the Earl of Salisbury and bequeathed to Scottish lore the heroic couplet:

Came they early, came they late,
They found Black Agnes at the gate.

Years later, this came to mind when a man in my congregation was
taken from us in middle life by the sudden onset of an incurable
disease. Laverne Bish was a quiet man when he was alive, but when
he died his absence left a hole that everybody noticed. One of the
tasks he had taken on each week, without being asked — he was also
a ruling elder and so had other things to do in the fellowship — was
to open the doors and make sure everyone who came to church was
greeted and handed the order of service for the day. 'Came they
early, came they late,' I thought to myself, 'they found Laverne at
the gate.' I have been in many an evangelical church since and found
nobody 'at the gate' to meet my eye and welcome me in.

G. N. M. Collins, the late Professor of Church History in the Free
Church College, Edinburgh, used to tell of preaching in Corrie, on
the Island of Arran, when he was a student for the ministry in the
1920s. He always felt a particular 'liberty' in the pulpit ministry in
that place, but never quite figured out why. One Sabbath before the
service, he discovered the reason. He had to go back to the house
where he was staying to pick up something he had left there and
needed for the service. As he went into the house, he heard a voice
praying aloud, asking the Lord to bless the service and the young
man who had come to preach the gospel to them. This was the blind,
bed-ridden matriarch of the family! She could not be 'at the gate' of
Corrie Free Church, but she could ascend to the gate of heaven and
serve the Lord's kingdom in a ministry of intercessory prayer!

When people have the heart to work for God, they will find that
task and do it.

Wicked, lazy servants (25:24-28)

The **'man who had received the one talent'** proved that his heart
was somewhere else. He did nothing. He sat on his responsibility.
He ventured nothing and inevitably gained nothing. He had an
opportunity to be productive, but could not bring himself to take the
risk.

Like everyone who has ever tried to 'dodge the column', he had
a ready excuse to offer: **'Master … I knew that you are a hard
man, harvesting where you have not sown and gathering where**

you have not scattered seed. So I was afraid and went out and hid your talent in the ground. See, here is what belongs to you' (25:24-25). There is no use trying to sort out any logic in this excuse. He was afraid of failure, so he did nothing. You might say that he failed as best he could. The excuse is just a lame attempt at damage-control, since all it really says is that at least he did not lose the original investment.

Nothing is static in this life. Money under the mattress doesn't earn interest or finance productive enterprise. It just slowly loses its value. Like muscles that get no exercise, it atrophies and becomes progressively useless. The one-talent man was not even conserving his master's money. He was wasting it. And because he was responsible for being productive, he was in fact robbing his master of his wealth. He was a thief. In terms of spiritual things and the service of the Lord, the meaning is surely plain enough. You profess Christ as your Saviour. You have his Word to instruct you, and the promise of the Holy Spirit to lead you. Yet your life is one of lukewarm commitment to the Lord, the gospel and the work of his kingdom. Does the Lord want you to have Sunday-only (or an Easter-and-Christmas-only) involvement with the church? Does the Lord want you to neglect bringing up your children in the nurture of the things of God? Is the Lord happy that you never thank him at the table for your daily bread, or worship him as a family day by day at home? Will he thank you on the Great Day that you never remotely approached giving a tithe of your income to support his work in the world, never cultivated your own walk in the Spirit by prayer and personal devotion, let the 'old faithfuls' do all the work at church, *et cetera … ad nauseam*? You know the answer, don't you?

But there is worse. The man who chose to be a wasting asset also implicitly blamed his master for his inaction. The master was a 'hard man'; that is to say, he was to blame. If he had been nicer, maybe it would have been possible to take the risk of investing the talent in some project, but as it was, his reputation just engendered too much fear to take any risks. How many will excuse themselves to the Lord in a similar manner? 'Lord, it was too hard. I didn't want to let you down. Anyway, you are pretty hard on failures. I was more likely to make a mistake (imperfect as I am, though no worse than the next man) and there are better, more qualified people than I who could do a better job. I am not that talented.' Perhaps you have heard these kinds of excuses. You may have used them yourself! Face it! They are a smokescreen to cover the fact that your heart was never in it. You had other priorities for your life. Is that not true? It sure is!

The master wasn't buying it, however. **'You wicked, lazy servant! So you knew that I harvest where I have not sown and gather where I have not scattered seed? Well then, you should have put my money on deposit with the bankers, so that when I returned I would have received it back with interest. Take the talent from him and give it to the one who has ten talents'** (25:26-28). Jesus is, of course, arguing from the lesser to the greater. The logic of the business world is clear and well understood. Money follows productivity and a good return. In spiritual matters the same principle applies with infinitely more profound results. God is patient with us, but he will never reward contempt for himself, his Son, his people or his kingdom. God sent his Son to die for sinners and those who have trusted in him for salvation can be expected to show some evidence that they actually love him for what he has done for them.

It is not even that the task of faithfulness is so hard, or that the Lord is a slave-driver. Jesus said, 'My yoke is easy and my burden is light' (Matt. 11:30) and generations of committed Christians have found this to be true. The work of simply serving the Lord in terms of the opportunities he opens up (putting God's 'money' in the bank) is less arduous than covering up your laziness (digging a hole and burying it)! The real task-master is your unbelief. The real bondage is your sinfulness. 'The open falseness' of the one-talent man, observes Lenski, 'here displays the slave's whole inner character and attitude. It completely blighted his soul.'⁴ Loving God, in Christ our Saviour, is freedom from all that.

Which way will you choose? (25:29-30)

Why did Jesus choose to use the one-talent man as his example of failure? Do men with five or two talents never fail? Yes, they do! People can neglect any kind of responsibility, great or small. What, then, is Jesus' point? Surely it is this: he uses the man with what seems to be the 'least' responsibility, precisely to show that it is faithfulness and not relative importance that is vital. No one can say,

'My task is so insignificant that it doesn't matter if I don't bother too much about getting it done.'

There are some people who have to be in the limelight or they will do nothing. They tell themselves (and never miss an opportunity to complain to others) that their 'gifts' are not being recognized. It is not unusual to hear of people who, when denied a teaching role in one church, go to another church and even tell the pastor they are looking for a fellowship that will give them scope to exercise their talents. This sounds so pious, but it is really just pride dressed up as willingness to serve Christ. The church and her pastors and people are treated as a vehicle for 'my gifts' to be exercised. My assessment of myself is the starting-point. Everyone should see that God has given me to the church for a ministry of great usefulness! And what is so sad is that people who think that way believe their attitude is right, spiritual and even humble! How easily we deceive ourselves! God, however, will not let any wool be pulled over his eyes!

The parable challenges us at the deepest level of our personal commitment. Jesus' application could hardly be more practical or more pointed.

The faithful will grow in grace (25:29)

Jesus' principle of spiritual growth is that **'Everyone who has will be given more, and he will have an abundance'** (25:29). Character deepens and blessings multiply in the arena of committed discipleship. The Lord promises to bless us when we 'walk according to the law of the Lord' (Ps. 119:1) 'Those whom [God] has once begun to form,' writes John Calvin, 'are continually polished more and more, till they are at length brought to the highest perfection. The multiplied favours which are continually flowing from him to us, and the joyful progress which we make, spring from God's contemplation of his own liberality, which prompts him to an uninterrupted course of bounty. And as his riches are inexhaustible, so he is never wearied with enriching his children.'[5]

The faithless will decline (25:29)

Doing nothing about the gospel and the claims of God has terrible consequences. A static neutrality is as impossible in spiritual things as it is in business and finance. **'Whoever does not have, even what he has will be taken from him.'** Jesus uses similar language in emphasizing how important it is to listen to God's Word and take it to heart: 'Therefore consider carefully how you listen. Whoever has will be given more; whoever does not have, even what he thinks he has will be taken from him' (Luke 8:18). The man with the one talent is parallel to the 'seed that fell among thorns' hearer of the gospel in Jesus' parable of the sower. He was given something but he didn't really have it. He had the illusion of having his one talent. He *thought* he had it, even though he had forfeited it by not using it faithfully. He had made it an illusion, by not mixing it with faith and so not responding to his God-given responsibilities with a living trust in the Lord. He only lost what he had already, in effect, rejected.

Further insight is afforded by the writer to the Hebrews, when he says that 'We also have had the gospel preached to us, just as they did [i.e., the Israelites who came out of Egypt and rebelled at Kadesh]; but the message they heard was of no value to them, because those who heard did not combine it with faith' (Heb. 4:2). When we do not act upon God's gifts — whether Christ and the gospel, the Word and holy living, or spiritual and temporal gifts — then they are of 'no value' *in our own eyes*. We may go on thinking that God is with us, Jesus has saved us and our lives are acceptable to the Lord, but the evidence of what we actually do proves our emptiness and self-deception. The life we think we have is gone! This is an awful judgement, for it means that the Lord has left us to ourselves, at least for the moment.

The incorrigibles perish (25:30)

Unless the sinner repents — in this case, the lazy, one-talent servant — he further regresses until he becomes incorrigible and perishes under the just condemnation of the God he has so steadfastly resisted. Jesus, speaking as the final Judge of all the earth, declares, **'Throw the worthless servant outside, into the darkness, where there will be weeping and gnashing of teeth.'** The 'darkness' is that which is 'outside' the final consummated kingdom of God. It is hell considered as a place devoid of the light of truth. 'It means', writes Calvin, 'that out of the kingdom of God, which is the kingdom of light, nothing but darkness reigns. By *darkness* Scripture points out that dreadful anguish, which can neither be expressed nor conceived in this life.'[6]

The parable of the talents calls us to believe in Christ as Saviour and to work for him as we await his return on the Great Day. He has given us great and precious promises. They will all be fulfilled in due course. In the meantime we have the boundless privilege of living for him in happy expectation of his 'Well done, good and faithful servant!'

27.
Final judgement

The parable of the sheep and the goats
(Matt. 25:31-46)

'Then they will go away to eternal punishment, but the righteous to eternal life' (Matt. 25:46).

The simplest truths in life are often the most difficult to talk about. It is very easy to know when you have no money, but so hard to tell the children that it means they cannot have new shoes. When a loved one dies, the fact is painfully obvious, but accepting its temporal and eternal implications can be tremendously difficult. The Bible's teaching about 'the Day of Judgement' has something of the same tension about it. It is a simple doctrine, set forth in Scripture with unmistakable clarity, yet it is one of the most difficult subjects to preach and teach and even to think about. Why is this so?

One reason, perhaps, is that there is a 'fairy tale' quality about how we think of the Day of Judgement. When we talk about biblical teachings on family life, ethical questions like adultery or drunkenness, or even death, we grasp their immediate relevance to the human experience. They are all part of daily life in the real world. By comparison, the Day of Judgement seems remote and unreal — a future event entirely comprehended by an act of faith, or else rejected in disbelief as a dark and unwelcome fantasy. Even believers often feel it to be of doubtful relevance to their own lives. We generally expect to die before the end of the world, so that the day of our death is for all practical purposes the day of our judgement — as it is for all who die before the Lord returns. So we feel specially vulnerable to the world's mockery when the subject of the Day of Judgement comes up, because we would prefer not to be labelled as 'fire-and-brimstone' fanatics. This is a wrong feeling, but it is, one suspects, widespread among Christian people.

Related to this is the frequently negative cast that seems to cling to the way Christians talk about the return of Jesus Christ. The leading motif is usually the wrath of God. So the salvation of God's people ends up looking more like a by-product of the condemnation of the wicked, instead of what it is — the glory and centrepiece of God's plan for humanity. A massive misreading of biblical prophecy has left millions — both Christians and non-Christians — with the notion that biblical eschatology is all gloom and doom. In reality, the redemption of believers, whether still alive or long since dead, is the reason for, and the focal point of, the last day of this present era.

The most important reason for being hesitant to deal with the Day of Judgement is probably the fact that this doctrine brings us face to face with eternity in a way that no other teaching in Scripture does. Today, death itself has been redefined as a 'normal part of life'. This is, for example, one of the tenets of the modern hospice movement. This cannot be done with the Day of Judgement. So the world has to laugh it off as the delusion of crazy religious fanatics and festoon it with jokes about 'prophets of doom'. The reason for this is clear enough. If you begin to take seriously what the Bible says about the last day of human history, you are forced to ask yourself the question: 'Where will I spend eternity?' The fact of death can do this, to be sure, but we are used to seeing death and inure ourselves to it in all sorts of ways. But a day of *judgement*? This calls us to ask, 'Who is my God?' and 'Am I saved or am I lost — for all eternity?' It is the most serious issues in life — not the trivial and frivolous — that people feel compelled to laugh off. They do so to cover their inner emptiness and drive away their deepest fears. 'Pack up your troubles in your old kitbag...' and pretend it won't happen to you.

Jesus will not let us off the hook. He *is* coming again. He *will* judge the living and the dead. Under the judgement of his lips, we shall all, one by one, go to our eternal destiny. He is coming to gather his believing people and in so doing he will also identify those who would never believe. There is no place to hide from this future assize. Yet, while there is life there is hope and the opportunity to flee the wrath to come, by answering his call to repentance and faith (Eccl. 9:4; 1 Thess. 1:10). We must face his parable of the sheep and the goats with biblical honesty, for ultimately it is a matter of life or death.

The parable presents four facts: the fact of a final judgement (25:31-33); the fact of eternal punishment for the wicked (25:34-40); the fact of eternal life for the righteous (25:41-45); and the fact that the parting of the ways is for all eternity (25:46).

Final judgement (25:31-33)

It is the straightforward and inescapable teaching of the Bible that there is a final act of divine judgement at the end of the history of this earth. Jesus Christ will return to judge 'the living and the dead' (2 Tim. 4:1). To claim to believe the Bible to be God's Word and deny this doctrine defies all rationality, but it happens anyway. The parable of the sheep and the goats actually consists of only two verses (25:32-33). These are embedded in, and illustrative of, a predictive prophecy of the judgement which will take place when Jesus comes again. This is not poetry or allegory, but sober history in advance. It shows us that there is a day appointed when Jesus Christ will return, bodily, to this world. He will judge the living and the dead, separating the righteous from the reprobate and exalting the Lord's people. You can deny this teaching, all you like. You will be there on the day, anyway, and Jesus will be your Judge!

There is a day when Christ will return (25:31)

A day is coming when **'the Son of Man comes in his glory'**. Christ, as risen Saviour and mediator King, will return to the world on a set day in the future, as the once and final Judge (Matt. 28:18; John 5:27; Acts 10:42; 17:31; Phil. 2:9-10).[1] The title **'Son of Man'** takes us to Daniel's vision of the latter-day glory of Christ: 'In my vision at night I looked, and there before me was one like a son of man, coming with the clouds of heaven. He approached the Ancient of Days and was led into his presence. He was given authority, glory and sovereign power; all peoples, nations and men of every language worshipped him. His dominion is an everlasting dominion that will not pass away, and his kingdom is one that will never be destroyed' (Dan. 7:13-14).

This glory remains to be revealed and will only become apparent to the whole human race on the last day of the history of the world as we now know it. Jesus will be exalted in triumph as King of kings and Lord of lords, **'and all the angels** [will be] **with him,** [and] **he**

will sit on his throne in heavenly glory'. The redeemed of the Lord
will all be gathered in; the reprobate lost will be subdued under his
feet and the kingdoms of this world will have become the kingdom
of the Lord Jesus Christ for ever (Rev. 11:15).

There will be a general judgement (25:32)

'All the nations', said Jesus, **'will be gathered before him.'** That
is to say, all people without exception will be there, both the dead
and the living, the believers and the unbelievers. All come together
for the public vindication of the kingly authority of Jesus Christ. The
picture in the story is of the flocks mixed up together in the fields —
the sheep with the goats — and their subsequent separation when
brought in to the fold. The sheep, which are more valuable than the
goats, are penned together in one place, the goats in another. **'And
he will separate the people one from another as a shepherd
separates the sheep from the goats.'** Jesus is seen as Judge. 'Every
eye will see him' (Rev. 1:7). The separation of the righteous and the
wicked will be seen by all. The absolute sovereignty and the
covenant faithfulness of God will be fully and finally demonstrated
to a watching world. Truth rejected will be vindicated. Truth
believed will be confirmed.

The Lord's people will be exalted (25:33)

'He will put the sheep on his right hand and the goats on his left.'
There will be no mystery as to who are saved and who are not. The
Lord knows his sheep and his sheep know him and recognize his
voice (John 10:14-18). Meanwhile, those who never knew Christ
will nevertheless recognize who he is, for they will be calling for the
mountains to hide them from the 'wrath of the Lamb' (Rev. 6:16).
There is a tendency to clothe the Great Day in an aura of dreadful
suspense, as if we will all arrive before Christ's throne in ignorance
of our eternal destiny — as if even Christians will have no assurance
that they are saved and will wait in nail-biting nervousness for the
word from the Lord. In fact, God's people will wait in wonderfully
heightened anticipation of the joy of their salvation. Their hearts
will be thrilled to see the Lord 'face to face' (1 Cor. 13:12). This is
their day — a day of deliverance, happiness and glorious
transformation!

Eternal life (25:34-40)

Jesus will first declare his judgement to **'those on his right'** — the 'sheep'. Here, he teaches us to anticipate the wonder and the joy of his second advent, for the Lord's people will not come to 'judgement' in the same sense as do the unbelieving. Believers are, rather, vindicated before the whole creation and raised to be kings and priests in the kingdom of heaven (1 Peter 2:9; Rev. 1:6). This is going to be the greatest of many great days in the lives of God's people. They have been saved by grace through faith. They have seen the goodness of their God in the land of the living. And now, the day dawns when they will see Jesus face to face and will enjoy for ever the perfect fellowship of heaven!

Believers experience the Lord's coming as *God's* 'sheep'. They are no longer *lost* sheep. They are 'his people, the sheep of his pasture' (Ps. 100:3). If this is reason for joy every day while the world lasts, how much more on the first great day of consummated heavenly glory? Furthermore, the 'sheep' are already assembled 'on his right' — theirs is the place of honour, because there are 'eternal pleasures at [his] right hand' (Ps. 16:11).

Invitation (25:34)

'Then the King will say to those on his right, "Come, you who are blessed by my Father..."' The first word the Lord utters captures the central theme of the Great Day. The summons to approach the throne of judgement is set in the context of grace already received from the Father. For the Christian, the Day of Judgement has no negative cast. Blessed by the Father, led by the Holy Spirit, called forward by the Son who died for them, believers enjoy their hoped for final transformation. The dead who died in the Lord are raised up in resurrection bodies. The living are transformed — this corruptible putting on incorruption (1 Cor. 15:53, AV). The day of the general assembly of the firstborn of Jesus Christ becomes accomplished reality (Heb.12:23, AV). All who love the Lord are together, united with their Saviour. Sorrows and pain are things of the past. There are not more tears, but only joy and praise in the consummated kingdom of God.

That they are in the position of coming to God at all is a testimony, not to any innate ability or merited award of their own, but to God's gift of grace. The ultimate reason for their being welcomed to glory is that they are, says Jesus, blessed 'by my Father'. 'There can be no doubt,' comments John Calvin, 'that Christ, in describing the salvation of the godly, begins with the undeserved love of God, by which those who, under the guidance of the Spirit in this life, aim at righteousness, were predestined to life.'[2]

Inheritance (25:34)

The first instruction for the newly installed inhabitants of the new heavens and the new earth is, **'Take your inheritance.'** The Greek is an (aorist) imperative. The sense is this: 'What you have hitherto known in part, now take in its fulness. I gave you the *right* to become children of God (John 1:12). You became, by grace through faith, the heirs of your Father God and co-heirs with Christ (Rom. 8:17). Take it. Lay hold on it. It is yours! The great work of redemption is now complete. The second Adam has overthrown the sin of the first Adam and more. The glory that was once still in the future is now *here* and it is *yours!*'

And what of the inheritance itself? It is **'the kingdom prepared for you since the creation of the world'** (cf. Eph. 1:4). Heaven, says R. C. H. Lenski, 'is a kingdom that is composed entirely of kings, a kingdom raised to the nth degree. And thus Christ shall be the King of kings (us) and the Lord of lords (us).'[3] Furthermore, this assurance of a kingdom *already* prepared is an encouragement to Christians as they grapple with the hard work of living. John Calvin is characteristically practical when he observes, 'It is no slight persuasive to patience, when men are fully convinced that they do not run in vain; and therefore, lest our minds should be cast down by the pride of the ungodly, in which they give themselves unrestrained indulgence — lest our hope should even be weakened by our own afflictions, let us always remember the inheritance which awaits us in heaven; for it depends on no uncertain event, but was *prepared for us* by God before we were born — *prepared*, I say, for each of the elect .'[4]

Interpretation (25:35-40)

On what basis is this favourable judgement applied to the righteous? Jesus gives neither a learned discussion on the doctrine of justification by faith alone nor a recitation of sound theology as talked about by the faithful. He fastens on what people *did* — pinpointing specific deeds that are indelible markers of living faith — the 'wedding clothes' of real personal godliness. Indeed, in all the passages in Scripture dealing with the basis of divine judgement the focus is kept relentlessly on actions rather than words.

The first point to grasp is that *actions* are the basis of the judgement. With God, it is *not* 'the thought that counts!' (See Matt. 16:27; Rom. 2:6-16; 2 Cor. 5:10). This concentration on deeds rather than declarations does not imply that people are saved on the basis of their own good works. In Scripture, salvation is always by God's grace, through faith in Christ — never by self-generated works-righteousness (Eph. 2:8-9 *alone* is decisive on that point!). It is simply that actions speak louder than words in assessing where a man really stands. What we *do* is the fruit and evidence of what we *are*! R. C. H. Lenski sets this out so clearly when he writes, 'These works are decisive in the final judgement, not because of an inherent meritorious quality, but because of their evidential quality. As in any proper court of law the evidence and the evidence alone decides in harmony with the law, so in this most supreme court at the end of the world this same procedure is followed.'[5]

Secondly, these actions bear an essential relationship to *Jesus himself*. What did the 'sheep' do? Jesus is their witness: **'For I was hungry and you gave me something to eat, I was thirsty and you gave me something to drink, I was a stranger and you invited me in, I needed clothes and you clothed me, I was sick and you looked after me, I was in prison and you came to visit me'** (25:35-36). You will notice that every action centres on Christ. What they did, they did for *him*. It is not that *anyone* was hungry and you helped *him*. These actions cannot be viewed in abstraction from Jesus Christ and apart from conscious commitment to him. It has been fashionable for years for these words of our Lord to be applied in an abstract way, as if any act of kindness in the world, whatever the religion (or lack of one) which motivated it, is the exact fulfilment of Jesus' words — and equivalent to being right with God (if there is a God). In Jesus' words, however, the goodness of the good deeds lies in their connection with him, not in the actions themselves, outwardly considered.

This is confirmed, in the third place, by the Lord's explanation of the response of the righteous to his description of their actions.

'**Lord, when did we see you hungry and feed you?**' they asked him (25:37-39). They could not think of any instance when they had personally done him any favour. So how could this be said of them? '**The King will reply,**' said Jesus, "'**I tell you the truth, whatever you did for one of the least of these brothers of mine, you did for me**'" (25:40). They had, as they said, never done any of these kindnesses for their Lord directly. Indeed, they were not particularly conscious of having accumulated a tally of major good deeds. That is to say, they had just lived their lives as Christians and attended to what came up in the normal course of things. They did not sit down and plan their good deeds — the way 'celebrities' are inclined to do (to become even more celebrated?). The believers can blink their eyes and honestly wonder when it was they did these kindnesses that Jesus is talking about, not because they did not actually do them, but because, as Herman Hanko observes, 'A good work which is genuinely a good work is done with complete self-forgetfulness.'[6] The same writer reminds us that 'Those works which are good are only those done to the glory of God. If the child of God does works for himself or his own glory, they cease to be good.'[7]

'Well,' says Jesus, 'however unaware you are of having done these things for me, I can assure you that you did them for certain "brothers" of mine — and that is the same as doing it for me!' The key to understanding what Jesus is saying is determining who these 'brothers' of his are. They are, of course, those whom he has saved and will yet save. 'Both the one who makes men holy and those who are made holy are of the same family. So Jesus is not ashamed to call them brothers' (Heb. 2:11). Jesus' brothers are those who believe in him and are saved by his work of atonement. Simon Kistemaker correctly points out that 'Jesus' self-identification with his brothers does not include all the poor and needy in the world. To see in the passage on the last judgement a basis for Christian love for the poor, indiscriminately considered, because the poor represent Christ, is reading something into the text ... The parable of the sheep and the goats and its subsequent portrayal of the judgement day accentuates the word *brother* (Matt. 25:40) ... [and] the term *brother* does not apply to everybody, but only to those who acknowledge Jesus as their Lord and Saviour.'[8]

There is accordingly a profound union between Jesus and believers. They are as one (John 17:23). This was why Saul of Tarsus could be asked, 'Saul, Saul, why do you persecute me?' (Acts 9:4-5). To persecute Christians was to persecute Christ himself. The converse is also true. To love those whom Christ loves, to value those he values, and to do them good, is to do the same for Christ. The ultimate and only real test of true righteousness is the Lord and his people. True righteousness is expressed in practical love for Christ, which is quintessentially applied to the people of his kingdom, the fellowship of those who love him. It is not that good deeds are not to be done to all people, whether or not they are believers. We are to 'do good to all people', but, as Paul reminds us, 'especially to those who belong to the family of believers' (Gal. 6:10). How people treat Christ's cause on earth — and that means principally Christian people and Christian work — reveals their deeper convictions. Those who love the Lord will always pass this test. It is impossible to love Jesus and not love those who also love him.

Eternal punishment (25:41-45)

When Jesus turns to the other side of the judgement, we have a mirror image of the Lord's transaction with his people. The King sentences them to eternal death, and then, against their protestations of pretended innocence, he tells them why they are being consigned to eternal punishment in hell. **'Those on his left'** are the unsaved, the unbelieving, the unrepentant, the lost, all who would not receive Christ as their Saviour. They are the nasty and the nice, the good and the bad, now all united in their common rejection of Christ and the gospel.

The endless end of the lost (25:41)

The lost will hear three words from the King, and they constitute a triple seal upon the awful destiny of the damned.

First he says, **'Depart from me'** (25:41). They will be separated from God and from all that is good and truly pleasurable. This reiterates the sentence of the parable of the talents: 'Throw that worthless servant outside, into the darkness, where there will be weeping and gnashing of teeth' (25:30). In spite of this rather clear teaching, Jesus' doctrine of eternal conscious punishment in hell has recently come under fire from some evangelical Christians. Even John Stott, the doyen of British evangelicalism, has declared himself to 'believe that the ultimate annihilation of the wicked should at least be accepted as a legitimate, biblically founded alternative to their eternal, conscious torment' and has argued strongly for the annihilationist position.[9] In his recent study of the subject of hell and its critics, Dr Larry Dixon shows with irrefutable clarity that Jesus taught that hell is a place (Matt. 24:51; Luke 16:28; cf. Rev. 21:8; Acts 1:25), to be avoided at all costs (Matt. 5:22,29,30). He taught that it will be a place of enforced separation from his presence (Matt. 7:23; cf. 2 Thess. 1:8-9). As a place of darkness, its only sounds will be weeping and gnashing of teeth (Matt. 8:12). Hell is a fate far worse than one's physical death (Matt. 10:28) and will contain punishments varying in severity (Matt. 11:22-24).[10]

Those who separated themselves from Christ in this life, and wanted God to leave them alone to live their lives as they saw fit, will get their wish in eternity. The Lord will no longer bother their consciences with the morality of his law or the spirituality of his worship. They will be left to themselves and to the imploding miseries of their wilful rebellion against heaven. Hell will be sin without the fun of sinning. It will be death without the hope of oblivion. It will in one respect be what its inhabitants desired and practised all their lives — freedom from God. But gone will be the Faustian illusion of the good life that was their guiding motive in this world. They will know they 'had it coming', but unrepentant to the last, they will continue to curse God from the pit and so continually and endlessly justify their condemnation. Those who are squeamish about the idea of God punishing people for ever always seem to assume that a touch of hell will change their minds. It doesn't and it can't. The lost in hell are reprobate in their alienation from God and incorrigible in their hatred for Christ, his kingdom and his people. He who 'does wrong continue[s] to do wrong', and he who is 'vile continue[s] to be vile' (Rev. 22:11). The awful reality is that every day in eternity unbelievers will earn afresh the just condemnation of a holy God. They will sin for ever and accordingly be punished for ever.

Secondly, Jesus declares the end of the illusions of impunity they entertained while indulging their chosen lifestyle in this life. He calls them, **'you who are cursed'**. John Calvin has the measure of the psychology of determined sinners when he says that they 'are so intoxicated by their fading prosperity, that they imagine they will always be happy.[11] Just like the people in the days of the prophets, they dream that they have 'entered into a covenant with death', and 'with the grave ... have made an agreement,' so that 'when an overwhelming scourge sweeps by, it cannot touch [them]' (Isa. 28:15). They gambled their lives on the powerlessness of God to call them to account. They practised what they preached. Sin was not sin and God was dead. What was there to risk? They looked at death and called it a normal part of life. They barely glanced at hell and laughed it off on the way to their self-indulgence! But the 'curse' of God's law eventually caught up with them. That 'curse' is simply the consequences, temporally and eternally, of breaking God's law. The wages of sin is death (Rom. 6:23).

Thirdly, Jesus tells them that they will be put **'into the eternal fire prepared for the devil and his angels'**. There is a kind of 'fellowship' in hell — the anti-fellowship of miserable, sin-sick souls in the terminal experience of endless spiritual death. The 'fire' is of the kind that torments both spirits (fallen angels) and people with bodies (reprobate humans). It has to be a good deal more subtle than the simple combustion of fireplaces and furnaces.[12] Whether 'eternal fire' or 'outer darkness', the Bible's language speaks of God's anger and human anguish. It is unimaginable, yet it is just. It is pain without relief and sorrow without repentance — all shared in a pseudo-fellowship of carnal minds that are at enmity with God and are devoid of the slightest inkling of love.

The reason why (25:42-45)

Anticipating protestations of innocence, Jesus gives the evidence for the prosecution. He was, he says, **'hungry ... thirsty ... a stranger ... [he] needed clothes ... was sick and in prison ... and you did not look after [him]'**. What the elect did in their lifetime, the reprobate did not do. They lived for themselves. What is perhaps most striking about this is that Jesus only mentions sins of omission — things they omitted to do! He could have listed all sorts of sins of commission — the 'works of the flesh' (Gal. 5:19-21). He could have pointed out that God is sovereign in salvation and had prepared the wicked as 'vessels of wrath fitted to destruction' (Rom. 9:22). He could have spoken about their lack of faith in him and repentance towards God (Acts 20:21). All their sins, not least the sin of unbelief, were relevant to their spiritual state and their eternal destiny. But the

Lord confined his remarks to what they did not do. Why? The answer is that all he had to do to demonstrate the justice of their condemnation was to mention quietly what they did *not* do. They ignored him. He did not figure in their lives. And in that undramatic fact the essence of their lives was exposed. They lived for themselves and God was not in all their thoughts.

Naturally enough, they protested their innocence of Jesus' charge and did so in almost the same words as the saints had earlier expressed their amazement at his commendation for them: **'Lord, when did we see you hungry or thirsty or a stranger or needing clothes or sick or in prison, and did not help you?'** (25:44). On the face of it, this appears to be an appeal to the proposition that they never had opportunity to do such things for Jesus personally. This is, of course, nothing less than an attempt to escape conviction on a technicality and sinners, like all good criminals, know exactly what they are doing when trying to cop out of a plea. They are guilty as charged. They know it. But any excuse will do!

Jesus simply gave the screw another turn: **'I tell you the truth, whatever you did not do for one of the least of these, you did not do for me'**(25:45) The parallel is clear: 'the least of these' are the same 'least of these brothers of mine' in the exchange with those on the right. Jesus was not around to be fed and clothed, but Jesus' people were. His body, the church, was represented in their neighbourhood. The work of the kingdom was in evidence, as believers lived out, witnessed to and worked for Christ and Christian principles and causes in their world. What was their attitude to the gospel and to believers? Did they worship the Lord daily in their homes and in the church on the Lord's Day? Were they concerned about the lives of the unborn and did they labour to save them from death by abortion? What did they do with the least of Christ's brothers? They knew very well where they stood. The truth is, they had no time for the gospel, the people of God or the Lord himself. The excuse didn't wash! The appeal was dismissed and the sentence would stand!

The great divide (25:46)

The last verse sums up with simple finality the issue of human history — yours, mine and everybody's. **'Then they will go away to eternal punishment, but the righteous to eternal life.'** There is no wriggling out of this one — not for universalists, atheists or even Bible-believing preachers who want to be annihilationists. Hell is yawning for lost people. There is an eternal parting of the ways. Rebellion against God and rejection of his Son, persisted in to the grave, will result in a conscious experience of punishment without end. There is certainly no 'second chance' for anyone after this life is over, for we are 'destined to die once, and after that to face judgement' (Heb. 9:27). Jesus confronts us with the starkest reality in the universe and in effect asks us where we want to spend eternity.

The purpose of this and every other parable — and the whole earthly ministry of Jesus from his incarnation to his death, burial, resurrection and ascension — was to fill up heaven, rather than hell. Jesus takes no pleasure in the death of the wicked, but delights in their coming to repentance and faith, to new life in him and to a heavenly hope that will come to full bloom in the great day of his coming. 'Heaven is life,' says Matthew Henry. 'It is all happiness … the heavenly life consists in the vision and fruition of God, in a perfect conformity to him, and an immediate uninterrupted communion with him.'[13] He calls us to be stop being goats and start being sheep: his sheep; the sheep of his pasture; the sheep who hear his voice and follow him; the sheep who rest in the safety of his fold — the sheep for whom he was about to lay down his life (John 10:11-18).

'Believe in the Lord Jesus Christ and you will be saved…' (Acts 16:31).

References

Chapter 1 — The secrets of the kingdom
1. NIV's 'dynamic equivalence' rendering has 'knowledge' — a noun. In the Greek, this is a verb! The Greek literally reads, 'Because to you it has been given to you *to know* the mysteries of the kingdom.' The verb 'to know'*(gnonai)* is an aorist, which indicates 'an actual inner grasp and appropriation' (R. C. H. Lenski, *The Interpretation of St Matthew's Gospel,* Augsburg, 1964, p.511).
2. W. Hendriksen,*The Gospel of Matthew,* Banner of Truth, p.553.
3. John Calvin (*Harmony of the Evangelists,* vol. II, p.106) sees parables as essentially obscure and thus expressive of God's intention *not* to reveal his truth clearly. Jesus spoke in parables, then, so that 'the form of an allegory might present a doubtful riddle'. This roots the difficulty in the parable, rather than in the hardness of the hearers' hearts — the exact opposite, I would suggest, of what Jesus is telling us about the purpose of his parables. Charles Simeon (*Expository Outlines on the Whole Bible,* Baker, 1988 (original edition 1847), vol. 11, pp.396ff.) is of the same opinion.
4. Herman Hanko, *The Mysteries of the Kingdom,* Reformed Free Publishing Association, 1975, p.8. Hanko cites Luke 16:14-15 as an example.
5. Edward J. Young, *The Book of Isaiah,* Grand Rapids, 1972, vol. I, pp.255-61.
6. As above, vol. I, p.259.
7. M. Henry, *A Commentary on the Whole Bible,* vol. 5, pp.182-3.
8. Norval Geldenhuys, *Commentary on the Gospel of Luke,* Eerdmans, 1968, p.307.

Chapter 2 —The message of the kingdom
1. J. A. Alexander, *A Commentary on the Gospel of Mark,* Banner of Truth, 1960 (original edition 1858), p.87.
2. Charles Simeon, *Expository Outlines on the Whole Bible,* Baker, 1988 (original edition 1847, vol. 11, p.402.
3. Henry, *Commentary,* vol. 5, p.186.
4. R. C. H. Lenski, *The Interpretation of St Matthew's Gospel,* Augsburg, 1964, p.523.

Chapter 3 — The two seeds in the kingdom

1. For example, in a homosexual 'Coming out Sunday' demonstration on the campus of the Pennsylvania State University, State College, Pa, a woman minister of a main-line American denomination and a member of the university's Religious Affairs Department carried a placard with the legend: 'If Jesus Came Back Today He'd Probably Come as a Poor African-American Lesbian' (*Centre Daily Times*, State College, Pa, Monday, 12 October 1992, p.2).

2. The 'weeds' were probably a species of darnel *(Lollium)*, a plant that is very similar to wheat in its early growth.

3. Lenski, *St Matthew's Gospel*, p.536.

4. H. Hanko (*Mysteries of the Kingdom*, pp.26-7) disposes of this viewpoint very effectively.

5. Ungodly harrying of true believers is out and out persecution in the interests of promoting heresy. But what of the efforts of orthodox Protestants to 'extirpate' error by the sword? The *Solemn League and Covenant* of 1643 between Scotland and the English Parliamentary side in the Civil War uses just such language and there is no doubt that an exclusively figurative application of this language was not in their minds.

6. The *preterist* school of eschatological interpretation views these passages as describing events now in the past ('preterism' = pertaining to the past). The tribulation of Matthew 24, the harvest of Revelation 14 and most Scripture references to 'the day of the Lord' and the *'parousia'* (Second Coming) of Jesus Christ are then interpreted as referring to the destruction of Jerusalem in A. D. 70 (Thus D. Chilton, *Paradise Restored*, Dominion Press, 1987, pp.138-9, and *Days of Vengeance*, Dominion Press, 1985, p.376). Most preterists believe there is a last Day of Judgement, but say that the only texts we can be sure refer to it are those associated with the general resurrection of the saints (e.g., John 6:38-40,44,54). This theory also assumes and requires an early date for the book of Revelation (*c.* A. D. 60 rather than A. D. 95) and has to telescope most of the Bible's eschatological language of universal judgement and destruction (conveniently dismissed as 'collapsing-universe terminology') into the A. D. 70 siege and destruction of Jerusalem. Needless to say, such folk are staunch postmillennialists — after all, the really bad stuff is behind us! It is, however, not good enough to explain away the apocalyptic language of Scripture as mere 'collapsing-universe terminology'. Preterist eschatological speculations violate the plain meaning of such language and are to be rejected as unsound. For the best, most readable, exposition of a sound view of prophecy in general and the book of Revelation in particular, see Graeme Goldsworthy, *The Gospel in Revelation*, Paternoster Press, 1984.

7. See Louis Berkhof, *Systematic Theology*, Banner of Truth, pp.728-34.

8. Simeon, *Expository Outlines*, vol. 11, p.410.

9. Berkhof, *Systematic Theology*, pp. 735-6.

10. Annihilationism is the (false) teaching that the wicked, having rejected Christ and his salvation, are not consigned to hell for ever, separated from God and under his undying wrath. This has reared its head in recent years in the writings of such well-known Anglican evangelicals as John Stott and the late Philip Edgcumbe Hughes.

11. Berkhof, *Systematic Theology*, pp.736-8.

Chapter 4 — The growth of the kingdom
1. Henry, *Commentary,* vol. 5, p.191.
2. The site is now a cleared, grassy site next to the Royal Museum in Edinburgh's Chamber's Street. Then it was a jumble of nondescript buildings called Brown's Square.
3. See my *Looking for the Good Life* (Presbyterian and Reformed, 1991) pp.164-5 for an account of my own conversion to Christ.
4. The church as an organization — in congregations, under pastors and elders — is instituted by Christ. In this sense, the institution of the church, organized according to God's Word, will always exist on earth. But there is no guaranteed permanence to *particular* church organizations, whether congregations or denominations (see the churches of Asia Minor in Revelation 2 and 3, or the plethora of extinct Protestant denominations), or their institutions (theological colleges or missionary societies).
5. Hanko, *Mysteries of the Kingdom,* p.42.

Chapter 5 — The value of the kingdom
1. Lenski (*St Matthew's Gospel,* p.542) and Matthew Henry (*Commentary,* vol. 5, p.192), think the 'field' is 'undoubtedly the Scriptures'. This is without support, however, and violates the analogy of Scripture, i.e., the meaning as made plain in the other parables, and indeed in Jesus' explanations of those of the sower and the weeds.
2. John Murray, *Redemption Accomplished and Applied,* Banner of Truth, is a clear and very understandable exposition of this 'order of salvation'.
3. *The Book of Psalms for Singing,* Selection119B, v.4.

Chapter 6 — The ministry of the kingdom
1. Hendriksen, *Matthew,* p.577.
2. *Westminster Confession of Faith,* 25, 5.

Chapter 7 — Forgiveness
1. See, for example, how Jesus deals with the woman of Samaria. First he talks of 'living water', then he hits her with her breaches of the Seventh Commandment (John 4:10,17). Some modern Christians would go to great lengths to persuade her from the Bible that she was actually sinning, before pointing to Christ as the only Saviour. I have known people who sat under Bible-believing preaching for years before they realized that Christ actually could save them from their sins, so great was the emphasis in the preaching on the 'law-work' as a precursor for a work of grace.

Chapter 8 — Caring about others
1. The Samaritans were a people, living around Samaria, who were descended from the intermarriage of the remnant of the people of the northern kingdom of Israel and the Assyrian settlers who came in after the fall of that kingdom in the eighth century B. C. Their religion was an eclectic form of Judaism, based on the acceptance of the Five Books of Moses only as the Word of God. To this day, they offer their annual sacrifices on Mount Gerizim.
2. Hanko, *Mysteries of the Kingdom,* p.78.

3. Dean Plumptre once remarked somewhere that the more the Pharisees lost the power to make proselytes, the more they 'dwelt with exhaustive fulness on the question how proselytes were to be made'. It is much easier to talk about being good than it is to actually do some good. Eventually the talking has to stop, or the whole thing is a fraud and a charade.

4. *The Book of Psalms for Singing,* selection 112A.

Chapter 9 — Prayerfulness

1. Hanko, *Mysteries of the Kingdom,* p.85.
2. From the hymn, 'Rock of Ages, cleft for me,' by Augustus Montague Toplady (1740-78).
3. The NIV omits this clause, on the strength of the third-century papyrus, *P45,* and the fourth-century uncial Codex Vaticanus (B), when there is abundant manuscript evidence for its validity. The AV is to be preferred.
4. R. C. H. Lenski, *The Interpretation of St Luke's Gospel,* Augsburg, 1961, p.630.

Chapter 10 — Rich towards God

1. R. C. Trench, *Notes on the Parables of our Lord,* 1841, p. 339.
2. Hanko, *Mysteries of the Kindom,* p.99.
3. Henry, *Commentary,* vol. 5, p. 711.
4. *The Book of Psalms for Singing,* Selection 119B.

Chapter 11 — Bearing fruit

1. Hanko, *Mysteries of the Kingdom,* p.104.
2. Geldenhuys, *Commentary on Luke,* p.372; Kistemaker, *Parables of Jesus,* p.186; Hanko, *Mysteries of the Kingdom,* p.104. Others see the vineyard as Israel but, in my view, have to resort to strained arguments to maintain this and adequately identify the fig-tree. For example, Matthew Henry (*Commentary,* vol. 5, p.721) says the vineyard is Israel / the church and the fig-tree is those who receive baptism, while Lenski (*St Luke's Gospel,* p. 726) thinks the fig-tree is Jerusalem.
3. John Owen, *The Works of John Owen,* vol. VIII, p.598. This is from Owen's exposition of Luke 13:1-5, entitled, 'An Humble Testimony unto the Goodness and Severity of God in His dealings with Sinful Churches and Nations...' (1681). This masterly treatise of some sixty pages is sub-titled: 'The only way to deliver a sinful nation from utter ruin by impending judgements,' and could hardly be more relevant to the state of Britain today.
4. As above, p.599.
5. As above, p. 605.

Chapter 12 — Humility

1. David Brown, *The Four Gospels,* Banner of Truth, p.283.
2. John Calvin, *Harmony of the Evangelists,* vol. 2, p.165.
3. As above.
4. Monte Williams, 'A buzzword for the '90s: self-esteem,' *Centre Daily Times* (State College, PA), 11 February 1993 (Originally in *New York Daily News*).
5. For a wonderfully illuminating exposition of this theme, see Donald McDonald, *Christian Experience,* Banner of Truth, 1988, chapter 13 ('The Marriage Supper of the Lamb') pp.124-33.
6. Hanko, *Mysteries of the Kingdom,* pp.124-5.

Chapter 13 — Reconciled to God
1. Kistemaker, *Parables of Jesus*, pp.196-7.
2. Calvin, *Harmony of the Evangelists*, vol. II, p.173.
3. Lenski, *St Luke's Gospel*, p.776. Calvin (*Harmony of the Evangelists*, p.168) regards it as less than truly pious, 'a remark about future blessedness' thrown out 'in order to draw out some observation in return from Christ'. It must be said that the Reformer reads all this into the man's words, when the evidence of the text is that it was an honest remark, which Jesus proceeded to answer in a straightforward way. The characteristic faults of Pharisees need not be ascribed to everyone who says something to Jesus.

Chapter 14 — Seeking the lost
1. Lenski (*St Luke's Gospel*, p.802), for example, emphatically upholds the view that the ninety-nine were true believers, but discreetly avoids dealing with those passages where Jesus uses similar expressions to expose the true state of the self-righteous and hypocritical.
2. Hanko (*Mysteries of the Kingdom*, pp.139-40) gives an excellent exposition of this understanding of the text.
3. Kistemaker, *Parables of Jesus*, p.212.
4. Lenski, *St Luke's Gospel*, p. 805. This always weighty Lutheran does a fine job of debunking some of the more fanciful interpretations.
5. Henry, *Commentary*, vol. 5, p.740.
6. Hanko, *Mysteries of the Kingdom*, p.145.

Chapter 15 — Welcoming the found
1. Hugo Grotius, quoted by Trench, *Parables*, p.384.
2. Lenski, *St Luke's Gospel*, p.807.
3. Kistemaker, *Parables of Jesus*, p.217. Since the firstborn received a double portion for his inheritance at his father's death (Deut. 21:17), and there were just two sons, the younger son's share would have been one third. Scholars surmise that the settlement *while the father was still alive* would have been less than this and a figure of two-ninths has been suggested.
4. Henry, *Commentary*, vol. 5, p.743.
5. As above, pp.743-4.
6. From a public opinion poll taken in March 1993.
7. Brownlow North, *The Rich Man and Lazarus*, Banner of Truth, 1979, pp.9-10.
8. John Richard de Witt, *Amazing Love*, Banner of Truth, 1981, p.138.
9. Lenski, *St Luke's Gospel*, p.807.
10. It is worth pointing out that this contrasts with the ninety-nine sheep in the parable of the lost sheep. These too would have had to be regarded as believers, safe in the Lord's fold, were it not for Jesus' own interpretation of the parable in Luke 15:7, where he characterizes them as self-righteous, unconverted Pharisees — 'righteous persons who do not need to repent'.
11. Lenski (*St Luke's Gospel*, p.821) makes verse 31 out to be no more than a rebuke of the son's lack of love and never addresses the question of the sense in which the older brother was *always* with the father and possessed *everything* that belonged to his father. Herman Hanko (*Mysteries of the Kingdom*, p.170) glosses over it, without attempting any interpretation, and J. R. de Witt (in a book of 160 pages on this parable alone) doesn't deal with it at all! It all illustrates that what

commentators don't say, or won't tackle, can be at least as revealing as what they do write about.

12. Lenski, *St Luke's Gospel*, p.822.

Chapter 16 — Commitment

1. Kistemaker, *Parables of Jesus*, p.233. This view that the manager had a sudden dose of honesty rests on the assumption that the original bills for the various goods supplied were inflated by the usurious application of interest and that what was being deducted was that excessive interest charge (and Kistemaker has a lengthy description as to how this was done in those days). There is, however, no evidence in the text that this was so in this case. That alone ought to explode the 'honesty' theory. A further, equally unwarranted assumption is that the master's commendation indicates that the steward's actions were morally upright — i.e., that he had for once acted honestly. Again, there is no evidence in the text for this. The parable is better read as a vignette of worldliness. The manager fiddled things to suit himself and showed how a 'wheeler-dealer' can get ahead in the world — and get away with it. See Lenski, *St Luke's Gospel*, pp.823ff. for a fine example of how to interpret this parable without wandering off into fanciful speculations.

2. Lenski, *St Luke's Gospel*, p.828.

3. As above.

4. 'Mammon' is to be preferred to NIV's 'Money'. The Syriac 'mammon' is equivalent to 'the world', of which 'money' is only one potentially idolatrous expression. Money as a materialist god is in view in this parable, but there is no implication that money, or turning a profit in business, are bad things. It is better to retain the original word 'Mammon' because it emphasizes the aspect of idolatry most effectively.

Chapter 17 — Heeding the Word

1. See Brownlow North, *The Rich Man and Lazarus*, pp.17-24, for a very searching discussion of the idea that earthly suffering procures salvation. North's 123-page exposition of the parable — originally sermons preached in the 1859 revival — is as gripping in the reading today as it must have been when preached over a century ago.

2. Henry, *Commentary*, vol. 5, p.762.

3. North, *Rich Man and Lazarus*, p.102.

4. As above, p.103.

5. As above, p.106.

6. Henry, *Commentary*, vol. 5, p. 763.

Chapter 18 — Dutiful service

1. Lenski, *St Luke's Gospel*, p.872.

2. Calvin, *Harmony of the Evangelists*, vol. 2, p.196.

3. As above.

Chapter 19 — Perseverance

1. Most recently, Edgar Whisenant, an American, predicted the Lord's return for September 1988. A Korean charismatic church set it for October 1992, and Harold

Camping, the founder of the highly regarded California-based Christian Family Radio, has set the date for some time in 1994.
2. Henry, *Commentary*, vol. 5, p.774.
3. Kistemaker, *Parables of Jesus*, p.255.
4. Hanko, *Mysteries of the Kingdom*, p.206.

Chapter 20 — The right attitude
1. Most churches sit for prayer today, but standing (1 Kings 8:22; 2 Chron. 6:12; Matt. 6:5; Mark 11:25) and kneeling (Dan. 6:10; 2 Chron. 6:13; Acts 9:40; 20:36; 21:5) are the appropriate biblical postures for public worship. Privately, David sat to pray in 1 Chronicles 17:16 and prayed when lying in his bed in Psalm 4:4.
2. From the hymn 'Rock of Ages' by Augustus Montague Toplady (1740-78).
3. Kistemaker, *Parables of Jesus*, p.260.
4. Simeon, *Expository Outlines*, vol. 13, p.34.
5. Henry, *Commentary*, vol. 5, p.777.
6. Thomas Manton, *The Complete Works*, vol. XXII, p.59 (From a sermon on 1 John 1:7).

Chapter 21 — The last and the first
1. These are as follows:

1. The labourers in the vineyard (Matt. 20:1-16).
2. The ten minas (Luke 19:11-27).
3. The two sons (Matt. 21:28-32).
4. The tenants (Matt. 21:33-46).
5. The wedding banquet (Matt. 22:1-10).
6. The wedding garment (Matt. 22:11-14).
7. The ten virgins (Matt. 25:1-13).
8. The talents (Matt.25:14-30).
9. The sheep and the goats (Matt. 25:31-46).

In this volume we shall cover these in seven chapters, by considering together, respectively, the two sons and the tenants (ch. 23), and the wedding banquet and the wedding garment (ch. 24).
2. Hanko, *Mysteries of the Kingdom*, p.223.
3. Henry, *Commentary*, vol. 5, p.283. Simeon, *Expository Outlines*, vol. 11, pp.485-6. This is appealing, and the psychology of the workers fits the later Jew-Gentile tensions in the apostolic church, but it ignores the immediate context of the parable, which is to do with attitudes in an exclusively Jewish context.
4. Cited by Kistemaker, *Parables of Jesus*, p.81 (footnote).

Chapter 22 — Living for the Lord
1. Archelæus reigned as ethnarch of Judea, Samaria and Idumaea from 4 B.C. to A.D. 6. He was responsible for the murder of 3,000 men in the temple area — hence the deputation to Rome opposing his accession — prior to his confirmation as ethnarch. His subsequent tyrannical rule led to his being deposed by the Romans.
2. Simeon, *Expository Outlines*, vol.13, p.54.
3. *The Book of Psalms for Singing*, Selection 98A.

Chapter 23 — Christ our cornerstone
1. Calvin, *Harmony of the Evangelists,* vol. III, p.14.
2. Kistemaker, *Parables of Jesus,* pp.93-4.
3. Lenski, *St Matthew's Gospel,* p.845.
4. As above.

Chapter 24 — Many are called but few are chosen
1. See chapter 13 above.
2. One version of which is in Manchester Art Gallery.
3. This involves the question of the order of salvation (the *ordo salutis*) — the order in which people are brought to saving faith. For a matchless discussion of this subject see, John Murray, *Redemption Accomplished and Applied.*
4. Young, *Isaiah,* vol. III, pp.465-6.

Chapter 25 — Watching for Christ's return
1. For the most thorough exegetical treatment of 1 Peter 3:18-20 see John Brown's classic exposition of *1 Peter,* pp.467-552, now available in a reprint from the Banner of Truth. For a modern discussion of the 'Descent into hell' doctrine see Larry Dixon, *The Other Side of the Good News,* Wheaton, Illinois, 1992, pp.97-120.
2. Kistemaker, *Parables of Jesus,* p.132 (footnote 13).

Chapter 26 — Working for Christ's return
1. Luke 19:11-27. See chapter 22 above for an exposition of this parable.
2. In Matthew 25:18, the Greek word *argurion* is used to describe the money the man with 'one talent' buried in the ground.
3. William Perkins: *Works,* (1612 ed.) vol. I, p.391 .
4. Lenski, *St Matthew's Gospel,* p.983.
5. Calvin, *Harmony of the Evangelists,* vol. 2, p.104 (Matt. 13:12; Luke 8:18).
6. As above, vol. I, p.384 (Matt. 8:12).

Chapter 27 — Final judgement
1. There is an extreme form of 'preterism' (the approach to apocalyptic prophecies, especially the book of Revelation, that sees them fulfilled in the events current at the time of writing) which views the Day of Judgement as associated with the destruction of Jerusalem in A. D. 70. This was promoted over a century ago by J. Stuart Russell, *The Parousia* (1871), recently republished by Baker Book House, and Max R. King, *The Spirit of Prophecy* (1971), published in Warren, Ohio, by an arm of the Church of Christ, a sect of the Campbellite movement.
2. Calvin, *Harmony of the Evangelists,* vol.3, p.177.
3. Lenski, *St Matthew's Gospel,* p.990.
4. Calvin, *Harmony of the Evangelists,* vol. 3, pp.177-8.
5. Lenski, *St Matthew's Gospel,* pp. 991-2.
6. Hanko, *Mysteries of the Kingdom,* p.303.
7. As above.
8. Kistemaker, *Parables of Jesus,* pp.155-6.
9. Stott, John R.W. and Edwards, David L., *Evangelical Essentials,* London: 1988, p.320.

10. Dixon, *The Other Side of the Good News*, p.145.
11. Calvin, *Harmony of the Evangelists*, p.181.
12. Lenski, *St Matthew's Gospel*, p.996.
13. Henry, *Commentary*, vol. 5, p.384.